OF SPIES AND LIES

MODERN

WAR

STUDIES

Theodore A. Wilson
General Editor

Raymond A. Callahan

J. Garry Clifford

Jacob W. Kipp

Jay Luvaas

Allan R. Millett

Carol Reardon

Dennis Showalter

David R. Stone
Series Editors

OF SPIES AND LIES

A CIA

LIE DETECTOR

REMEMBERS

VIETNAM

John F. Sullivan

University Press of Kansas

© 2002 by the University Press of Kansas

Published by the University Press of Kansas (Lawrence, Kansas 66049), which was organized by the Kansas Board of Regents and is operated and funded by Emporia State University, Fort Hays State University, Kansas State University, Pittsburg State University, the University of Kansas, and Wichita State University

The paper used in this publication meets the minimum requirements of the American National Standard for Permanence of Paper for Printed Library Materials Z39.48-1984.

Library of Congress Cataloging-in-Publication Data

Sullivan, John F., 1939–
Of spies and lies : a CIA lie detector remembers Vietnam / John F. Sullivan.
p. cm. — (Modern war studies)
Includes bibliographical references and index.
ISBN 0-7006-1168-1 (cloth : alk. paper)
1. Vietnamese Conflict, 1961–1975—Secret service—United States. 2. United States. Central Intelligence Agency. I. Title. II. Series.
DS559.8.M44 S85 2000
959.704'38—dc21   2001007223

British Library Cataloguing in Publication Data is available.

Printed in the United States of America
10 9 8 7 6 5 4 3 2

To Lee

CONTENTS

A photo gallery follows page 136.

PREFACE

．　　．　　．　　．　　．　　．　　．　　．　　．　　．　　．　　．　　．

This book presents a picture of the war in Vietnam as I saw it—a picture that others who were there can perhaps relate to and laugh and cry over. To understand why and how the United States lost the war, the CIA's role must be told from the perspective of those who served in the trenches. My perspective is not that of a scholar, historian, military tactician, or CIA decision maker who saw the big picture, but that of a civilian grunt who went to Vietnam naive and pure of heart and came home with touches of guilt, cynicism, and disillusionment.

I am grateful to my many colleagues in Vietnam who became my friends and made the experience tolerable. Also, I thank those who were part of the problem rather than the solution. They made it possible for me to appreciate the "good guys" and were instrumental in providing documentation for many of the points I make in this book. On a more personal note, my two tours in Vietnam greatly enchanced my polygraph skills, helped forge a bond between my wife and me that is still going strong, and gave me a perspective on the functioning of clandestine operations that has served me well. The birth of our son, John, in December 1973 was the highlight of the events that occurred during my time in Vietnam.

Author James Michener in his book *Hawaii* refers to the first missionaries there, whose progeny later became the wealthiest families in Hawaii, as those who "came to do good and did well." Many of my colleagues and I went to Vietnam to do good and also did well. In doing well, however, we lost sight of why we were there. It numbed us to the reality of what was happening and helped perpetrate the myth that Vietnamization was working. For allowing myself to become a part of it, I will forever be guilty. This book is a mea culpa that I hope will expiate my role in some of the events. It is also an attempt to provide a broader perspective of the Vietnam War that will be of use in assessing why we lost.

ACKNOWLEDGMENTS

∎ ∎ ∎ ∎ ∎ ∎ ∎ ∎ ∎ ∎ ∎ ∎ ∎ ∎

Many former colleagues were very generous with their time and advice in helping me with this book, and I am deeply grateful. Among them are Greg Collins and Chris Hanlon, two colleagues from Vietnam. They are the only Agency people to whom I showed the manuscript before trying to get it published, and they were of tremendous help in making sure that I got it right.

Bob Pickell, a former colleague and the best examiner with whom I ever worked, regularly validated my faith in the polygraph process and convinced me that a book such as mine could help clear up some misperceptions the public has, not only about polygraph, but also about the CIA.

Merle Pribbenow, a colleague from Vietnam and the most knowledgeable person I know regarding postwar Vietnam, was particularly helpful in bringing my thoughts on the FIREBALL operation to some kind of closure.

Paul Frandano, a former colleague and one of the truly bright people I met in the Agency, was one of my first sounding boards for ideas about the book. He also helped me get through some problems I had with the introduction.

Jim Parker, author of *Last Man Out* and *Code Name MULE* and another former colleague, was a constant source of advice and encouragement. He referred me to Terry Belanger, who helped turn my words into readable text. More importantly, Terry and Jim referred me to Mark Gatlin of the Smithsonian Institution Press.

Mark was a catalyst. I submitted my manuscript to him, and although he turned it down, he suggested that I try Mike Briggs at the University Press of Kansas. Throughout the process, Mark has been a constant source of encouragement. After a harsh (but pretty accurate) review of the manuscript, I was very discouraged, and Mark got me back on track.

Tim Lomperis of St. Louis University, in a prepublication review of my manuscript, was generous with his praise, honest, as well as accurate, with his criticism, and played an instrumental role in helping me turn disjointed meanderings into a readable text. I will be forever grateful.

No first-time author could do better than to have the University Press of Kansas accept his or her manuscript for publication. Mike Briggs, Susan Schott, Jessica Pigza, and Melinda Wirkus are consummate professionals and the friends I have yet to meet. Their ministrations have made *Of Spies and Lies* a reality.

Maureen Van Popering, my high school English teacher, taught me that words are things of beauty. In 1952, Mrs. Van recommended Nicholas Monserrat's *The Cruel Sea* to me and thus began my love of reading. To this day, she is a source of counsel and encouragement.

Diane Woodward Sawyer, another of Mrs. Van's students, an accomplished author in her own right and my oldest friend, has been a sounding board as well as a steady source of support and advice.

Joan Cali Pecore gave me a superb history teacher's perspective on Vietnam, which helped me articulate some of my thoughts about the country and the war.

Lucia Staniels, the wife of a high school classmate and longtime publishing professional, reviewed a contract I was offered prior to hearing from the University Press of Kansas. Her advice: "Kansas is first rate. If they offer you a contract, jump on it." That is just about the best advice I've had.

Last, and most important: Lee. Without Lee, *Of Spies and Lies* would not be. Each night, after I finished with the manuscript, Lee would wait until I went to sleep and then get up and work until the wee hours correcting my errors.

On at least three occasions, I lost a day's work by hitting a wrong key (or something) on the computer. Each time, I would go a little crazy. Lee would take my jumbled, barely legible notes and reconstruct what I had lost.

Having been in Vietnam with me, Lee was invaluable in helping me recall the details of events that I described. She was also a tough but very fair critic.

Whatever success *Of Spies and Lies* has will be due to Lee's painstaking and tireless efforts. For that and so many other reasons, *Of Spies and Lies* is to, for, and because of Lee.

ACRONYMS

. . . .

ARVN   Army of the Republic of South Vietnam
CAT   Civil Air Transport
CIA   Central Intelligence Agency
C/OPS   chief of operations
COS   chief of station
DCI   director of central intelligence
DI   deception indicated
EA   East Asia (Division)
FBI   Federal Bureau of Investigation
FNG   fucking new guy
IB   Interrogation Branch
ICCS   International Commission of Control and Supervision
ID   identification
IRD   Interrogation Research Division
JIC   Joint Interrogation Center
MAAG   Military Advisory Assistance Group
MAAGV   Military Assistance and Advisory Group, Vietnam
MACV   Military Assistance Command, Vietnam
MIA   missing in action

MR   military region
MSS   Military Security Service
NIC   National Interrogation Center
NVA   North Vietnamese Army
OS   Office of Security
PD   Polygraph Division
POIC   province officer in charge
POW   prisoner of war
PRU   provincial reconnaissance unit
ROIC   regional officer in charge
ROK   Republic of Korea
R&R   rest and recreation
SAM   surface-to-air-missile
SOB   Saigon Operational Base
TDY   temporary duty (assignment)
USAID   United States Agency for International Development
VC   Vietcong
VNAF   South Vietnamese Air Force
VNO   Vietnam Orientation

OF SPIES AND LIES

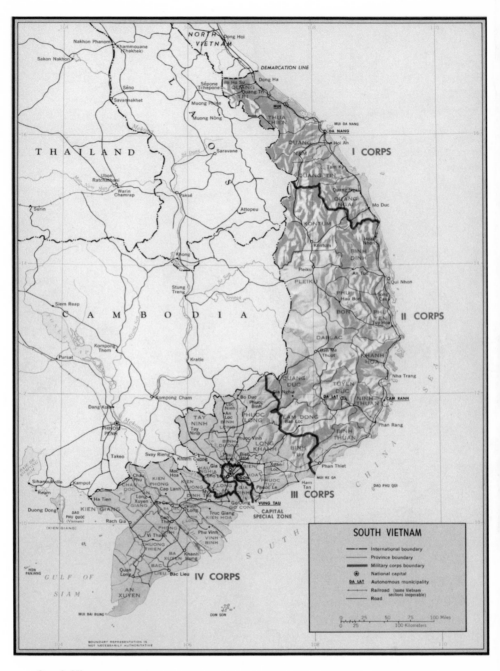

South Vietnam.

INTRODUCTION

■ ■ ■ ■ ■ ■ ■ ■ ■ ■ ■ ■ ■ ■

From April 10, 1971, until April 10, 1975, I was a Central Intelligence Agency (CIA) polygraph examiner in South Vietnam. When I arrived in Vietnam, I believed that winning the war was possible. I also thought that we were on the right side and that I was going there to do good. Four years after my arrival, almost to the hour, I was taking the station files out of Saigon to keep them from falling into the hands of the North Vietnamese Army (NVA).

During that four-year period, I traveled to every province in South Vietnam, spent a lot of time in Cambodia, and took occasional trips to Laos and Thailand. I tested more Vietnamese than any polygraph examiner in the history of the CIA: Vietcong (VC) prisoners, NVA prisoners of war, assassins, Chieu Hois (VC who rallied to the South Vietnamese forces and were ultimately called *ralliers*), Cambodian and Montagnard reconnaissance teams, and drug dealers. I also know of no CIA employee serving in Vietnam during the war who met or worked with more CIA officers than did I.[1] That experience gave me a unique perspective on the

---

1. In discussing CIA personnel with whom I worked, I use aliases (indicated by quotation marks at first mention), except for those employees who have been identified by their actual names elsewhere.

CIA's performance during the last years of the war. Chronicling the negative aspects of the CIA's role during the Vietnam War is essential for a more complete assessment of the Agency's performance.

Many books about the military's role in Vietnam are available.[2] Every battle has been dissected, leading personalities profiled, and strategies analyzed. Conversely, there have been few books documenting the CIA's role in Vietnam's demise, perhaps because the military's role was much more heroic and better lends itself to literary description.

Another reason might be that, by design, less is known about how we so-called spooks performed. The press and other media did not have the same access to the CIA that they had to the military. Also, by law, as well as by condition of employment, CIA employees encountered problems in documenting or airing most of their experiences in Vietnam. In 1977, former CIA analyst Frank Snepp published a book without the prior approval of the CIA, as required.[3] Snepp was taken to court and had to relinquish his royalties. Since then, much of the material dealing with Vietnam has been declassified, and the CIA has loosened its strictures on employees who wish to narrate their wartime and clandestine experiences.

CIA case officers in Vietnam worked with handicaps that the legendary James Bond could not have overcome. Three months after arriving in Vietnam, I concluded that my CIA colleagues and I were unprepared to conduct intelligence operations that would enable us to either recruit VC agents or penetrate the VC infrastructure. The way the CIA conducted its business in Vietnam was an aberration of its procedures in other parts of the world. Case officers did not speak the language; they found it impossible to work clandestinely; and, in many cases, they had not gone willingly to Vietnam. Orrin DeForest, a CIA employee with whom I served in Vietnam, uses the term "intelligence failure" to describe the CIA's performance in Vietnam.[4] DeForest is half right. In

2. David Chanoff, "Expert's Picks: Books on Vietnam," *Washington Post*, April 30, 2000, lists twenty-five books that he considers the best books on the Vietnam War. None of the books cited deals specifically with the CIA's role in the war. *Decent Interval* and *Slow Burn* (see notes 3 and 4, respectively), two books written by CIA colleagues with whom I served in Vietnam, are not listed and, in my opinion, are too narrow in scope regarding the CIA's role.

3. Frank Snepp, *Decent Interval, an Insider's Account of Saigon's Indecent End Told by the CIA's Chief Strategy Analyst in Vietnam* (New York: Random House, 1977).

4. Orrin DeForest, *Slow Burn* (New York: Simon and Schuster, 1990).

terms of penetrating the VC infrastructure, the CIA failed miserably. However, in terms of providing accurate information on the military, political, and economic conditions in South Vietnam, the CIA produced some good information. The fact that the information was not disseminated was more a policy failure than an intelligence failure, and it negated the efforts of some very good officers.

Washington's (State Department, CIA, and military) policy—from before I arrived in Vietnam until everything started to go downhill—was that no negative news, all evidence to the contrary notwithstanding, would be coming out of Vietnam. For example, in 1963, the Army of the Republic of South Vietnam (ARVN) was humiliated by a much smaller VC force in the battle of Ap Bac (in military region 4 [MR/4]). The position of the U.S. Military Assistance Command, Vietnam (MACV) was that the ARVN had won because the VC had ultimately retreated. Exaggerated body counts of enemy soldiers in conjunction with a policy of not giving specific numbers of American casualties were additional examples of the "no bad news" policy.

President Richard Nixon's comment a month after the ARVN had been routed out of Laos—"Tonight I can tell you that Vietnamization has succeeded"[5]—was a misrepresentation of the facts and a continuation of the "no bad news" policy. The positive spin put on this debacle in its Vietnam Orientation (VNO) course made the CIA complicit in this policy.

Gen. Charles Timmes's Pollyannaish approach to the war and the assurance by Thomas Polgar (the CIA's last chief of station in Saigon) to "Chris Hanlon," an MR/4 province officer in charge (POIC), on April 24, 1975, that there would be a negotiated settlement flew in the face of reality and seemed an almost fitting end to the "no bad news" policy.

Vietnam was a great tour for the wrong reasons and a bad tour for the right reasons. It was a great tour because many CIA personnel in Vietnam lived better and made more money than ever before in their lives. Although war is hell, Vietnam was an enjoyable and profitable respite from the real world for many of us. CIA people permanently assigned to Saigon seemed oblivious to the war, and the creature comforts extant in Saigon made the war easy to forget. For those CIA employees who never left Saigon—and there were many—the war was an abstraction.

5. Quoted in Stanley Karnow, *Vietnam, a History* (New York: Penguin Books, 1991), p. 645.

Vietnam was a cash cow for CIA employees with financial concerns, a refuge for those trying to escape bad marriages, a last chance for poor performers hoping to resurrect failing careers, the ultimate watering hole for those with a penchant for imbibing, a sexual playground for those so inclined, and a dumping ground to which CIA Headquarters in Langley, Virginia, exiled problem employees. Alcoholism, debauchery, fear, fraud, divorce, and incompetence were as much the elements of the Vietnam scene that I observed as abandoned babies, desertions, fragging incidents,[6] race riots, drug use, venereal disease, and prison riots were for our military.

Vietnam was a bad tour because the CIA allowed itself to become politicized and abetted the administrations from Kennedy to Ford in the betrayal of the South Vietnamese. Polgar commented during an interview with author Larry Engelmann, "I thought we did a miserable job for these people, and they would have been much better off if we had not gone there in the first place."[7] In retrospect, I tend to agree with Polgar, although we came to our epiphanies via different routes. In reflecting on the CIA's presence in Vietnam, I cannot come up with one positive effect that our being there had on the Vietnamese people. Twenty-five years later, I still feel that we betrayed the South Vietnamese, but my opinion about whether we could have won the war has changed. If winning meant keeping the NVA out of South Vietnam, we could have done that by staying in Vietnam, but if it meant winning the hearts and minds of the South Vietnamese, we could not have done that.

6. The killing of officers by their soldiers, usually by throwing fragmentation hand grenades into their tents.

7. Larry Engelmann, *Tears Before the Rain: An Oral History of the Fall of South Vietnam* (New York: Oxford University Press, 1990), p. 74.

1

. . . .

PERSPECTIVES ON VIETNAM

My first recollection of the word *Vietnam* is from 1954, during my freshman year in Greenport High School on Long Island, New York. I was reading the *New York Daily News* and saw a headline trumpeting the fall of Dien Bien Phu. People of short stature, the Vietminh, who were wearing conical hats and living in a place called Vietnam, had defeated the French in a major battle.

William J. Carruthers, my history teacher, did not seem to think this was worthy of a headline, and at the time, neither did I. During the next few years, I read occasional news articles about Vietnam, but the mid-1950s were the "Happy Days." The Korean War had ended less than a year before the fall of Dien Bien Phu, and ignoring the situation in Southeast Asia was easy to do.

In July 1962, when I arrived for army basic training at Fort Dix, New Jersey, what had been an abstraction became more real. I did not know the exact location of Vietnam, and the only two Vietnamese names I recognized were Ngo Dinh Diem, president of South Vietnam, and Madame

Nhu, his sister-in-law, notorious for her insensitive comments after the self-immolation of some Buddhist monks and for her jet-setter lifestyle.

SFC John Koun, a drill instructor, welcomed us new recruits with these words: "We are slipping into a big, fat, juicy war in Vietnam, and I may be unfortunate enough to have to take some of you dickheads there with me. Be advised, if you screw up here and end up on the boat going to Vietnam with me, I will save the 'gooks' the trouble of killing you by throwing you off the boat myself."

During the next five years, I continued to hear more about the war as it escalated. At each post, I encountered GIs going to or coming from Vietnam. During the early months, most of them talked about Vietnamese women, how much money could be made on assignments to Vietnam, and how much fun a tour could be. To many of the GIs with whom I spoke, it was not a real war.

While at the army's language school in Monterey, California, from May 1963 to May 1964, I noticed a significant change in the soldiers' attitudes toward Vietnam. They were beginning to see Vietnam as a dangerous assignment that was not so much fun after all. The majority of the soldiers at the school were taking a six-week immersion course in Vietnamese prior to going to Vietnam. There was also a twelve-month course in Vietnamese, and it occurred to me that Sergeant Koun had been right—the war was getting big.

On several occasions, I saw GIs crying in their beers at the noncommissioned officers' club and predicting that they would not survive Vietnam. GIs returning from Vietnam appeared to have been sobered by their experiences, and they spoke of the Vietcong as more than worthy adversaries. The VC were primarily South Vietnamese members of the communist movement.

In November 1964, while I was assigned to the U.S. Army Intelligence School at Fort Holabird, Maryland, we received word of a VC attack on the U.S. air base at Bien Hoa, which was only twelve miles from Saigon. Five Americans were killed, and six B-57s (twin-jet light bombers) were destroyed. Most of the GIs at Holabird were surprised and alarmed. They saw this attack as a major escalation of the war, as well as a harbinger of things to come. For me, a tour in Vietnam now seemed much more likely than it had prior to the attack on Bien Hoa.

As a Russian linguist, I was ordered to Germany for an assignment with the 513th Military Intelligence Group. During my two and a half years in Germany, Vietnam was the main topic of conversation. The war was escalating in quantum leaps, and units in Germany were depleted to meet levies for Vietnam. Then assigned to Bremerhaven, the port from which GIs shipped their cars back to the States, I saw the line of cars waiting for shipment grow longer each day.

I first encountered antiwar sentiment in the military among the GIs in Germany. A couple of friends told me that there was no way they would ever go to Vietnam. They contended that the war was immoral as well as illegal, and they would refuse to go. GIs returning from Vietnam were describing the enemy as "kicking our asses" and not likely to fold anytime soon.

Special Forces Sgt. E-5 Anthony Batastogne, a classmate at the language school in Oberammergau, had just returned from Vietnam and described his experiences there as chaotic. "The longest firefight I was ever in was with our own troops," he said. "We were shooting at each other all day long when one of our guys heard someone yell in English. We yelled back, and the fight was over."

Batastogne described another incident in which his team heloed (arrived by helicopter) into an area where it was to hook up with an ARVN unit: "As we went from the landing zone to the meet point, I saw some guys in black pajamas in the trees. When we hooked up with the ARVN, I asked this captain about the guys we saw. I thought they might have been with the ARVNs. The captain told me they had to be VC."

More memorable to me was his description of an incident during which a suspected VC woman had been tortured by American troops. "We stuck field telephone wires in her box, cranked the handle, and watched her go nuts. She ended up telling us where some VC supposedly were, but when we got there, they ambushed us, and we lost three men."

Batastogne was killed during his second tour in Vietnam. He was my first friend killed in the war. Capt. George Hoffman, one of my bosses in Bremerhaven and a fine young officer, was also killed in Vietnam. He left a wife and two children. William Boone, a young man I had met when he starred on the Bremerhaven American High School football team, was also killed in Vietnam. He was nineteen and much too young to die.

Frankfurt was my last post before being discharged, and I had some guilt feelings about spending five years in the army without having served in Vietnam. I rationalized by telling myself that there was not much demand for a Russian and German linguist in Vietnam. What could I contribute there? In terms of being a real soldier, I was closer to the comic strip character Beetle Bailey than to the World War II hero Audie Murphy, and I felt that I might have been more of a liability than an asset.

Hundreds of Vietnam veterans were processing out of the army with me at Fort Hamilton, New York. Combat Infantry Badges and Bronze Star and Purple Heart ribbons were displayed in abundance on the chests of these young soldiers, and they spoke respectfully of their VC enemies. I never heard one of them use a derogatory term such as "gook," "slant eye," or "slope." It was, "Mr. Charles kicked our asses that day," "Mister Charles is one tough little motherfucker," or "Kicking Mr. Charles's ass ain't gonna happen."

One private first class from the Big Red One (an American infantry division) told me that, at one point, half the men in his company had venereal disease. He also told me how terrified he had been and that getting stoned was the best way to get through it. On the day before I was discharged, some of us were watching the news when the announcer used the term "light to moderate casualties" in characterizing U.S. losses in Vietnam that day. The soldier sitting next to me said, "You never hear them give the numbers. Light to moderate means we got beat up bad."

With those thoughts in mind, I was off to Michigan State University graduate school to pursue a master of arts/teaching in German. There, the antiwar movement was in full bloom. As a returning veteran and a conservative by nature, I was initially offended by the "armpits with eyes" who were running around burning flags and criticizing values that I held dear. I particularly resented their attacks on our GIs. Referring to terrified young kids as baby killers and war criminals was, to me, obscene. This was before the My Lai massacre.[1]

The Tet Offensive of 1968 had a significant impact on my attitude about Vietnam. Up until that point, I thought that we were winning the war and could not believe that what was essentially a guerrilla force was giving America's military might all it could handle. I reflected on what

---

1. On March 16, 1968, American troops entered the hamlet of My Lai in Quang Ngai province, rounded up all the civilians, forced them into a ditch, and began shooting them. Estimates of exactly how many were killed are as high as 500. First Lt. William L. Calley, Jr., was court-martialed for his part in the event and initially sentenced to life in prison. After two appeals, his sentence was reduced to ten years. In 1974, President Nixon pardoned him.

the GIs at Fort Hamilton had said about how tough the VC had been and, for the first time, thought, "We could lose this war."

I never could work up any sympathy for the protesters, but when Vietnam veterans started to join their ranks, I paid a little more attention to what they were saying and became a little less hawkish.

2

. . . .

THE AGENCY

While at Michigan State, I did a lot of substitute teaching in East Lansing junior and senior high schools. The apathy I encountered among the students caused me to rethink my decision to spend the rest of my working life teaching German to high school students.

When a CIA recruiter visited the campus during the fall of 1967, I talked with him and applied for a position. In April 1968, I went to CIA Headquarters in Langley, Virginia, for interviews and was asked if I would be interested in becoming a polygraph examiner. William Osborne, chief of the Interrogation Research Division (IRD), as the Polygraph Division (PD) was then known, made it sound interesting, and I said yes. Having been trained as a case officer while in the army, I had had some exposure to the use of polygraphs, and while in Germany, I was a close friend of my unit's polygraph examiner. My impression was that the work would be interesting, and I was amenable to Osborne's suggestion.

I had to return to Langley for one more interview before being hired. On the second visit, Michael Tirpac met me in the lobby of the headquarters building. He was from the Office of Security (OS) personnel office and said that I would be brought on staff as a GS-9 ($8,054 a year). After that conversation, a distinguished-looking, white-haired gentleman picked me up and brought me to his office for my first polygraph examination. The test itself went very well, but I found the examiner to be quite abrasive and confrontational. For example, he asked me, "Has drinking ever been a problem for you?"

"I don't drink," I said.

His reaction, in a loud, harsh voice, was, "That's not what I asked you! Do you think there is something wrong with people who take a drink?"

I almost reached the point of telling him that I did not need the job badly enough to put up with him.

At the conclusion of the test, he asked, "Do you have any comments?"

My answer was to tell him that I did not like the way he had conducted the polygraph test. More to the point, I said, "Until I came in here, everyone I met has treated me professionally as well as courteously, and I find it very disconcerting to be spoken to in an abrupt, to the point of being rude, manner."

I could have left it at that, but his response was, "You can't expect everyone to be nice to you."

Not able to let it go, I said, somewhat heatedly, "Until I am rude to you, the very least I expect is courtesy, and it goes up from there."

Somehow, but I do not remember how, I extricated my foot from my mouth. The CIA offered me a job with the OS as a polygraph examiner. Later, I became good friends with the examiner who had tested me. One positive result of my first polygraph examination was my decision never to conduct an examination in the same way.

Before coming on board with the CIA, I returned to East Lansing for final examinations. During finals week, I witnessed the Students for a Democratic Society riots and became even more disgusted with the antiwar protesters. I left East Lansing three days after the riots and, on the following Monday, began working for the CIA.

I was very excited about joining the *Agency* (the term most employees use when referring to the CIA). During my first day on the job, however, I was given a shot of reality that dampened my initial enthusiasm. "Jon Kirk," IRD's training officer, brought me a notice of employment that welcomed me on board as a GS-7 ($6,734). When I saw the entrance grade, I immediately went to Osborne's office and suggested that an error had been made. I told Osborne of my conversation with Tirpac.

"Mike had no right to make you that offer, and there isn't anything we can do about it," Osborne said.

At no point in my initial interviews with either Osborne or Kirk had grade and salary been discussed. Tirpac had been the only person to mention salary, and I had assumed that he was authorized to make the offer.

As soon as I finished with Osborne, I sought out Kirk. He laughed in my face.

"You goddamn fool, we would have given you anything you asked for," he said.

"You son of a bitch!" I thought. "You sat in the polygraph room with me for an hour after my test and never said a word about salary."

I had assumed that Tirpac's offer was a sure thing. I would have accepted a GS-6 at that time, but I had been offered a GS-9. I should have gone to the mat on this one and told them, "No GS-9, no me," but that was not my way.

While having lunch that day, I heard a loud voice say, "John, what are you doing here?"

The person asking the question was "Larry Cook." I had served in the army with Cook in Germany, knew him very well, and could not believe that he was working with the CIA. Cook, who had serious drinking, financial, and gambling problems, was a foul ball. I had caught him stealing money from the office coffee fund and, on many occasions, had bought him meals because he was broke. More to the point, I could not believe that he had survived a background investigation and polygraph test. Suddenly, the CIA was not as elite as I had thought it to be.

Before beginning my polygraph training, I had to take the week-long "Introduction to the CIA" course, during which the function of each of the Agency's four directorates was explained: the Directorate of Plans (or Clandestine Services), the Directorate of Intelligence, the Directorate of Science and Technology, and the Directorate of Support.

During the section on the Directorate of Plans, we were asked to review a case in which a KGB officer had defected in Berlin and decide whether the man was a legitimate defector. When I read the handout we were given on the case, I noticed that there was no mention of a polygraph test. The man had defected over a year ago, and I was certain he would have been polygraphed.

"How did he do on his polygraph test?" I asked the woman leading the discussion of the case.

"That really doesn't matter, because they are trained to beat the polygraph," she answered.

"Was he tested?"

"I'll check, but it really isn't important," she reiterated.[1]

That an instructor lacked such knowledge bothered me, but her attitude about polygraph testing bothered me even more. It was something I would get used to in my dealings with the clandestine services.

I was the first new CIA employee without any previous polygraph experience hired by IRD. IRD's policy had been to recruit only trained examiners or OS officers who requested IRD assignments and were trained in-house. After five weeks of training, I went "on-line" and, for the next thirty-one years, was a toiler in the OS vineyards of truth and justice.

No aspect of the CIA's security process is more controversial than polygraph testing. How does it work? Is it art or science? How valid is the process? How reliable is it? Can people beat it?

The following is a brief description of the mechanics of a polygraph test. The polygraph instrument itself is called "the box." Three measurements are taken during a polygraph test: (1) rate of respiration, (2) heart rate, and (3) electrodermal conductivity. Five attachments are required. Two pneumograph tubes are put around the upper and lower chest to measure the subject's rate of respiration, a blood pressure cuff is wrapped around the upper left arm to measure the subject's heart rate, and two finger plates are attached to the tips of two fingers to measure sweat gland (electrodermal) activity. The measurements are recorded on paper, and, at the conclusion of testing, the charts produced are scored and a decision rendered. The decision can take three forms:

1. "No deception indicated," meaning that there is no polygraphic evidence that the subject practiced deception.
2. "Deception indicated," meaning that there is polygraphic evidence that the subject was not truthful.

---

1. It turned out that the defector had been tested and had passed the test, and he proved to be a great source of information on KGB operations in West Germany.

3. "Inconclusive," meaning that readable charts could not be obtained, and a decision could not be rendered.

Other factors considered in determining whether an individual's test results are deceptive, nondeceptive, or inconclusive are the subject's behavior (verbal and nonverbal) and the facts of the case (whether the story makes sense).

"He failed his polygraph test and didn't get the job [or was fired]" is a comment heard in the CIA when employees discuss polygraph testing, but it is not quite accurate. One can pass a polygraph test, be completely truthful, and not be offered a job. For example, if the person being tested is completely honest but provides disqualifying information, that person has "passed" the test. *Pass* and *fail* are not terms that CIA polygraphers like to use.

In my opinion, polygraph is about 92 percent art and 8 percent science. Robert J. Pickell, the best polygraph examiner I ever worked with, is my Rembrandt of polygraph and concurs with this opinion. Pickell is currently the sheriff in Genesee County, Michigan, prior to which he was a CIA polygraph examiner for five years. Before coming to the CIA, Pickell served for twenty-two years as a police officer and investigator for the district attorney in Flint, Michigan.

The validity and reliability of polygraph testing are very much dependent on the circumstances under which the examination is conducted. For the purpose of resolving a single issue, I believe that polygraph is quite reliable; the more issues to be resolved, however, the less reliable the process. Intangibles and extraneous factors such as language, cultural differences, the ability of the examiner, the chemistry or interaction between the subject and the examiner, and the emotional state of the subject all impact validity and reliability. The fact that intangibles cannot be quantified or scientifically measured challenges the claim that polygraph is a science. I do not believe that it is possible to put a percentage on the reliability of polygraph testing, but under optimal conditions, it is very reliable. I have caught enough liars to know that polygraph testing does work, and I have been beaten by enough liars to realize that it is far from perfect.

So much of the negative perception by CIA personnel as well as the general public about polygraph testing is, in my opinion, due to the fact that a very personal experience (the polygraph examination) has been depersonalized in the guise of making the process appear to be more objective and scientific. But based on my observations of hundreds of CIA examiners conducting thousands of polygraph examinations and my own experience conducting approximately 6,000 examinations, I have concluded that polygraph testing works more often than not and that CIA polygraph examiners, as a group, are the best trained, most carefully recruited, and most closely supervised of all polygraph examiners utilized by the U.S. government.

Upon completion of training in August 1968, I spent the next eight months testing prospective employees. Except when taking training courses, I would test two applicants each day.

In February 1969, I was sent to "the Farm," the CIA's covert training facility, to take the Operations Familiarization (Ops Fam) course. The course was designed to familiarize newcomers with how the Directorate of Plans conducted its clandestine operations and was an abbreviated version of the Field Operations Intelligence course I had taken at Fort Holabird in 1964–1965.

Upon my completion of Ops Fam, Osborne told me that I would be going on a training trip in April. A senior examiner would take me to several foreign cities, where he would supervise me as I interacted with case officers and tested their assets.

Apparently, I did well. On the day I returned from the trip, I was asked if I would be willing to go to Latin America the following Monday. This would be the first of what would turn out to be more than 100 foreign temporary duty assignments (TDYs).

Being the only single guy in the office and wanting to travel, I was almost constantly on the road for the next two years. The shortest trip I took was one week; the longest, seventy days. As a GS-7 and then GS-8, money was a little tight, and the travel was a great way to save money. I was living on my per diem and rarely had to cash a check. For the most part, the hospitality I encountered during these trips was outstanding, and I was loving life. Among those trips, two stand out: a five-week TDY to Laos in May and June 1969, and a seventy-day TDY to Latin America in the summer of 1970.

As little as I knew about Vietnam in 1969, I knew even less about Laos. There was nothing in the media (at least the media I was reading and viewing) about Laos. I knew that IRD had an examiner there and that his primary responsibility was conducting polygraph tests on the road-watch teams the CIA was using to monitor NVA traffic on the Ho Chi Minh Trail. I was uninformed regarding the political significance of Laos and had no geographical knowledge of the country. Two Special Forces sergeants with whom I attended language school told me that they had had extensive combat experience in Laos, so I knew that Americans were being shot at, but I had no grasp of the extent of American involvement there.

Since I had never been to the Far East, when "John Bauer," chief of covert operations in IRD, asked me if I would be interested in a TDY to Laos, I jumped at the chance.

Bangkok, Thailand, was my first stop en route. I landed at Don Muang airport shortly after midnight, and as I walked from the plane to the arrival lounge, I thought I was walking through a steam bath. The thermometer over the entrance to the lounge registered 111 degrees, and by the time I cleared customs and immigration, I was sweating profusely.

"Rob Meehan," the number-two security officer in Bangkok, was waiting for me. He was the perfect ending to what had been a very long day. He took me to the Oriental Hotel, one of the most beautiful hotels I have ever seen, got me settled in, and could not have been more hospitable.

"I'll pick you up tomorrow morning, take you to the office, and give you a briefing on Laos. Have a good night." And with that, he was off.

"Laos is the Agency's Wild West," was the way Meehan began the briefing. "The guys up there aren't Boy Scouts but are great to work with. They work hard and play even harder. Don't go up there and play cop/security officer. Just do your job, and you'll be fine."

That was it. After the briefing, Meehan took me to his home to have lunch with his wife, Agnes, and their three children. He also arranged for my flight to Udorn the next day. "Rob Creed," the examiner assigned to Laos, would meet me there. Kay, Rob's wife, was waiting for me when I got off the plane.

"Hi, John. I'm Kay. It's good to have you here. Rob's in Vientiane and wants you to wait here. He'll be back tomorrow. You can stay at our house tonight."

Thus a friendship began that is still ongoing. But waiting in the Creed house that night was not to be.

When Kay took me to meet the chief of support, "Bob Perry," he said,

"Rob wants John in Vientiane right now. I already laid on a plane. Get him down there."

Kay tried to dissuade Perry, but to no avail. Without further ado, she took me to the flight line, where a Pilatus Porter, a short takeoff and landing aircraft, was waiting. Our flight from Udorn to Vientiane lasted about twenty minutes, and we arrived at about 6:30 P.M. I had assumed that Rob would be there to meet me, but there was no one. When I went into the terminal, there were a few locals cleaning up and a Thai who noticed the confused look on my face. When I told him that Mr. Creed was supposed to meet me, he made a call, and about twenty minutes later, "Larry Michaels," the CIA's security officer in Vientiane, showed up.

"John, I'm really sorry. We didn't know you were coming. Rob is working and will get together with you tomorrow morning."

Michaels then took me to a place called the TV House. This was a facility in downtown Vientiane where TDYers were put up.

"I told Kay to have you stay at our house last night, and I'm sorry for the inconvenience," were Rob's first words to me the next morning.

We went to breakfast, exchanged office gossip, and took another flight back to Udorn. Back in Udorn, Rob introduced me to the base personnel, checked out an instrument for me to use, went over the type of test I would be doing, and told me that I would be working in Long Tieng, a focal point of road-watch team activity. The next morning, I took a Porter flight into Long Tieng and began what I consider the most exciting and interesting five weeks of my CIA career.

"Jim ('Stonewall') Forrest" was waiting for me when I got off the plane. Stonewall was a paramilitary officer assigned to the CIA's Special Operations Division and had been assigned to Laos after completing a tour in Vietnam. He was a true, down-home, good old southern boy from Alabama and one of the finest people I have ever met, in or out of the CIA.

"Hey, John, Rob told me you were coming. I'm Jim Forrest. It's good to meet you." As we walked across the tarmac, Stonewall commented, "John, you really need a haircut."

I didn't think I did, but I didn't mind getting one. At the end of the runway, an old Chinese had a chair, a set of clippers, and a pair of scissors. When he finished with me, I could comb what was left of my hair with a washcloth.

Tom Clines was the chief of base and greeted me warmly when Stonewall brought me into his office. "We've got a lot of guys to test, and any help you can give us will be appreciated."

Stonewall introduced me to "Vic Scanlan," Clines's deputy, and "Jerry Bond," his chief of support. Bond would coordinate my test schedule and arrange for any travel I had to do.

Testing began the very next day. My first subject was the leader of a road-watch team that had just returned from a mission. I am not sure what I expected, but the best words I can use to describe this subject are primitive and unsophisticated. I had an excellent interpreter, but communication was in very simple terms. The poor man had absolutely no understanding of what a lie detector was all about and looked at the instrument in wide-eyed wonder.

Prior to actually running the test, I reviewed the questions I would ask him. I asked him if he and his team had traveled to the Ho Chi Minh Trail, if they had reported seeing vehicles they had not seen, or if they had claimed to see NVA soldiers they had not seen. He claimed that he and his team had traveled to the trail, staying in the area for five days, and had not reported seeing vehicles or enemy soldiers they had not seen.

But as soon as I inflated the blood pressure cuff and the interpreter began asking the test questions, the subject did a 180-degree turn.

"Did you and your team travel to the trail?"

The subject answered, "No."

"Did you report seeing vehicles you did not see?"

The subject answered, "Yes."

"Did you report seeing enemy troops you did not see?"

The subject answered, "Yes."

I immediately stopped the test and asked the interpreter, "What's he saying?"

"Mr. John, he saying he didn't do mission," he said. "He say if he and his men did mission they all get killed."

Variations on this scenario would occur with each test. Some road watchers did attempt to do the missions but did not stay on site as long as they claimed. Almost all of them admitted to falsely reporting sightings of vehicles or enemy troops. The strangest aspect of these tests was that in the pretest, they all claimed to have done the mission as ordered, but once the test began, they reversed their stories. As I was to learn, many of the road-watch teams would get their assignments, venture out a few miles from Long Tieng and hole up for the length of the mission, and then report that they had done the mission.

There were two sites where I conducted tests: Long Tieng and the interrogation center at Pha Khao. On days when I worked at Pha Khao, Stonewall and I would take a fifteen-minute Porter flight just over the mountain to the site.

The cast of characters at Long Tieng was something the likes of which I had never seen. They were a composite of Robin Hood's merry men, Hogan's Heroes, the A-Team, the Magnificent Seven, and the Dirty Dozen. Most were contract employees who had been hired to work in Laos. Many were former Special Forces sergeants, and some were former smoke jumpers who had worked for the U.S. Forest Service. All were adventurers.

Among them, none was more notorious than "Tony Poe." "Mr. Tony," as he was known to the Lao and the Meo and Hmong tribesmen, had been in Laos since the early 1960s and had gone completely native. He had been a virtual warlord in Nam Yu, in northwestern Laos, and was known for paying his troops a bounty for proof of having killed enemy soldiers. The proof he accepted was the ears from the corpses.

I met Tony once during my TDY and on another occasion when I traveled on assignment from Saigon to Laos. He was drunk and a little out of control on both occasions. Between the first and second occasion, I asked some of the guys at Long Tieng about him. The consensus was that in his early days in Laos, he had been a brave and valuable asset, but obnoxious. He had since outlived his usefulness and was now more a liability than an asset. When I saw him in Udorn in late 1972, he impressed me as being a burned out, almost pathetic figure, and he seemed well aware that he was an embarrassment to the CIA.

At Long Tieng, the days seemed to just run together. There was a real sense of camaraderie, but also a sense of futility. Tom Clines once commented to me, "These guys [the road watchers] are such a gentle people. They aren't warriors, and there isn't much we can do to change that. Trying to turn them into combat soldiers is a mistake. We can monitor the trail, blow up a few trucks, and even capture an NVA soldier once in awhile. B-52s aren't going to get it done. If we are serious about stopping traffic on the trail, American ground troops are going to have to do it, and that ain't going to happen as long as [Ambassador William H.] Sullivan keeps American ground troops out of Laos."

Gentle though the road watchers might be, they were capable of violence. They absolutely hated the Thais, and the feeling was mutual. Thai forces were working with the road-watch teams, and I was in Long Tieng when a team departed with a Thai lieutenant in charge. The next day they returned, claiming that they had had to abort the mission because they had been ambushed. The only casualty was the Thai. He had several bullets in his back.

"Sullivan wants us to adhere to the Geneva Accords while the North Vietnamese violate them every day. We [the CIA] don't want the [U.S.] Army stealing our thunder, but if the NVA ever get serious, they'll go through us like a hot knife through butter. Vang Pao [the Hmong general and leader of the pro-American forces] is one very brave and tough little fucker, but there is no way he and his army can take on the NVA." Every day in Long Tieng, I would hear variations on these comments.

Getting shot at was a common occurrence for many of the men at Long Tieng, and despite Ambassador Sullivan's directives to the contrary, going armed was de rigueur. I remember Clines giving a briefing in which he said, "You guys know what you are facing out there. There is no way I am going to tell you not to carry weapons."

The war in Laos was referred to as the "Secret War." Laos was one of the most heavily bombed countries in the world, and more bombs were dropped on Laos than were dropped on Germany during World War II. Yet the American people were totally unaware. Much of this, I thought at the time, was due to the fact that very few American troops were being killed in Laos, and those that were, were reported as being killed in Vietnam.

On the three occasions I went into Vientiane, I was advised to stay away from the embassy. "The ambassador is a little nervous about having up-country people in the embassy where they might run into a reporter."

When I ran into "Don Herring," the number-two security officer in Vientiane, at the TV House, he noticed that I had a camera around my neck and reminded me that I should not be taking pictures up at Long Tieng. I had been, but no one up there had seemed to mind.

Early on in my stay in Long Tieng, a *New York Times* reporter showed up and tried to interview Vic Scanlan. I was in the dining room when one of the team advisers said, "Some guy who says he is a reporter for the *New York Times* is trying to interview Vic down on the landing strip."

I do not know how they got the reporter out of Long Tieng, but I do know that he made a lot of people nervous.

Supposedly, there were no American combat troops in Laos, but there were some U.S. Air Force personnel. They wore civilian clothes and kept pretty much to themselves, but their presence was an open secret. I did meet one U.S. Army officer in Long Tieng. He was the only U.S. soldier I saw in uniform while in Laos.

He introduced himself to me in the bar one night. "I'm Captain Nelson. I hear you're the polygraph guy. I have a guy at Pha Khao that I would like you to test when we finish debriefing him. Do you think you can do it?"

I told him that I was available anytime he wanted me to do the test. Over the next few weeks, we ran into each other occasionally and came to be casual friends. He was a West Point graduate, clean-cut, and a very nice guy. The test he wanted me to do never came about, and shortly after I left Laos, he was killed in a plane crash. There were several bullet holes in his body, but exploding ammunition on the plane may have caused them.

U.S. military involvement in Laos was an open secret, but there was nothing secret about Laotian officials' involvement in drug trafficking. Laos, Thailand, and Burma were the countries of the Golden Triangle, one of the world's main sources of raw opium, and opium was Laos' only export. Growing poppies, processing the seeds into opium, and trafficking the opium were a way of life for the Laotian tribes. Rumors about CIA involvement in or support for Vang Pao's involvement in drug trafficking were rampant. Supposedly, there was a large opium processing plant near Vang Pao's residence in Long Tieng, but I never saw it. However, on many occasions, I did see old men smoking opium pipes.

On another occasion, I was in the operations center when "Frank Olson," one of the team advisers, yelled, "Hey guys, get a load of this!"

He then showed us a message he had just received from his team that was out on a mission: "Sir, please use some of ops funds to buy opium. We are addicted to near dead."

Whether Vang Pao was directly involved in the drug trade, I haven't a clue. Based on what I saw and heard during my tenure in Laos, my assumption is that the CIA was aware of the drug problem but impotent to do anything about the involvement of our Laotian allies.

Long Tieng was the closest I had ever been to a war zone. It was exciting seeing air force helicopters take off to rescue downed pilots or wounded troops, the road-watch teams depart on missions, and the Ravens (Hmong who flew "back seat" in U.S. 7th Air Force planes to help the American forward air controllers coordinate strikes) take off. These events were observed from the periphery and had little impact on me. Two incidents did occur, however, that gave me a more personal view of what war was all about.

"Bob Dorn" was the medic at Long Tieng, and on most days when I was there, I would sit with him at lunch. We were eating lunch when the air operations officer (air ops) called from down on the landing strip.

"Bob, we've got a couple of pretty badly shot up kids down here. Can you come down?"

"Be right there," was his answer. I asked Dorn if I could accompany him, and he said, "Let's go."

When we got down to the flight line, there were two bodies on pallets, lying next to a Porter. Neither of the wounded could have been more than sixteen years old. They had been on patrol, triggered a mine, and had their legs nearly blown off. The foot of one of them was completely gone. I could see the thighbone of the other, and the legs of both boys were like ground beef mixed in with the camouflage of their fatigue trousers.

Neither boy made a sound. They didn't appear to be glassy eyed or in shock, and I asked, "Bob, are you going to give them morphine?"

"They don't need it," he answered. The Laotians had a reputation for being stoic, but I found this situation hard to believe.

Dorn stopped the bleeding and prepared them to be medevaced. I later learned that both had survived, albeit without functioning legs. Seeing those wounded boys evoked a feeling of nausea and a sense of sadness. At sixteen, I had been a kid enjoying life. The two boys I had just seen had no life.

The second incident evoked excitement and fear. Long Tieng was not only Vang Pao's headquarters, it was also the home of "Union of Lao Races," the radio station used to broadcast Vang Pao's messages to the Lao people. I was in the operations room when Tom Clines and Vic Scanlan came in and made an announcement: "We just intercepted a PL [Pathet Lao] radio message saying they are going to hit the radio station tonight."

Most of the guys in the room seemed nonplussed by Clines's announcement, but I felt a twinge of fear. Stonewall pulled me aside and told me to look for him when the attack started. "Find me and stay with me, and you'll be okay," were his words to me. A little later, he came to my room and gave me a Colt Python pistol. "Just in case, John," he told me. That was the first time as a CIA officer that I carried a gun.

That night, a bunch of us gathered in the main office. A communications technician and a support officer were playing "quick draw," and the nervous tension was thick as a London fog.

Trying to be unobtrusive, I was sitting at a desk when Jerry Bond stuck a KA-Bar knife (a World War II marine combat knife similar to a Bowie knife) under my chin and said, "What would you do if someone did this to you?"

With the point of the knife pricking my chin and without thinking, I took the Python from under my fatigue jacket, stuck it under his chin, and said, "Blow his fucking head off."

The blood drained from Bond's face, and he said, "John, I'm just kidding. Don't fuck around with that thing."

Never before had I pointed a gun at anyone. Twice, in the army, I had had to carry a gun while guarding prisoners, but on neither of those occasions did I actually point the gun I was carrying.

"Paul Ingalls" was one of the really strange people I met in the CIA. He was assigned to Long Tieng, and my impression of him was that he was, in modern parlance, a Rambo wannabe. He was the butt of many jokes, and on one occasion, he was walking down to the airstrip when "Jack Arden," a team adviser, shot him in the butt with a BB gun.

Stonewall, Ingalls, and I were in Pha Khao when air ops radioed to tell us that clouds were moving in and that if we did not leave within the next half hour, we would have to spend the night there. I packed up the equipment, and Stonewall told Ingalls that a plane would be there in fifteen minutes to pick us up. Ingalls told Stonewall not to worry about it, because they would send another plane for him. Stonewall tried to convince Ingalls to come with us, but Ingalls would not listen. Stonewall and I left. By the time we got to Long Tieng, heavy clouds had closed in, and it was pouring rain.

As we checked in with air ops, we could hear Ingalls screaming over the radio, "Goddamn it! Get a plane over here. I'm not going to spend the night here!"

"Toby Mack," the number-two air ops (and former offensive lineman for Ole Miss) responded by turning off the radio.

During the night of the expected attack on the radio station, Ingalls paced around like an expectant father. At one point, he announced that he was going to go out and check the perimeter. No one paid any attention to him, but when he came back less than ten minutes later looking as though he had been in a fight with a leopard, he got some attention. He had tangled himself up in the concertina wire near one of the perimeter fences and sustained a lot of superficial cuts. No one said a word.

Not wanting to be alone should an attack take place, I stuck around until 3 A.M. and then went back to my room. I was awakened by the sound of an M-2 carbine being emptied into the overhang of the porch in front of my room. It scared the daylights out of me but turned out to be "Don Spruiel," one of the commo[2] guys. As he was shooting, he was yelling, "It's all over! It's all over!" The alert status had been canceled; the attack never materialized.

For the next few days I ran tests, but about a week later, Stonewall sat down next to me while I was eating dinner and said, "Look, John, this place is going down the tubes, and there isn't much point in staying here. No one is going to think any less of you for leaving, and if I were you, I'd do it."

I had been thinking along the same lines, but hearing Stonewall's words convinced me that it was time to go.

Jerry Bond arranged for a flight to Vientiane, where I caught another plane to Udorn. After briefing Rob Creed, I caught the 50 Kip[3] to Bangkok, where I overnighted. The next day, I caught a Pan Am flight back to Washington.

Laos was my first exposure to the Far East, and I enjoyed it. The CIA people with whom I worked in Laos turned out to be some of the best I would meet over the course of my career, and the experiences I had in Laos proved useful in Vietnam.

I spent most of that summer in Latin and South America, and in the fall, IRD sent me to the CIA's interrogation course. The course lasted for three weeks—one week in headquarters, one week at the Farm, and a week in Miami, debriefing Cuban refugees. Most of November, including

2. Shorthand for telecommunications.
3. The C-46 airplane that traveled between Udorn and Bangkok.

Thanksgiving, was spent in Europe, but I got to spend all of December at home.

January 1970 was a busy month. I was on the last leg of a three-week trip when I received a cable asking me to make one more stop. I arrived in country on a Friday afternoon and called the office to let them know I had arrived. "Harry Lutz," the station's finance officer, told me to just relax until Monday morning and invited me to a cookout at his house on Sunday.

"Hi, I'm Lee," a petite, beautiful woman dressed in a yellow pantsuit said. Lee was Leonor Estela Tijerina. Eight months later, almost to the day, she became Leonor Sullivan. Lee had been recruited by the CIA as part of a program that sought out Spanish-speaking women to take positions as secretaries in Spanish-speaking countries.

Between January and July, I managed to get down to see her on two occasions. In early July, we decided to get married at the end of the TDY. I was scheduled to finish the TDY in the Caribbean, and we thought we could combine business with pleasure by honeymooning after my last stop. On August 29, 1970, we were married. After doing my last test, we left for Jamaica for a week's honeymoon. Of all the TDYs I have been on, that one was the best. Lee had to return to the station after the honeymoon to wait for her replacement. I returned to headquarters, and just before Thanksgiving, Lee joined me.

At the time I joined the Agency, I had no idea I would be going to Vietnam, nor did I know the extent of the CIA's involvement there. It did not take long to find out that the CIA's role in Vietnam was dramatically expanding as the military's role shrank. Many of the people I was testing were being hired for the express purpose of going to Vietnam, and many case officers with whom I worked on my overseas trips were telling me that their next assignments would be Vietnam. IRD had assigned two polygraph examiners to Vietnam, where they were kept busy.

Among the CIA population in general, and the Directorate of Plans officers in particular, Vietnam was not an assignment of choice and, if possible, was to be avoided. This idea began to change, however, when Ted Shackley took over as chief of station in Saigon in December 1968. Shackley was a rising star in the CIA, and some people wanted to hitch a ride on his rocket. Director of Central Intelligence (DCI) Richard Helms had handpicked Shackley to run the show in Vietnam. He had carte blanche to manage the transfer of the war from the military to civilians, and he began to build what would become the largest station in the world.

No one in the CIA with whom I spoke considered Vietnam a dangerous assignment. Case officers (CIA officers who recruit and handle indigenous agents) with whom I worked in Europe and Latin America and who had not been to Vietnam spoke of it as a career dead end and did not want to be assigned there. Many case officers who had been to Vietnam felt that those tours had done nothing for them professionally and had been a waste of time. While they were in Vietnam, officers (other than those who had been assigned to East Asia Division before going to Vietnam) were temporarily out of sight, out of mind, and out of the loop in terms of being able to position themselves for advancement in their home divisions.

"How would you and Lee like to go to Vietnam? Bo Mooney's tour is up in April, and we need to find a replacement for him." On a cold morning in early December 1970, Bill Osborne's question caught me completely by surprise.

I told Osborne that I would talk it over with Lee and get back to him. Although apprehensive, Lee was willing to accept the assignment, and the next day, I told Osborne that we would go. He said that we would be leaving in April and added that I would get a promotion to GS-10 before I left. Then I heard nothing further about the assignment until mid-January. I had no real grasp of how the CIA's Office of Personnel functions (and to this day, I still don't), but I have concluded that the most guarded secrets in the CIA are personnel policies, because no one seems to know what they are.

Opinion on whether the United States was winning the war was mixed. "Bo Mooney," my predecessor in Vietnam, was the only person who actually said that we were winning. He came home for Christmas in 1970 and stopped by the office. By that time, I had already been named to replace him, and I talked to him about the situation.

"John, it's really looking good, and you and Lee will love it there," was the way he put it.

Most of those with whom I spoke were less sanguine. "I don't think we can win the war, but at this point, we aren't losing it," seemed to sum up their comments.

Rarely, during those first three years with the CIA, had I given any thought to an assignment in Vietnam. I felt that I was too junior an examiner to be considered, and had had no experience in Asia (except for my TDY to Laos). I was almost constantly on the road and thought that I would be more useful in headquarters than in Vietnam.

3

. . . .

ON THE ROAD TO SAIGON

In mid-January 1971, I received a call from an officer in East Asia (EA) Division's Office of Personnel, which was responsible for processing assignees to Vietnam. The person with whom I spoke seemed a bit upset that I had not started my processing and suggested that I begin forthwith.

"Just tell me what I have to do, and I will get to it," I said. I then asked about Lee's processing.

"We have no knowledge of Mrs. Sullivan going to Vietnam and are processing your assignment as an unaccompanied tour," was the disturbing answer.

Things went downhill from there. I refused to begin processing until Lee was approved to go. Both EA Personnel and OS management became irritated with me, and processing stalled.

"Harry West," the number-three man in OS, called me in for a discussion and told me that I would be letting the office down and passing up a good opportunity if I did not take the assignment.

"If they had asked if I wanted to go on an unaccompanied tour, I would have told them I wouldn't go without my wife," I said. "But they didn't. Bill Osborne asked me if Lee and I would like to go. It's a matter of principle."

West's answer is one that I will never forget: "I've seen a lot of people around here hurt their careers over matters of principle."

"No Lee, no me," I reiterated.

I am not a confrontational person, and this response was out of character. It seemed to work, however, but it turned out to be another case of winning the battle but losing the war. Some OS people never forgot that I had made waves, and they thought I might not be a team player.

Lee and I were called into EA Personnel and told by a rather nasty woman that if Lee wanted to accompany me, she would have to resign from the Agency and go to Saigon on a contract basis, even though a job was already lined up for her. In addition, she would have to take a pay cut and could not be guaranteed a job when we returned from Vietnam. The woman seemed to take some pleasure in telling us this, and my inclination was to tell her to take the assignment and shove it. Lee did resign, but under protest, and we began processing.

A major part of that processing was Vietnam Orientation (VNO), a two-week course designed to familiarize assignees with the situation in Vietnam and what they could expect to encounter. One week was spent at headquarters and one week at the Farm.

During our week at headquarters, we were briefed on the political situation, the military aspects of the war, the economy, the living conditions, and other topics related to service in Vietnam. Employees who had served in Vietnam and others who were back on leave spoke to us and offered much useful information. Course content was presented via the "accentuate the positive—eliminate the negative" approach. No negative aspects of the war were included in the curriculum. The positives— making money and creature comforts—were stressed, whereas the negatives—the failure of Vietnamization[1] and the deteriorating military situation—were omitted.

One of the VNO lecturers said that Lam Son 719 (an ARVN incursion into Laos in February 1971) had shown that the ARVN was capable of launching an offensive outside of South Vietnam and had put the fear of

---

1. *Vietnamization* was a term coined by Secretary of Defense Melvin Laird and referred to the Nixon policy of turning the war over to the South Vietnamese.

being invaded into the NVA. At the time, however, the ARVN had been routed from Laos. My take from what I had been reading in the *Washington Post* and seeing on the news was that the ARVN had been mauled, and the debacle was a repudiation of Vietnamization.

Of the people who spoke to us during the course, Donald P. Gregg stood out. He was the regional officer in charge (ROIC) in MR/3 and provided us with an assessment of the situation that contrasted with what we had been hearing from the VNO instructors. He told us that he did not know where the war was going and that he saw no reason for optimism. I later worked with Gregg in Vietnam and considered him to be the best ROIC I was associated with during my four years there.

During the headquarters phase of the course, I read a quote from Gen. David M. Shoup, Medal of Honor winner, U.S. Marine Corps commandant from 1960 to 1963, and a harsh critic of the military buildup in Southeast Asia. He strongly suggested that the United States not get involved in a ground war in Indochina, as it was not winnable. When I mentioned this quotation in class, the moderator said, "It is interesting how after people retire, they suddenly become experts." I thought this was somewhat of a nonsequitur and, in retrospect, feel guilty about letting it pass.

Our week at the Farm was more fun than anything else. Ever since my five weeks of training there in 1969, I tried to return whenever possible. I loved the place and had put on fifteen pounds there in 1969. The food was great and much too plentiful.

"Glen Talley," a former marine lieutenant who had been severely wounded at Khe Sanh (site of the biggest battle of the Vietnam War), was also taking the course. He told us that he had survived at Khe Sanh by playing dead and recalled North Vietnamese troops walking among the bodies and killing anyone who was still alive. Talley put on a show when we were firing the "grease guns" (U.S. Army M-4 submachine guns). He could make a small matchbox jump from side to side without hitting it.

By the time we finished VNO, I had some reservations about who was winning the war. Based mainly on Don Gregg's comments and the disparity between media accounts of Lam Son 719 and what we had been told in VNO, I thought that we were in a stalemate but could win.

Three days before we were to leave for Vietnam, I still had not been promoted. I went into Osborne's office and reminded him of the promotion to GS-10 that he had promised.

"Excuse me, John. I'll be right back," he said.

Ten minutes later, he came back and handed me a promotion notification. What Osborne had failed to tell me was that I could not go to Vietnam unless I were promoted to GS-10. The position I was taking was that of a GS-13 and could not be filled by anyone at a grade lower than GS-10. Osborne had made it appear that he was doing me a favor.

I had one final protocol to take care of before leaving—my meeting with the director of security, Howard Osborne (no relation to Bill Osborne). I had never met Osborne but knew him by sight. He was a large and imposing man with a leonine head, and he had the reputation of being hard-nosed. My meeting was scheduled for 10:30 A.M. At about 9:00, I was on the fourth floor, where his office was located, when one of his assistants saw me. "John, Mr. Osborne has an appointment at 10:30. Could you see him now?" the assistant asked.

Osborne did not recognize me. I had the impression that he did not even know that I was a polygraph examiner, and he apparently did not know that I was taking Lee with me.

"John, we send only our best people overseas. This is a great opportunity for you. Enjoy!" And that was all he said.

On April 2, 1971, we left for New York, where we stopped to visit my brother Bill before leaving for San Francisco. While I was there, I called a former student I had taught in high school. I told him that I was en route to Vietnam and would like to stop in and say hello to his parents.

"Louie [his younger brother] was killed last year in Vietnam, and Mom hasn't gotten over it. John, if you do stop in, don't mention Vietnam," he said.

I remembered Louie very well, and the news saddened me. I did not go to see his parents.

Our flight to Saigon was not called the "red-eye special" for nothing. Early on the morning of April 9, 1971, we were up and away for our grand adventure. The plane landed at 10:30 the following day on the sun-drenched tarmac of Saigon's Tan Son Nhut Air Base. That flight was one of the most uncomfortable I have ever taken, perhaps by design, so that any destination would look good to the bleary-eyed passengers.

CIA tradition, if not protocol, dictated that the officer in place meet his or her replacement at the airport. When Lee and I descended from the plane, Bo Mooney was waiting at the foot of the stairs. As we made our way from the plane to the terminal, a jeep with three Vietnamese military policemen and a .50-caliber machine gun mounted on a tripod was traversing the runway. That sight reminded me that we were entering a war zone.

Cong Ly, the street leading into Saigon from the airport, was jammed with traffic—mopeds, bicycles, minicabs, military vehicles, and cyclos (three-wheeled motorbikes that served as taxis). When I recall my first impression of the capital of South Vietnam, Neil Diamond's song "Beautiful Noise" comes to mind. Saigon was bustling, vibrant, and, at least at first glance, not war torn.

The first stop for almost every CIA officer arriving in Vietnam was the Duc Hotel, located at 14 Tran Qui Cap and the corner of Cong Ly. The CIA leased and operated the five-story hotel as a residence for new arrivals until they completed in-country processing and received their assignments.

"John, welcome to Vietnam!" Getting out of the car in front of the Duc, I saw "Paul Daly," a young man I had tested when he first came on duty.

He looked weather-beaten, dressed in dusty camouflage fatigues, jungle boots, and a floppy bush hat. Daly said that he was a provincial reconnaissance unit (PRU) adviser in Quang Ngai province in MR/1. He was on his way to Tan Son Nhut to catch a flight up-country, so we did not have much time to talk. I introduced him to Lee, and he asked me to come up to Quang Ngai, as he had some work for me.

In the lobby of the hotel, we ran into Harry Lutz, chief of support in MR/4, and someone with whom Lee and I had previously worked. After cursory greetings, Lutz told me that MR/4 had a real backlog of cases and asked me to fit a trip there into my schedule as soon as possible.

Lee and I checked into the hotel at about 11:00. We were eager to begin processing, and after we had lunch in the Duc restaurant, a chauffeur drove us to the embassy. My first stop was to check in with my office chief, "Jack Gordon." I had previously met Gordon at headquarters and had taken an instant liking to him. He was one of the best bosses I had at the CIA. Gordon was over six feet tall and occipitally bald. He had a basso profundo voice and was in perpetual motion. I walk fast, but compared with Gordon, I crawl. He was also incorruptible and, in my mind, incapable of telling a lie.

Gordon's office was in the Norodom Complex, an annex adjacent to the embassy. He extended a warm greeting to Lee and me and introduced us to the rest of the personnel. His deputy was another Jack—"Jack Dorne," who was a Red Skelton look-alike and very laid back. In addition to Bo Mooney, "Mel Heath" (the other examiner), and two secretaries, the staff included security officers "Mark Verity," "Tom Wirth," "Terry Reese," "Phil Durr," and "Lee Borne," who were responsible for providing personal protection for the chief of station, as well as physical and technical support for the station and its personnel.

On Saturday, which was a half workday in Saigon, Lee and I went to our respective offices, and Bo took me around to meet people. I discovered that I already knew a number of the people from other stations. Six of those I met that morning I had previously met in Latin America.

James E. Parker, a former CIA staff employee, wrote a book titled *Code Name MULE*, in which he refers to himself as an FNG (fucking new guy) and mentions the problems frequently incurred by FNGs. Because mine was a familiar face to many people there, being an FNG was not a problem. Also, as Lee's husband, I had a certain amount of cachet, because she had also worked with some of the people I was meeting.

Another reason why I was welcomed, at least outwardly, was that case officers needed my services. Their assets (indigenous agents) had to be polygraphed in order to be authenticated, and they did not want to get on the wrong side of anyone who would have an impact on this process.

Sunday was the day for socializing at the Duc. The swimming pool on the roof, a gathering place for station personnel, was half affectionately called the "Bay of Pigs." Although I considered the term insulting to our female employees, I never heard any of the women mention it. The socializing usually started with brunch and Bloody Marys. After brunch, people swam, sunbathed, and socialized for the rest of the day.

Our first Sunday at the Duc did not go very well. Lee and I attended mass, had brunch, and then went out to the pool. We were introduced to a lot of people, and "Lena Romano," a finance officer, introduced us to "Hugh Berry," the chief of support for Saigon Station. Berry was Jack Gordon's boss and, in the station hierarchy, ranked only behind Ted Shackley and "Alan Freeze," the deputy chief of station.

Berry seemed pleased to meet us. He told Lee and me that we would be housed in a villa in Cholon (the Chinese section of Saigon) because the CIA had an operation being run from the villa and wanted someone there at all times.

"I'm not sure that's going to work," I replied. "I'm going to be on the road half the time I'm here, and I don't know if I want Lee alone under those circumstances."

Berry took umbrage and told me that if I did not like it, I could go back home. He further told me that the decision had been made and that was where we would be living.

I took exception to his attitude and riposted brilliantly with, "I found my way in from the airport. I guess I can find my way back."

Romano was shaking her head, and Lee was squeezing my arm. It could have gotten out of hand, but somehow Berry and I disengaged with no more harsh words.

"Olga Alvesa," who had known Lee in Latin America, was also there. After welcoming us, she said, "The VC could take this place [the Duc] anytime they want to. Who's going to stop them, the unarmed Nung guards we have outside?"

Prior to leaving Washington, our friends Jo and Jim Griffin had told us to look up Dana Meigs in Saigon. Dana was Shackley's secretary, and she and Jo were good friends. She was at the pool that day, so Lee and I introduced ourselves. Dana had a distinct southern drawl, bespeaking her Asheville, North Carolina, heritage. She was totally devoted to Shackley—or "Daddy," as she called him—and her only interest outside of work seemed to be her dog.

In the government, as in the private sector, the boss's secretary is often perceived as a real power broker, and Dana was no exception. At times, she was known to rub some people the wrong way, but she could not have been kinder or friendlier to us, and I felt that meeting her was a good counterpoint to my introduction to Berry. Later, when she hosted a party for Sir Robert Thompson, the British insurgency expert who had master-minded the defeat of the communist guerrillas in Malaysia, she invited us.

First thing Monday morning, I told Gordon about my conversation with Berry. He laughed and said that Berry had called him. I was not to worry about it.

That day, Lee and I talked with the station housing officer, "Ray Lomax." He told us that there were several houses available, but Lee and I had talked it over and decided that we wanted to live in the Duc Hotel. With my traveling much of the time and with Lee not driving, it would be practical and less expensive. Lomax was a little surprised but concurred.

By our third day in Vietnam, Lee and I had decided that we were glad to be there, even though Lee cringed every time she heard a loud noise in the street. We liked the people we met, thought the Duc was a great place, knew that we would live well, and felt optimistic about our tour.

During those first days in Vietnam, I also saw people I had tested back at headquarters. Some of their recollections of me were definitely not warm and fuzzy. One of Lee's supervisors in the station's finance office made a point of telling me that I had tested him and that he did not have good memories of the event.

Despite my brief set-to with Berry, Lee and I ended that first week in Saigon believing that we had made the right choice in coming to Vietnam.

In addition to newly assigned CIA officers entering Vietnam, those going home on leave or to Taiwan for family visitations overnighted at the Duc. Many officers coming in from Cambodia for rest and recreation (R&R) also stayed at the Duc.

Located one block from the presidential palace and four blocks from the U.S. embassy, the Duc had about fifty rooms, plus five apartments for permanent residents. Nung (ethnic Chinese) guards stood at the front and rear gates with unloaded weapons. Although far from luxurious, the hotel was comfortable. Besides the restaurant, bar, and swimming pool, the amenities included a small theater, liquor store, and recreation room.

Behind the pool was a room used for playing poker. The poker games were not penny ante. Serious money was won and lost. I once heard of a $3,000 pot, and it was not unusual for $1,000 to be on the table. Gambling was a problem for some of our employees. Perhaps by decree from on high (I never heard), the games suddenly died out.

Except under extraordinary circumstances, only CIA people were allowed in the hotel. On a couple of occasions, confrontations occurred when some of our stalwarts tried to bring in ladies of the evening.

More than 600 officers staffed Saigon Station in the mid-1960s, and by the time Lee and I arrived, that number was down to approximately 400, but it was still the biggest CIA station in the world. Hundreds of officers were constantly coming in and going out of the Duc. On the last Wednesday of each month, an elaborate "hail and farewell" party was held in the Duc dining room. Thanksgiving and Christmas were celebrated at the Duc with great buffets, and although *la vita* at the Duc was not as *dolce* as it was in Rome, it wasn't bad.

The Duc more than met our needs. Lee and I eventually acquired a two-bedroom apartment with a living room, kitchen, and bath. We ate most of our meals in the restaurant. When we entertained, one of the Duc cooks prepared the food, and a couple of the waitresses served it. A dinner party for six, including drinks and labor, cost less than $50. We did hire a maid to clean the apartment and do our laundry, but we lived simply compared with most of our colleagues. Although entitled to a car, I did not accept one because I had never owned a car and was a poor driver. Also, there was no need. The Duc's chauffeurs were available to take us wherever we wanted to go.

As a result of Lee's two previous tours in Latin America, she was more in tune with the protocol and social amenities of overseas living than I was. Even so, she was surprised at Saigon Station's social environment. Although the Duc was the focal point for much of the social activity, dinner parties were held in private homes on an almost nightly basis. As enjoyable as many of them were, I eventually felt that we were fiddling while Rome burned.

On Sundays at the Duc, it was hard for me to believe that we were in a war zone. I soon concluded that, for some unknown reason, the Duc was not on any VC target list. At first, I thought perhaps an accommodation had been reached, but I later decided that the VC did not see us as a threat. As I was doing laps in the pool, I often thought of what two VC with B-40 rocket launchers or a satchel charge could do to the Duc. On any given Sunday, they could have eliminated quite a few Americans. A lot of classified information was discussed in the Duc bar and around the swimming pool. Perhaps the availability of that information was one of the reasons the Duc was never attacked. Had the NVA or VC wanted the CIA out of Vietnam, an attack on the Duc, combined with a few selected attacks on our province personnel, would have been a good start.

One of our neighbors at the Duc was Edwin Moore, a brooding, taciturn loner. We always greeted each other at the hotel but never had a real conversation. He was an embittered employee because he had been passed over for promotion many times and was considered to be a "terminal GS-9." After retiring, he threw a bag containing classified documents, and an offer to provide more of them, over the wall of the Soviet embassy in Washington. The Soviets thought the bag contained a bomb and called the police. Moore was subsequently arrested and sent to prison.

Most of my memories of the Duc Hotel are good ones. Our son John first swam in the Duc pool. We never had so much as a dime stolen from us, Lee and I made lots of friends there, and, most important, we felt safe.

4

- - - - - - - - - - - - - -

PRIME-TIME PLAYERS

During my tour in Vietnam, the major players were Ellsworth Bunker, U.S. ambassador to South Vietnam, 1967–1973; Theodore G. Shackley, Jr., CIA chief of station (COS) in Saigon, 1968–1971; Maj. Gen. (Ret.) Charles Timmes, liaison between the CIA and the ARVN's top commanders, 1964–1975; Graham Anderson Martin, U.S. ambassador to South Vietnam, 1973–1975; and Thomas Polgar, COS in Saigon, 1972–1975.

Ellsworth Bunker

President Lyndon B. Johnson appointed Ellsworth Bunker as the ambassador to South Vietnam in April 1967. Before that, Bunker had served as the ambassador to Argentina, Italy, and India.

My only personal contact with Ambassador Bunker occurred on July 10, 1971, at his reception for newly arrived employees. Lee and I went to the ambassador's residence, where we joined a long line of those waiting to be presented to him. On that occasion, his wife, Carol Laise, the U.S. consul general in Nepal, was not with him.

"Larry Wolf," Saigon Station's personnel chief, introduced us to Bunker as we came through the line. My previous experiences in similar situations had always been perfunctory: "Nice to see you. Thanks for coming." This time, it was a little different. Bunker talked to Lee and me and seemed genuinely interested in us. If I were to use one word to describe him, it would be patrician. He was tall, white-haired, and bespectacled and carried his seventy-seven years as though they were fifty.

More than 200 guests attended the reception. After passing through the reception line, Lee and I mingled for a couple of hours. When we decided to leave, Bunker was talking to guests on the other side of the room, and we did not want to interrupt him to pay our respects. As we approached the exit, however, I heard a voice, "Mr. and Mrs. Sullivan." We turned, and there was the ambassador. He had crossed the room to wish us good evening and to thank us for coming. I was pleasantly surprised that he had remembered our names, and I appreciated the gesture.

"Clay Corning," one of Bunker's bodyguards, told me the story of what happened when the ambassador took a letter from President Nixon to Do Lap Palace. The letter directed South Vietnamese President Nguyen Van Thieu to sign the Paris Peace Accords. According to Corning, after Thieu read the letter, he told Bunker, "Stick the letter up your ass."

On the way back to the embassy, the ambassador was not nearly so put out by Thieu's reluctance to sign the accords as he was by the fact that Thieu had insulted him. "He told me to stick the letter up my ass," was Bunker's refrain. In his world, gentlemen did not use such language.

As much as I admired the ambassador, I thought he was a bit naive in not expecting such a reaction from Thieu. The Paris Peace Accords were the death warrant for Saigon. Thieu, as well as most people, knew that the accords were America's way of getting out of the war and a betrayal of the South Vietnamese. Certainly, Bunker knew what the accords proposed, and in my opinion, he should have been embarrassed to present Nixon's letter to Thieu. The fact that he demonstrated no discomfort in carrying out his errand cost him some points on my admiration scale.

Theodore G. Shackley, Jr.

Ted Shackley arrived in Saigon in December 1968, after DCI Richard Helms named him to take over the CIA's largest station. Saigon was still recuperating from the Tet Offensive, and the security situation was tenuous.

I first saw Shackley on April 15, 1971, when he gave newly arrived employees their welcome briefing. I do not know what I had expected, but my first thought was, "How nondescript he is." The author Ian Fleming, with his fictional James Bond, created an image of how a super-spy ate, drank, dressed, spoke, and made love. Shackley did not fit this image. Tall, slender, bespectacled, pale, and dressed in a light gray suit, he was more reminiscent of the Peter Sellers character in the movie *Dr. Strangelove*. But no one could spend more than five minutes with Shackley and not recognize his intelligence. In the briefing, he gave an interpretation of the situation in Vietnam that was full of what appeared to be facts, seemingly made sense, and left us newcomers with a feeling of optimism.

Except for that briefing, the only other contact I had with Shackley was at a luncheon he hosted for a visiting dignitary from headquarters. Although he was not much for small talk, when Shackley found out that Lee had served in Latin America, he discussed many people she knew and had worked with. I was impressed with his knowledge of the goings-on in the Latin America Division. Talking about Latin America seemed to loosen Shackley up, and he shared an anecdote about Gen. William C. Westmoreland, commander of U.S. forces in Vietnam. Shackley commented that when he visited General Westmoreland, the general was usually in his bathrobe, as he did not like to get his uniform wrinkled.

Shackley also said that he would be going back to CIA Headquarters soon and would have to start house hunting. The main criterion was that the house be less than thirty minutes from headquarters. Shackley practically lived in his office in Saigon and, workaholic that he was, would probably continue to do so at headquarters.

Shackley's wife, Hazel, was safe-havened in Hong Kong with their daughter, but she visited Saigon during the summer of 1971. I saw Mrs. Shackley at a party during that visit and found her to be very impressive. She was striking—of moderate height with long, lustrous dark hair and dressed in a purple pantsuit. One of the women attending the party commented that she had never seen Mrs. Shackley in anything but purple and that she was called the "lady in purple."

Jack Gordon, my boss, worshipped the ground Shackley trod on. He had served with him in Berlin and thought he was a great case officer. One of my predecessors in Saigon, "Lou Falcone," had also served with Shackley in Germany and Vietnam and had the same opinion.

Before I left for Vietnam, I spoke with Falcone, and he told me, "John, you're going to love Ted Shackley. He is brilliant. When we were in Berlin, he was so organized, he would write his contact reports before he met with his agents."

That last statement gave me some concern, and I told Falcone that writing contact reports before meetings smelled of fabrication.

All the members of Shackley's protective detail in Saigon thought—or at least said they thought—very highly of Shackley. He was totally focused and did not have any sympathy for those who did not share his motivation. To be a member of Shackley's team, it had to be all or nothing.

"Steve Varney," our best man when Lee and I were married, had worked for Shackley in Miami. Although Varney liked Shackley, he turned down Shackley's request to join him in Vietnam. Varney told me that working for Shackley meant that nothing comes before the job—it is a 100 percent commitment.

Alan Freeze, Shackley's deputy, was a dapper, aloof man with CIA experience primarily in Latin America. He was short, weighed about 150 pounds, was silver haired, and had a ruddy complexion. To me, he seemed a bit of a Napoleon. Except for being a much better dresser, Freeze somewhat imaged Shackley. He was demanding and intelligent. But being Shackley's deputy was similar to being the vice president of the United States. In the Latin America Division, Freeze had the reputation of being a dynamic go-getter. I doubt that he enjoyed playing second fiddle to Shackley.

On one occasion, he and Mrs. Freeze invited some of us over to watch a movie at their residence. The movie was *Carnal Knowledge,* starring Candice Bergen and Jack Nicholson. Mrs. Freeze got pretty upset, because she thought the movie was too risqué.

The only professional contact I ever had with Freeze was secondhand. I had been asked to work on a high-profile case involving two alleged assassins who were in the custody of the South Vietnamese police. Freeze sent a note to Jack Gordon stating that I was not to be present during any mistreatment of the two alleged assassins.

Neither Shackley nor Freeze was a "press-the-flesh" type and did not seem to have much to do with the lower echelons. I thought this created a gulf between management and labor that was detrimental to the "forward-leaning" posture that Shackley espoused.

Shackley had an accountant's personality, and apparently his philosophy was numbers, numbers, and more numbers. Everything had to be quantified. Unfortunately, numbers can lie, and many of the numbers that he (vis-à-vis Saigon Station) put out did. It seemed to me that Shackley was of the "quantity over quality" persuasion. His credo appeared to be: "If we recruit enough people, sooner or later, one of them will be good."

One measurement of the success of Shackley's reign in Saigon was the number of reports disseminated. Any month that the reports section of Saigon Station disseminated 300 or more reports, a champagne celebration was held. This emphasis on numbers not only put a great deal of stress on case officers but also resulted in their being less cautious, and perhaps less scrupulous, than they should have been in assessing their agents and operations.

One of Shackley's first attempts to up the numbers involved beefing up the province offices. Song Be was the test site for his plan. The six officers he sent there were greeted by a huge mortar barrage and were out of there the next day, never to return.[1] That seemed to stall his "more is always better" policy.

In June 1969, members of the U.S. Army's 5th Special Forces in Nha Trang killed one of their own agents, Thai Khac Chuyen, because they suspected that he was a double agent. When those involved were subsequently arrested and indicted, they claimed that they had acted with the approval of the CIA. The CIA in Vietnam in 1969 was Ted Shackley. According to the indictees, they had approached the CIA's chief of operations (C/OPS) in Nha Trang, "Hank Cole," for guidance as to what to do with a double agent. When none was forthcoming, they assumed (or so they claimed) that they had the CIA's tacit approval to execute Chuyen.

Civilian attorneys for the accused wanted to call Shackley to testify during the court-martials of the men. DCI Helms ordered CIA people not to testify, and Secretary of the Army Stanley Resor ordered that the charges be dropped because the men could not get a fair trial without CIA testimony.[2]

I do not believe that Shackley was involved in the execution of Chuyen, but I think Cole may have inadvertently put Shackley in a tenuous

1. Orrin DeForest, *Slow Burn* (New York: Simon and Schuster, 1990), pp. 60–61.
2. David Corn, *Blond Ghost* (New York: Simon and Schuster, 1994), p. 201.

position. This case was the closest thing to a scandal to occur during his tenure.

Shackley insisted on approving every cable transmitted from the station. A lot of cables went out of Saigon, and waiting for Shackley to sign off on a cable could be tedious. The closest I ever heard Jack Gordon come to criticizing Shackley was when he commented that he wished Shackley would delegate a little more.

Shackley did inspire loyalty, however, and no one exemplified that better than Dana Meigs, his longtime secretary. Dana was untiring in her efforts on Shackley's behalf, sometimes to the point of excess. Be that as it may, Dana's relationship with Shackley typified the loyalty he inspired and demanded.

Authentication was Shackley's answer to bringing order to the way the CIA's agents in Vietnam were recruited. He espoused a series of steps that were to be taken before an asset could be authenticated as a recruited agent. My impression of his authentication process was that it was more form than substance. It was great for paper shufflers but did not seem to improve case officers' recruitment numbers. His departure heralded the shelving of the authentication process.

My final comment on Ted Shackley is that I do not understand how a man of his intellect and capability could expect our people in Vietnam to run successful, clandestine operations against the VC.

Charles Timmes

On one of my first flights from MR/2 back to Saigon, I was a passenger in the twin-turbo Volpar that Air America used for some of the CIA's more senior people. The only other passenger on the plane was a pleasant man who introduced himself. "Hi, I'm Charlie Timmes." Over the next four years, our paths would cross time and again, and no one in Vietnam logged more Air America miles than did Charlie Timmes.

I learned later that he was Maj. Gen. Charles Timmes, U.S. Army (retired). He had first come to Vietnam in 1961 as the commander of the Military Assistance and Advisory Group, Vietnam (MAAGV) and deputy to Gen. Paul Harkins, commander of the first MACV. When he finished his tour and subsequently retired, he was hired by former EA Division chief William Egan Colby to serve as a liaison between the CIA and the upper echelons of the South Vietnamese military.

General Timmes was a short man—no more than five feet, six

inches—weighed about 140 pounds, was in his early sixties, and, although quite energetic, was not at all imposing. I never saw Timmes on a flight without his tennis racket. When he arrived in a regional headquarters or province, he played tennis with the local Vietnamese commander, wrote a report based on the information his contact gave him, and was quickly on his way.

His wife, Marie, was a lovely and gracious lady. During our first few months in Vietnam, each time that Lee and I ran into General and Mrs. Timmes, she had to remind the general who we were. He finally remembered me, but it was a little disconcerting for someone with his clout to have such a poor memory. At one of the parties at the Duc, Mrs. Timmes anxiously remarked to us that the general had just had a birthday and that his contract might not be renewed.

On a personal level, I was an admirer of General Timmes, but on a professional level, I had some real problems with him. Although the general had introduced himself to me as Charlie, I never called him by his first name. He was more than thirty years older than I, and I would have felt uncomfortable. It also would have been a mistake to do so. Once, at a happy hour in Da Nang in MR/1, a new ROIC made the faux pas of calling him Charlie. Some senior ARVN officers were present, and it was apparent that General Timmes did not like it. After the Vietnamese left, Timmes made it very clear to the ROIC that he was "General Timmes." "My stock in trade is being a general," he said. "That's who I'm paid to be, and that is how I want to be addressed."

Timmes was mild mannered and quite unassuming on most occasions and did not fit the image of him created by John Wayne in the movie *The Longest Day.* He had been awarded the Distinguished Service Cross for his actions during the Normandy landing, and I realized that there was more to him than met the eye.

My negative feelings about the general arose from my belief that he was an apologist for the South Vietnamese military and was blind to its shortcomings. He never had a bad word to say about the ARVN and did his best to make sure that no one else did. General Harkins, when he had been MACV commander, decreed that only optimistic reporting would go out of Saigon, and perhaps General Timmes was merely carrying on a long-established tradition.[3]

3. Harry G. Summers, Jr., *Vietnam War Almanac* (New York: Facts on File, 1985), p. 187.

Because Timmes knew so many ARVN generals professionally and had personal friendships with many of them from his MAAGV days, his lack of objectivity might be understandable. When it inhibited the flow of accurate reporting on Vietnamese military performance, however, I perceived him as a liability. One of the more egregious examples of this occurred in MR/4. I was on a Porter flight when we stopped in Vinh Long to pick up "Jack Lehr." Lehr and I were friends, and he had been a deputy COS and Lee's boss in Latin America. Lehr had served in North Vietnam during the 1950s, and he was not a novice when it came to Vietnam. During the flight, Lehr told me that an ARVN colonel had just given him figures on the desertion rate in his division and that he was taking the information to the MR/4 reports officer.

I had to go to My Tho the next day, and I overnighted in Can Tho. At dinner that night, I ran into the MR/4 reports officer, "Jean Herrick." She and I had joined the CIA at the same time and were longtime friends. She was furious.

"John, do you know what Timmes did today?" she said. "I was getting set to send out Jack's report when Timmes brought me a report he had gotten from one of the generals down here. I told him about Jack Lehr's information, and he told me not to send it. He said he had just talked to one of the ARVN generals, and he [the Vietnamese general] said there was no desertion problem. Jack's report did not get out. General Timmes's did."

I was in Bac Lieu (MR/4) one morning when "Dick Mills," who had also served in Latin America, returned from the daily ARVN briefing. There had been a VC ambush that morning just outside of Bac Lieu, but, according to Mills, it was not mentioned during the briefing. General Timmes was at the briefing, Mills said, and the ARVN general giving the briefing spoke directly to him: "General Timmes, my troops can't make any progress without air support. Please tell the air force to give my troops cover."

According to Mills, a Vietnamese Air Force (VNAF) general then stood up and said, "General Timmes, unless his troops protect my airfields, we can't support him."

Mills expressed amazement that Timmes did not seem to catch on to how the Vietnamese were playing him. Later that morning, General Timmes stopped by the compound, and I asked him about the action on the road outside of Bac Lieu.

"What action? There was no VC activity around here today," he replied.

The general's Pollyanna approach to the Vietnamese military was the subject of many discussions among CIA people in Vietnam. I remember one in particular that I had with "Cal Moran," a C/OPS in MR/2. Moran said that, prior to coming to Vietnam, he had been told that General Timmes had virtual carte blanche and that no one was to interfere with him—what he wanted, he got.

Regardless of his misplaced optimism, General Timmes was not afraid to go where the war was. About a month after the ARVN retook Quang Tri (after having lost it during the NVA's 1972 Easter offensive), "Brian O'Malley," the POIC in Hue, asked me to test an asset he had in Quang Tri. Timmes was on the flight with me from Da Nang to Hue.

"John, what is Brian's wife's name?" Timmes asked me just before we landed.

"Joan," I said, and he wrote it down in his little notebook.

I had worked with O'Malley in Europe and in the States and had met his wife. I considered him to be an excellent case officer. He was waiting at the airstrip when we landed.

"Brian, how are you? And how is Joan?" Timmes inquired when he deplaned.

When O'Malley mentioned the test in Quang Tri, Timmes asked to tag along on the drive up there. O'Malley, Timmes, an interpreter, and I left at around 4 P.M. and arrived in Quang Tri about two hours later. That trip was one of the few occasions during my Vietnam tour when I was armed. Unfortunately, all the M-16s we had were rusty and obviously had not been cared for or fired in a while.

Quang Tri was surreal. Except for my test subject, the only living creature I saw there was a dog looking for food. The place was permeated with a smell that I could not identify. At risk of being melodramatic, I would suggest that it was the smell of death. I was more than just a little nervous and was frankly impressed with General Timmes's aplomb.

Given his extensive combat experience, I had trouble believing that Timmes was as naive as he sounded. One night at dinner in Chau Doc (MR/4), Timmes was extolling the strength of the ARVN and predicting its success. "Dominic Rossi," a case officer assigned to Chau Doc, took exception. Rossi had had a previous tour in Vietnam and seemed to have a good grasp of the current situation.

"General Timmes, they couldn't win the war when we had 500,000 American troops here. What makes you think they can do it without them?" Rossi asked.

The general's answer was a classic: "Have you ever seen how the Vietnamese maneuver in traffic? They are very devious. They can do it!"

In February 1975, I was talking to Timmes and some American pediatric surgeons outside church. The doctors were part of a program whereby American physicians volunteered to go to Vietnam and perform plastic surgery on Vietnamese children. (The mayor of Da Nang sold appointments to see the doctors.) When one of the physicians asked Timmes if he thought Congress would approve more funds for Vietnam, Timmes commented that he was sure Congress would.

"There's no way that is going to happen," I said.

"John, if they don't, the war is over," the general insisted.

"You're right, and it is over," I responded.

Just after Da Nang fell and the rout began in earnest, I was present when Timmes tried to put a positive spin on that debacle. I do not remember exactly to whom he was talking, but his words, in effect, were, "But 20,000 ARVN troops got out!"

"Yeah, 20,000 got out, but they weren't troops; they were rabble. They left their weapons and equipment and just ran," the other person answered.

That was the last time I saw Timmes before I left Vietnam.

Graham Anderson Martin

Graham Martin, who succeeded Bunker as U.S. ambassador to South Vietnam, was the most significant player during the last twenty-two months of the war. He arrived in Saigon on June 24, 1973. His most recent post had been Rome, and he had had a tour in Bangkok. The word in Saigon was that Martin was an ardent anticommunist but a little crazy.

Until February 1975, he was somewhat of an enigma, at least to me. I had no contact with him whatsoever—never saw him at any official or social function—and the only personal knowledge I had was that he and Frank Snepp were fellow North Carolinians.

On February 24, 1975, a congressional delegation arrived in Saigon to assess the situation. Shortly afterward, I heard that Martin was having trouble convincing the delegation to support his request for more financial aid for South Vietnam. When he could not sway the delegation, he flew back to Washington to make his case in person. Martin was still in the States when the NVA launched its attack on Ban Me Thuot on March 10. By March 14, when Ban Me Thuot fell, he was in the hospital recovering from oral surgery. Five days later, when it looked as though things were starting to fall apart, a cable was posted on the door of the embassy communications room. "What the fuck is going on? Martin."

On the day before Da Nang fell, March 28, Martin returned to Saigon with a delegation headed by Gen. Fred Weyand. Ted Shackley was also in the entourage. Al Francis, the last consul general in Da Nang, tried to tell Martin how bad things were in Da Nang and that the prognosis was very bad. Martin blew him off.

That afternoon, I was cashing a check in the embassy when I heard two State Department people comment, "He [Martin] thinks Da Nang will be retaken. He's insane." I doubt that there was another person in Vietnam who believed that Da Nang would be retaken.

Over the next week, the NVA juggernaut picked up momentum, the ARVN was in a rout, refugees were pouring into Saigon, and I was getting nervous. Between March 29 and April 10, when I left, Martin gave no briefings on the situation to the troops. There had been no precedent for him to do this, but Saigon in late March and early April was in crisis, and I thought that Martin should have been more forthcoming.

Thomas Polgar

Prior to replacing Shackley, Thomas Polgar came to Saigon for a visit in November 1971, after making stopovers in Thailand and Laos. There was a glitch in Polgar's arrival, in that (according to station gossip) Shackley did not meet his plane. I don't know whether Polgar's nose was out of joint or there was a communications breakdown, but Shackley arranged a reception for him at the Duc, and Polgar did not attend. Instead, he went to Bangkok to spend the weekend with his family. Polgar spent a couple of weeks in Saigon before returning to headquarters via Hong Kong. He spent Christmas back in the States and returned in early January 1972 to take over as COS.

Before coming to Vietnam, Polgar had been the chief in Buenos Aires, and many of the people at Saigon had known him in Latin America. Consensus was that he was "a pretty good guy." He had attracted some attention by foiling a plane hijacking in Buenos Aires and had a generally good reputation. One concern of the CIA people in Vietnam was that

Polgar was taking over the largest station in the world, which was many times larger than any he had ever managed.

When I first saw Polgar, I thought, "What a contrast to Shackley." Although both had Eastern European ancestors (Shackley, Polish; Polgar, Hungarian), any similarities stopped there. Shackley's tall, blond, almost Aryan appearance was in sharp contrast to Polgar, who was short and stocky, with Semitic features and a heavy Hungarian accent. In *Decent Interval*, Snepp describes Polgar as looking "more like an overgrown gnome than 'Special Assistant to the Ambassador.' "[4]

Polgar's and Shackley's managerial styles were also in sharp contrast. Most notable, at least to me, was that Polgar delegated authority. Nothing had gone out of Saigon without Shackley's stamp of approval. Polgar's word to his senior staffers was that they were paid to make decisions, and until they made a bad one, he would let them do their jobs. He also allowed his officers to send their reports directly to headquarters without his approval. Saigon Station sent follow-up rebuttals when necessary, but Polgar's policy afforded the military regimes much more independence than they had known under Shackley.

Another difference was that Polgar's wife, Pat, eventually lived in Saigon, and their three children, two girls and a boy, spent their summers there. Mrs. Polgar was a tall, attractive, and gracious woman.

There were some complaints from the marine guards and lower-echelon people that Polgar was aloof and never said good morning. But rather than aloof, I found Polgar to be shy.

Polgar seemed to have arrived in Vietnam with the view that the war, at least in terms of military action, was over. He opened up the station by allowing more nonworking husbands and wives to accompany their spouses to Saigon and initiated discussions about opening a school for dependent children. Many of us felt that these actions were a bit premature and that Polgar either did not know what was going on or knew something that the rest of us did not. Granted, major military activity had significantly decreased, but my own observations during my travels throughout Vietnam indicated that the war was far from over.

Whether Polgar felt that the war was over or that he preferred quality to quantity, I do not know, but the pressure to recruit diminished under

4. Frank Snepp, *Decent Interval, an Insider's Account of Saigon's Indecent End Told by the CIA's Chief Strategy Analyst in Vietnam* (New York: Random House, 1977), p. 85.

Polgar, which I saw as a positive change. Another characteristic of Polgar's administration was his accessibility. Neither he nor Shackley was a social lion, but Polgar mixed with the troops more than Shackley had. I saw Polgar at the pool and at parties, and he seemed to be making an effort to get to know his people. He did not utilize the bodyguards as extensively as Shackley had and tried to appear less imperious.

Shackley's Asian experience included a tour in Laos, and his predecessor, "John Latham," had been an experienced Asia hand. Both of them had a "feel" for Vietnam that Polgar would have to acquire. And looking back, I do not think he ever did. Saigon Station was a monolith created for the most part by Shackley. No COS could significantly change it, and I think Polgar knew it.

Polgar was a classic as well as an accomplished operations officer, but he never became accustomed to the way things were done (or, frequently, not done) in Vietnam. He had spent the previous thirty years in environments where case officers, for the most part, spoke the language of their assets and shared other ethnic and cultural commonalities. Vietnamese operations, with rare exceptions, were the antithesis. Paramilitary operations were another aspect of the operational climate in Vietnam with which Polgar had limited, if any, familiarity.

Perhaps Polgar's biggest handicap was not speaking the language. When I saw Polgar interact in Spanish with some Argentine generals visiting Saigon, he exuded confidence. In similar situations with the Vietnamese, he seemed to be a different person.

Shortly after Polgar's arrival, I did a test in which I called an asset "bad" but was unable to get an admission from him. The case officer requested approval from headquarters to run the asset and defended the man's failure to pass the polygraph test by saying that polygraph results were not admissible in court. Polgar wrote a rather scathing memorandum in which he defended polygraph testing and said that our assets would pass their polygraph tests or they would not be authenticated. My impression was that Polgar saw the polygraph as a useful tool and appreciated its utility. In contrast, Shackley saw the polygraph as useful only when it helped boost his numbers.

About three months after Polgar arrived, I began to have stomach problems and thought I might have ulcers. I had to take some time off to have tests run at the Seventh Day Adventist Hospital. The day after the tests were completed, I was at the Duc pool when Polgar approached me and asked me how the tests had gone and how I was feeling. I had never met Polgar and was surprised that he even knew who I was.

Polgar made a change in staff policy that endeared him to the wives who had had to resign from the CIA and go on contract in order to accompany their husbands: he restored their staff status. In addition, Lee received a promotion to GS-7. She and two other employees were called to Polgar's office, where he personally notified them of their promotions and offered his congratulations.

From the beginning of his tour, Polgar pushed the idea that there would be a negotiated settlement of the war, and he gave every impression that he thought Vietnamization was working. I often wished that I knew the source of such information.

In retrospect, I do not think that anyone could have solved the problems of Saigon Station or done anything that would have had a positive impact on the war. The war was lost before Polgar arrived in Vietnam. That conclusion begs the question: When Polgar came to Vietnam, did he know that he was there to maintain a guise of American support until the United States could extricate itself from that quagmire?

Until the very end, however, he posited that there would be a negotiated settlement. Until recently, I thought that he was just quoting the party line. I have now come to the conclusion that he actually believed it. Chris Hanlon, the POIC in Chau Doc, told me that he had been in Saigon on April 20, 1975, trying to arrange for the evacuation of key indigenous personnel who worked for the CIA in MR/4, when he ran into Polgar.

"What are you doing up here?" Polgar asked him.

Hanlon told him, and Polgar replied, "You can go ahead, but there really isn't any need. There will be a negotiated settlement."

In Vietnam, I did not hear much about Polgar's involvement with the Hungarian members of the International Commission of Control and Supervision (ICCS). I did hear that he and Col. Janos Toth, chief of the Hungarian delegation, were close, but I heard nothing about Polgar being unduly influenced by him. In their books, Snepp and DeForest imply that Polgar was led down the primrose path by Colonel Toth.[5] Shortly after the ICCS delegation arrived, one of the Hungarians tried to defect to the Americans. Because of potential problems with the ICCS,

5. DeForest, *Slow Burn*, p. 255; Snepp, *Decent Interval*, p. 326.

the CIA rejected his overtures and asked the Australians to take the defector, which they did.

Vietnam went down the tubes on Polgar's watch. I think he came to Vietnam to promote Nixon's "peace with honor" policy that had been initiated three years earlier. Midway through Polgar's reign, the Paris Peace Accords were signed, South Vietnam's fate was sealed, and Polgar became a pallbearer-in-waiting.

5

. . . .

THE OFFICE

The Office of Security in Saigon was responsible for providing bodyguards for the chief of station, physical security for all our facilities, and
polygraph support for covert operations and personnel screening and for
conducting investigations of security-related incidents—thefts, deaths,
altercations, and so forth. There was a chief, a deputy chief, three polygraph examiners, four to six security officers, and three secretaries assigned to the office. Polygraph examiners were called examiners or "box
men." All other officers assigned to Saigon's Office of Security were referred to, and referred to themselves, as security officers.

Norodom Complex was the home of the Office of Security in Saigon.
The chief, the deputy, and each examiner had his own office. There was
a vault in which to store files, and a room was set aside as a repair facility
for equipment.

Security officers in Saigon took on duties that no one else was clearly
assigned to do. For example, at one point, a polygraph examiner was running the nightly movie at the Duc. When a CIA VIP was arriving in Saigon, a security officer would usually meet and greet the individual. On

many occasions, when a CIA person ran into difficulty with immigration or customs at Tan Son Nhut, a security officer had to respond and deal with the situation. Security had a multifaceted role in Vietnam that was carried out by a diverse group of officers, including Bo Mooney, "Amos Spitz," "Keith Barry," "Art O'Leary," "Bill Evans," Mark Verity, and Rob Creed.

Bo Mooney

Bo was the most junior examiner in the office when I first entered on duty. Married, with a large family, he had started on the fast track as a career trainee but had been drummed out of the Directorate of Plans for botching an operation in which some agents had been killed. According to Jon Kirk, Bo was the only one of his students who had failed the polygraph course.

My early contacts with Bo were limited, but he came across as a genuinely nice guy and the epitome of what a good family man should be. Although it was hard not to like him, his reputation as an examiner was not good. When he was sent to Vietnam, the office scuttlebutt was that he could do less harm there than elsewhere.

Bo had an ebullience and childlike naiveté that seemed out of place in the polygraph environment. He had a real problem confronting people and rarely developed derogatory information about his subjects. Bo saw a tour in Vietnam as an opportunity to get his career back on track.

During the twenty-minute ride from Tan Son Nhut Air Base when Lee and I arrived in Vietnam, Bo had been upbeat. He assured us that "the war is going well, and the tide of the Red menace had been stemmed. The Vietcong ralliers [Chieu Hois] keep telling me they see their only future as ending up dead on a barbed wire fence, and they are worn out," he added. Bo also mentioned recently testing a VC security cadre who was providing us with great information. This woman, according to Bo, was working for us because we (the CIA) had arranged for her mother to have a cataract operation. "She believes the VC will win, but because we helped her, she will help us," he said.

Without getting argumentative, I told Bo that I found that hard to believe.

"Oh, no, John, she is the real thing. Family is everything to these people, and she is really grateful," he said.

That same day, Jack Gordon, my boss, called me into his office and asked me to look at some polygraph charts. He did not indicate who had conducted the test, but the minute I saw the charts, I knew that Bo had been the examiner. I had seen his charts in headquarters and recognized his chart markings.

I told Gordon that the quality of the charts was very bad, but if I had to make a call, I would say that the issue of homosexuality was unresolved. The charts were from a polygraph test of one of our contract employees. According to Gordon, Bo had told him that the guy was good. We later learned that the man was a homosexual and had been importuning the Nung guards for sex.

Later that same day, Mel Heath called me into his office and said that deception indicated (DI) determinations, especially without admissions, did not go over well in Vietnam. If I made a DI call, it would be a good idea to have an admission. Mel then dropped a bomb on me. He said that Bo had just tested FIREBALL, the number-one agent in Vietnam, and fabricated the test results. Mel said that FIREBALL had failed his test and that Bo had passed him. Mel also implied that Bo had been afraid to call the station's best asset deceptive.

Mel went on to say that Shackley had been the chief in Miami who had kicked Bo out of the Directorate of Plans, and when Bo's name had been submitted to EA Division for an assignment to Saigon, there was some doubt as to whether Shackley would accept him. Mel suggested that there was a quid pro quo involved. A final comment seemed to sum it up when Mel told me that the case officers loved Bo, but he was one fucked-up polygraph examiner.

On this, my first day in-country, I had seen evidence that Bo had passed an individual who clearly should not have been passed and been told that Bo had fabricated the results of another test. The next day, I wrote a memorandum for the record about my conversation with Mel about FIREBALL and put it in FIREBALL's polygraph file.

Later that week, Bo took me with him when he tested a Vietnamese who had applied for a job with our logistics office. From the time the subject came into the room until he left, no more than thirty minutes passed. During the test, the man fidgeted around, and the charts he produced were barely interpretable. After Bo passed him, I questioned him about the results.

"That's about as good as you're going to get with the Vietnamese," Bo said.

Shortly after Bo rotated back home, one of the U.S. Army examiners stopped by. His unit was closing down, and he asked me if I could use a brand-new polygraph instrument. Gordon overheard the offer, came out of his office, and gratefully accepted it.

"Bo lost one of our instruments, and we can really use this one," Gordon said when the army examiner had left.

The legacy of Bo caused me some problems. Chiefs of operations and POICs would schedule more cases than I could possibly handle, and some case officers would ask me to tell subjects that they were taking not lie detector tests but medical tests. When I objected, I was told that Bo had had no problem doing these things.

In December 1973, Bo wrote and asked me to request his assignment to Saigon to help us with our caseload. Mark Verity, Rob Creed, and I declined his offer. When Bo's boss, "Ray Lenihan," asked me why we did not want Bo back in Saigon, I blew the whistle on Bo. This would haunt me for the rest of my career.

Amos Spitz

In July 1971, Gordon told me that Amos Spitz would be coming out to Saigon in August to fill the second polygraph examiner slot opened up by Mel Heath's departure. After three months more or less on my own, I was getting a little ragged around the edges. Although I was loving it, I was ready to slow down and get into a saner routine. As much as I needed help, however, I viewed Amos's arrival with a lot of misgivings. I had never met him, but everything I had heard about him was negative, and I was anxious about working with him.

When Amos arrived in mid-August, I went out to Tan Son Nhut to meet him. Amos was a rather big man, about six feet tall and probably close to 200 pounds. He was from Illinois; spoke in a flat, almost atonal, voice; and seemed to be a little hard of hearing. Amos had a wife and three daughters back in the States, but I never heard him speak of them.

My first words after our initial greeting were, "Am I glad to see you! It has been really busy around here."

Amos made it quite clear that he would let me know when he was ready to start doing tests. After getting him settled in at the Duc, I took him over to the offices. Two offices had been set up for us. Both were the same size and similarly furnished. Each had a gray, government-issue metal desk, but Amos's glass desk cover had a crack in it. That afternoon when I came back from lunch, I noticed that Amos had switched desk covers. In retrospect, I should have called him on it.

Gordon and I briefed Amos on how we did business. Amos had been a polygraph examiner for a long time, had had a tour in Okinawa, and was experienced in testing Asians. I felt as though we were preaching to the choir. He found an apartment directly across the street from the U.S. embassy and in a week was on-line.

Amos was a bright man, but stolid and taciturn. In terms of personalities, we were complete opposites, and I had trouble communicating with him. Amos was blunt to the point of being rude, and he assumed an offensive posture when speaking to most people. He reminded me of Judd Frye as portrayed by Rod Steiger in the motion picture *Oklahoma.*

One day after coming back from Tay Ninh, I described how my helicopter had come under fire. The words "I was sitting behind the right-side door gunner" were no sooner out of my mouth when Amos enthusiastically jumped in.

"That's a lie right there. The door gunner is on the left side," he pontificated.

Tact was not Amos's strong suit. When "David Carey," a POIC in Tay Ninh, committed suicide, Bill Evans conducted the investigation. After Evans briefed us, Amos implied that he had done a shoddy job and covered it up. I thought that Evans was going to tear off Amos's head. When I told Amos that Lee would need a cesarean delivery because the baby's head was too large, he said, "You have a ready-made nickname, 'Bubble Head.' "

As an examiner, Amos did some good work, but he alienated a lot of case officers. The POIC in My Tho told me that Amos was the rudest man he had ever met and that he never wanted Amos there again. "He ordered the maid to do his laundry and treated us like he was doing us a favor by being here," the POIC said.

One of the POICs in Bac Lieu took the occasion of one of my visits to vent his feelings about Amos. A Boston Irishman who had spent much of his long career in the Arab world, this POIC was easygoing and competent, a good man to have around. "Do you know what that son of a bitch [Amos] did?" he asked. "He was testing one of my guys, and before he ran the last chart, he cocked a gun behind his ear and asked him if he wanted to change any of his answers. He then ran the chart with the cocked gun behind his ear. What an asshole!"

One newly arrived ROIC, in a cable to Saigon, transmitted, "Keep that goddamn Hitler out of my region." Apparently, Amos had tested a husband-and-wife team recruited by this ROIC. When Amos found out that the woman had had an abortion, he told her that she would go to hell. She and her husband quit.

Bill Osborne, my first CIA boss, had told me before I left headquarters on my first operational trip, "Don't be another Amos Spitz. On one of his trips, he passed four people, and they all quit."

Amos did take some of the load off me, but I sometimes questioned whether it was worth it. A case officer in Da Nang told me about a test that Amos had conducted. The subject was a suspected VC, and he did not seem to be paying attention during the test. Amos grasped the arms of the subject's chair, picked it up with the man in it, dropped it, and said, "I need your undivided attention."

Telling jokes and talking sports are two of my passions. During the two years that I worked with Amos, I never told him a joke (or heard him tell one), discussed sports, or had a pleasant conversation with him. Amos's primary topic of conversation was the wealth of OS people. "How much do you think so and so is worth?" he would ask. "Who do you think is the richest man in security?" We were never hostile to each other, but we never found a common ground on which to meet.

He offered to help me on sensitive cases, but he never discussed any of his cases with me or showed me any of his charts. Being junior to and less experienced than Amos, I thought it odd that I was getting the more high-profile cases, but I did not complain.

His pigheadedness once caused Amos to have a serious problem. He was in Chau Doc when he came down with "Ho Chi Minh's revenge" (the Vietnamese equivalent of "Montezuma's revenge"). He had to catch a flight back to Saigon, and because there was no restroom on the plane, the POIC gave him some paregoric pills. Instead of taking one pill, as directed, Amos took several pills. By the time he reached the Air America terminal in Saigon, he was almost comatose.

"Douglas Lemon," the Air America security officer, saw Amos sitting in the terminal and thought he looked out of it. He approached Amos to see if he was okay. According to Lemon, Amos became belligerent. Lemon was quite concerned and called the medics. When Amos told the doctor at Seventh Day Adventist Hospital about the pills, the doctor said that Amos could have killed himself.

"It would have been terrible if I had had an accident on the plane," Amos said when he told me what had happened.

In early 1972, I began conducting seminars in each region on how to make better use of polygraph testing. All the C/OPS with whom I discussed this project seemed to think that it was a good idea. On prearranged days, case officers came in from the provinces of each region, and I met with them collectively for give-and-take discussions. Apparently, nothing like that had been done before, and the discussions seemed to go over well. I did not tell Jack Gordon or Keith Barry, his successor, about them, but I told Amos and showed him the outline of my presentation.

In December 1972, a conference of security officers took place in Seoul, with Barry and Amos representing our office. When they returned from Seoul, Barry told me that Amos had made a great presentation at the conference on the idea of conducting seminars on polygraph testing in the regions. I am not aware of Amos ever conducting a seminar or giving a briefing on polygraph testing, and I resented his taking credit for something I had done.

Amos saw the assignment in Vietnam as the road to a GS-14. He told me that he had written a letter to John Bauer, the new IRD chief, to inform him that he was ready to come back and take one of the GS-14 slots. Amos had no idea that he did not have a prayer.

When I was on home leave in June 1973, "Henry Kurasaka," C/OPS of IRD, called me to his office. Kurasaka told me that there would not be a place for Amos in IRD when he finished his tour and suggested that I be the one to tell him. I felt very uncomfortable with Kurasaka's request, and since I do not like to be the bearer of bad tidings, I never told Amos. He probably would not have believed me anyway, or he would have thought that I had some part in the decision. When he returned to headquarters in August 1973, he was forced into early retirement.

Bo made my job more difficult because he was incompetent, and Amos made my job more difficult because he offended people. Many of those he offended not only refused to have their assets tested by him but also vented their frustrations with him on me. Like me, Amos had been assigned to Vietnam because IRD could not find anyone else willing to go. To a certain extent, I was an unknown quantity, in that I was the least experienced examiner in the division. Amos and Bo were known quantities but held in very low regard by IRD. Obviously, Saigon Station was not getting the best IRD had to offer.

Keith Barry

Keith Barry arrived in Saigon to take Jack Gordon's place as chief of security in the spring of 1972. Barry was a dapper man—suave, well spoken, and energetic—in his early forties, five feet, five inches tall, about 145 pounds. A former polygraph examiner and career security officer, Barry was married and had three children. His knowledge of polygraph testing made him more of a hands-on boss than Gordon had been, and I found that discussing polygraph cases with him was a real plus.

I had the impression that Barry saw me as naive and as someone who might rock the boat over the drinking and sexual escapades I encountered. At least during his early months in Vietnam, Barry thought that I was doing a great job. When word came that OS Director Howard Osborne planned to visit Saigon in the fall of 1972, Barry wrote him a personal letter extolling my performance and asking that Osborne do everything in his power to give me an overdue and well-deserved promotion. I saw the letter and was very pleased with Barry's laudatory comments.

On the downside was an incident that occurred regarding overtime. One of the perks of my service in Vietnam was that I received "premium pay," which amounted to 15 percent of my base salary in addition to the 25 percent differential. Because I was traveling so much and a lot of my work was done after hours, management had decreed that I, along with several other officers, was entitled to that extra 15 percent. In the summer of 1973, "Horace Lake" became the new chief of support, and one of his first edicts was to do away with the 15 percent premium pay. He told employees who had been getting it to submit claims for overtime whenever we felt we had earned it.

The first and only time I submitted a claim for overtime, Lake wrote across the memo "RIDICULOUS," and sent it back. That claim was for work I had done in Da Nang over a weekend. I had gone up there on a Saturday morning, worked Saturday night and all Sunday afternoon, and taken the plane back to Saigon on Monday. When Barry showed me Lake's rejection of my claim, I said, "Keith, I worked those hours and earned the overtime." Barry told me that there wasn't much he could do about it, and I let it drop. It would not have been career enhancing for him to fight Lake on this, but I wish he had.

Barry was a stickler for the rules. During a test of one of our Vietnamese employees at the Yendo Logistics Compound in Saigon, the employee told me that his boss, "Harry Lamont," had taken a Pentax camera without signing it out. "I asked him to sign a receipt, and he wouldn't do it. He went back home without turning it in," the man said.

After reading my report, Barry called me into his office and asked if I were sure of the information. I told him that I was, and he sent the report to headquarters. Headquarters subsequently sent us a cable advising that Director of Security Howard Osborne had personally interviewed Lamont regarding the camera and had found no cause for action. According to the cable, Lamont could recall no such incident. Lamont was a very senior officer, and I was surprised that Barry had sent the report to headquarters, but I also admired him for doing it.

Barry left Saigon in August 1974. In my thirty-one years in security, Barry was one of the most competent people I worked with.

Art O'Leary

In the spring of 1973, Art O'Leary arrived to replace Jack Dorne as Barry's deputy. Tall and distinguished, O'Leary reminded me of General Westmoreland.

I doubt that O'Leary would admit to it, but we shared some commonalities. We were both East-Coast Irish Catholics, we had the same "mother fixation" as most Irish males, and we were both avid sports fans—O'Leary from the perspective of an accomplished college football player (as center for Saint Bonaventure University), and I from the perspective of a jock wannabe. The only times that I really felt comfortable with O'Leary were when we were talking sports.

Although we never had any real disagreements, my relationship with O'Leary was never warm. I thought that he was a well-intentioned but totally uninformed cog in the Saigon Station bureaucracy. Misguided paternalism is the term I would use to describe his attitude toward me. One night at a party, when he was a little bit in his cups, I heard him tell Lee, "Lee, I really love this kid," referring to me.

When I told O'Leary that I had played football in high school, he kind of scoffed. I am convinced that he never believed me and that his skepticism colored his perception of me. He probably saw me as a lovable little Walter Mitty type who needed to be saved from himself.

By the time everything started to fall apart, Barry had left, and

O'Leary was then chief of security. On March 29, 1975, the day Da Nang fell, I told O'Leary that I wanted Lee and John out of there.

"John, this too shall pass," was his condescending retort, and a reiteration of what he had told me when the NVA offensive had started. "In a month, things will be back to normal. If you want Lee and John out of here, that's okay, but I think you are overreacting."

"Art, in another month, there won't be a South Vietnam," I said. (I missed it by one day.) Lee and John left on April 3.

By March 1975, I had forgotten more about South Vietnam than O'Leary would ever know. His failure to recognize the gravity of the situation was not a good sign. Did he really believe that the NVA would stop its offensive? If so, he was dangerously misinformed. If he did not believe it, his pissing on my shoes and telling me it was raining was an insult.

After Lee and John left, I spent most of my time helping to destroy files. I had figured on being in Saigon until whatever happened, happened. My intentions notwithstanding, I was asked to escort the station files back to the States, and on April 10, I bid O'Leary farewell and was on my way to Tan Son Nhut Air Base.

Bill Evans

When Bill Evans arrived in Saigon in February 1972, he was assigned to the Office of Security. Evans was on the COS's protective detail and was also responsible for conducting physical security inspections of the CIA's twenty-six sites throughout Vietnam and investigating security-related incidents (e.g., thefts, vehicular accidents, physical altercations, and deaths, including suicides).

Evans was an impressive young man at six feet five inches and well over 200 pounds. He had played defensive end for Florida State University in the 1964 Gator Bowl, but he did not fit the preconceived notions that many people have about football players. Evans was articulate, sensitive, and compassionate. He was a great writer, a genuinely good guy, and one of the better security officers I encountered. Because of Evans, Vietnam became a better place for CIA employees. He organized basketball, rugby, and softball teams, and he did not project the "cop" image favored by many security officers.

Two months after his arrival, Evans was on Polgar's protective detail for a trip to My Tho in MR/4. They were going to drive, and Evans brought a Swedish K submachine gun along with him. Polgar told him,

"You can put that in the trunk. The roads are safe." Evans demurred. On that particular trip, Polgar met with the "Coconut Monk," a seer who lived on a barge on the Song Tien River. The monk said that all Americans should leave Vietnam, because they could not win the war. That was not what Polgar wanted to hear.

Bill did some outstanding investigations while in Vietnam and was a tremendous asset to the office. A real vacuum was created when he left in 1974.

Mark Verity

Mark Verity was one of the best polygraph examiners I worked with during my thirty-one-year career. Mark arrived in Vietnam in 1970. During his first tour, he was on Shackley's protective staff and was responsible for security surveys throughout the country.

A native of Illinois, Mark had joined the army after high school and had been a paratrooper with the 82nd Airborne Division. Later, he attended Long Beach State University in California. A real nature lover, Mark had also been a ranger in Yellowstone National Park. He was a Bjorn Borg look-alike, but with short hair, and was sought after by many women looking for husbands.

Just before he rotated to the States in late 1972, Mark asked me about becoming a polygrapher. I thought that he would be a good examiner and told him so. Following his polygraph training, he returned to Vietnam in 1973.

Once he came on-line, he quickly established himself as a superior examiner, primarily by getting admissions from those he called deceptive. Mark was also a great supervisor and training officer, and on at least two occasions, he bailed me out of tough cases. He was unflappable and never raised his voice, yet his steely silences could be intimidating.

Rob Creed

As mentioned in chapter 2, I had worked with Rob in Laos. He was respectfully and affectionately called "Bobby Box" by some of the EA Division case officers. On a previous tour in Vietnam, Rob had been severely wounded in the bombing of the American embassy in 1967. He had also had two tours in Thailand and Laos and was transferring laterally from Thailand to Saigon when he replaced Amos in August 1973.

When I characterize people, I have a tendency to compare them with celebrities. Rob reminded me a little of Don Adams, of *Get Smart* fame, particularly his voice. His wife, Kay, reminded me of Sandy Duncan, of Peter Pan fame—slender, very attractive, and always upbeat. Kay accompanied Rob on this second tour in Vietnam. She had a terrific reputation in EA Division, as both a secretary and an administrator, and most managers in Saigon who knew her jumped at the chance to have her in their offices.

In terms of grade, Rob was the most senior of the examiners in Saigon. I was a GS-10, Mark a GS-12, and Rob a GS-13. Rank notwithstanding, Rob did more than his share of the work, and I found him to be a real workaholic. He never pulled rank or avoided a case and was always available when I needed advice.

Rob's arrival was a tremendous plus for the polygraph program in Saigon. His first tour in Vietnam, as well as the experience accrued from an army tour in Korea and tours in Thailand and Laos, qualified him as a real expert on CIA operations in Asia. There was not a case officer in Saigon who knew more about clandestine operations in Asia than Rob did.

Another plus was that my workload decreased. Case officers, ROICs, and POICs wanted Rob to test their agents. Rob also knew many of the old Asian officers we were working with in Vietnam and Cambodia, and on several occasions, he gave me a "heads up" on how to deal with a particular officer.

I left Saigon a week before Rob, Kay, and the two South Vietnamese children they had adopted left. My association with the Creeds is another one of my good memories of Vietnam.

6

. . . .

TOTAL IMMERSION

Jack Gordon wanted Bo Mooney to take me up-country before he left for the States, and Bo arranged for a weeklong trip to MR/1. On Monday, April 20, at 7 A.M., a Duc driver took me to the Air America terminal to meet Bo, and we boarded an Air America C-47 that would take us to Da Nang.

Da Nang was the second largest city in Vietnam, and the American air base there was very active. The air ops officer in Da Nang told me that, at the height of the war, there were more jet takeoffs and landings at Da Nang than at any airport in the world. Even in 1971, the roar of the F-4 Phantoms seemed never ending.

Bo and I checked in with "David Benson," the C/OPS in Da Nang. Benson gave us our test schedule and an office where we could meet with the case officers. Bo knew all of them, and it was like old-home week for him.

I conducted my first test there on a Chieu Hoi who would work with the provincial reconnaissance units if he passed the test. His case officer was "Laurence Patton," the PRU adviser. Patton wanted to know if the subject had been ordered to rally to South Vietnamese forces and if there had been any contact between him and the VC since he had rallied. The test went well, and Patton and I were both pleased.

Afterward, Bo told me that "Thomas Bourne," a case officer assigned to Special Branch, had a "very sensitive case" he wanted Bo to do. Because of its sensitivity, Bo thought it best that I not observe. I was sleeping when Bo came into my room at about 11:30 that night and woke me. He was on the verge of being a knee-walking, commode-hugging drunk, but he wanted to tell me that the test had gone well. Then he asked, "John, why can't we test people on their *intentions*? Why isn't it okay to ask them do they intend to do something?"

One of the basic rules of polygraph is that you cannot test people on their intentions, simply because they can change their minds. I explained this to Bo, but I knew that it went over his head. It was hard to believe that an experienced examiner would ask such a question.

Bo said that he had passed Bourne's agent based on the agent's claimed intention to go on a mission for the Special Branch. When I asked him if I could take a look at the charts, Bo said that he had already sealed them for transmission back to Saigon. He would have had to go into the office to do that. I knew that he was lying, but I did not push the point.

The next morning, Bo was so hung over he could not get out of bed. When I tried to get him up, he told me that he was too sick to stick around and was going back to Saigon. That left me with one case to do in Da Nang and one in Hue. My first test went well, and afterward I took a Porter to Hue. The POIC in Hue, "Bill Garrett," was an experienced East Asia hand and an all-around good man. Although the test in Hue did not go smoothly, Garrett took it well.

The most memorable moment of my first visit to Hue occurred the next morning. As I was doing my morning ablutions, I looked in the commode, and staring up at me was a large rat. Thank God, I had not sat down.

During that first trip to MR/1, I had two conversations about Lam Son 719 that were disquieting. One was with a U.S. Army helicopter pilot in Da Nang, the other with a retired U.S. Marine Corps warrant officer in Hue.

The army helicopter pilot said that he had helped evacuate ARVN troops from Laos during Lam Son 719, and he described what had happened as a disaster. "As bad as it was, it would have been a lot worse if we hadn't been here. The NVA is just waiting for all of us to leave, and they are going to stomp these poor bastards into dog shit," he said.

The retired warrant officer told me, "The NVA were using rear echelon troops and had no air support, but they slaughtered ARVN. ARVN can't do it without us, and when our troops are gone, so is South Vietnam."

The day after that conversation, I went back to Da Nang to do another test and, on Friday, back to Saigon and Lee. By the time I got back to Saigon, Bo had started to pack up and was not spending much time in the office. I was in MR/4 when Bo left, and I missed his farewell party.

When I went into the office on Monday morning, I did not say anything to Gordon about Bo getting drunk. He would be leaving in a week and was not doing any testing, so I saw no point in it. Mel Heath was also on leave. That same morning, "Ivan Serov" came into the office. Serov, an intense man and an interrogator of renown, was known as the Rasputin of the Directorate of Plans. At that time, he was involved in debriefing a high-level North Vietnamese defector and wanted the man polygraphed. He proceeded to give me a list of more than eighty questions on which he wanted the man tested. I negotiated the list down to about ten questions and made arrangements to conduct the test later that week at the National Interrogation Center (NIC).

"Frank Celic," our liaison officer at the NIC, gave me a briefing during which he told me that I would be encountering some pretty hardcore VC and that I should not be overly optimistic about getting admissions from them. As an example, Celic told me of an incident that had recently occurred during the interrogation of a Vietcong woman. According to Celic, the woman had put the tip of her tongue between her front teeth, slammed her hand into her chin, and spit the tip of her tongue in the face of her interrogator.

The defector I was to test for Serov was a North Vietnamese government official, articulate and very bright. This would be my first contact with a North Vietnamese communist, and I looked forward to doing the test. One of our psychologists had given him a battery of tests and described him as "egotistical, grandiose, and hostile."

In my initial contact with him, I found him to be a bit arrogant. As the interview went on, he told me that he had deeply resented the psychological testing. "They treated me as if I was a dunce. I have a Ph.D., and I was insulted." Once we got into the test, he seemed to warm up, and the test went well. He clearly had not been foisted on us by the North Vietnamese and had not provided us with information he knew to be false. During my time in Vietnam, I never concluded that a defector I tested had been directed by the North Vietnamese to defect.

Mai, the interpreter during this examination, was outstanding. A young, attractive woman, she could interpret simultaneously and spoke English as well as I did. Over the next few years, we would work together on several occasions. Each time, she would ask me, "Mr. John, I am really looking for a nice American man. Could you find me one?" I never took her seriously, but during a break from one of the tests, she asked me, "Mr. John, if you can't find me a nice American, how about you?"

I was pretty surprised, because I had told her that I was married, and I answered, "Mai, I really don't think my wife would like it."

"You don't do it because your wife wouldn't like it, you do it because it is fun."

That was the only time I was propositioned in Vietnam.

During my third week in Vietnam, I had my first run-in with a case officer, "Chris Heil" from Saigon Base (MR/5). He had scheduled a test for one of his assets, and it fell to me to do it. When it came time to do the test, Heil said that he wanted to sit in, and I told him that I would prefer that he didn't.

"What happens if I insist?" Heil asked.

"I don't do the test," I said. The truth is, I was being a pompous ass and could have handled it better. Heil was a good officer, and I was just too full of myself. After the test, I told Gordon what had happened and that he might be hearing from Heil. Gordon then did something that endeared him to me. He called Heil in to his office and made it quite clear that his examiners set the conditions as to how tests were conducted.

MR/4 put in a request for polygraph support, and I arranged to go down there for a few days. On May 3, 1971, I arrived in Can Tho. Chief of Support Harry Lutz was waiting for me in the Air America terminal, and the first words out of his mouth were, "Good to see you, John. We have seven guys lined up for you to test. They're here and ready to go."

"Harry, what are you talking about? There's no way I'm going to test seven people today," I said.

"How many can you test?" Lutz asked.

"Two, maybe three, but that's it!"

"Bo had no trouble testing this many."

"I'm not Bo, and I don't work that way," I said. But I was thinking, "Bo, what have you done?"

At that point, I began thinking that if I were going to function in Vietnam, I would have to educate my clients about polygraph testing. In the operational arena, scheduling one case a day was optimal. Two cases could be done on rare occasions, but more than two was discouraged. Normally, the examiner had to read files, work out questions with an interpreter, and take care of other details. But as I was to learn, that was not the way it was done in Vietnam. Files were negligible, if they even existed at all, and even the files that seemed to be well documented were of little value because there was no way to verify the biographic information in them.

At headquarters, when we were given an applicant's file, it included a background investigation that verified much of the information in the personal history statement completed by the applicant. There were no background investigations or, for that matter, any extensive biographic data on the subjects we tested in Vietnam. A lack of biographic data is a characteristic of many operational tests, but in Vietnam, that lack was more significant because it occurred in conjunction with no language capability and an absence of cultural, historical, and geographical awareness on the part of the case officers.

Composing the questions to be used on a test is usually a collaboration between the examiner and the case officer. During Bo's reign, that had changed. Apparently, Bo had used a standard set of questions for most of the Vietnamese assets, and the whole process had become "canned."

I agreed to do three tests that day. Of those, two went well and one not so well. Between tests, C/OPS "Carl Toner" told me that I would be going to Chau Doc, Ben Tre, My Tho, and Rach Gia during my stay in MR/4.

Can Tho was not a pretty city, but the CIA compound was well organized and more than adequate. The TDY quarters were comfortable, and the club, containing a restaurant and bar, was well run. A lot of Americans, including military personnel, State Department officials, U.S. Agency for International Development (USAID) employees, and construction workers, frequented the club. The food was good, at least to my unrefined palate, and inexpensive. The POICs in most places did not charge me for the food I ate, and that was another way to save money.

After Can Tho, my next stop was Chau Doc, which would become one of my favorite places to visit. Located on the Bassac River, it was very scenic, and the office was in an old French villa. Nung guards manned the gate, and a .50-caliber machine gun on the roof faced the river. "Al Cullen," the POIC, had been a C/OPS in Latin America, and I had worked with him in the past. Cullen's assistant was an officer with whom Lee and I had gone through the VNO course. Before dinner, the POIC and any other Americans present would meet on the roof for cocktail hour. Watching the sunset from that roof is another pleasant memory of Chau Doc.

John Cassidy, a former POIC in Chau Doc, wrote a book titled *A Station in the Delta*. Although fictionalized, it is a rather good account of the life of a province officer in Vietnam. In the book, the protagonist rescues two navy nurses from a compound under siege. That incident is based on the actual deeds of S. Sgt. Drew Dix and Jim "Stonewall" Forrest (see chapter 2), who was then a PRU adviser assigned to Chau Doc. For their efforts, Dix was awarded the Medal of Honor and Forrest the CIA's Intelligence Star.

My first test in Chau Doc was scheduled for 8 P.M. I did most tests in the provinces at night. Since no American could meet clandestinely with a Vietnamese in the provinces, darkness was the best we could do to maintain a modicum of secrecy. The subject of my test was a Cambodian refugee who supposedly had information on NVA troops in that area. He said that he did, but the test results did not support his claim.

After the test, Cullen told me that with so many refugees from Cambodia coming through Chau Doc, it was easy to gin up a lot of reports. The staff sometimes took information from one debriefing and turned it into several reports that were disseminated over a couple of weeks. That way, they exceeded Shackley's expectations for reports. I saw this scheme repeated in every military region. Under Shackley, numbers were the name of the game, and recruitments and disseminated reports were the measures of success.

Cullen's successor, "Ross Donaldson," was a huge man, standing over six feet six inches and weighing over 250 pounds. He brought a water bed to Chau Doc, and on one occasion, I conducted a test in his room. The Vietnamese man I tested was fascinated by the water bed. He sat on it, bounced up and down on it, and seemed more interested in the bed than in the test.

Of the POICs I worked with in Vietnam, Donaldson's successor, Chris Hanlon, was one of the best. He was also a truly honorable man. A tall, slim, urbane New Yorker (without the accent), Hanlon was a thirty-five-year-old Georgetown University alumnus who wore a Vandyke beard. He and his number-two man, "Jeff Starrett," a banjo-strumming Tennessean, spent most of their time in weeding out the bad operations of their predecessors. Hanlon's two predecessors had been promoted to GS-14 while they were in Chau Doc. Their promotions were based, for the most part, on fabricated operations. Starrett, the last POIC in Chau Doc, did a superlative job in closing down the office. Neither Hanlon nor Starrett was promoted.

When Hanlon and Starrett began having Chau Doc's assets tested, the number of recruited agents went down dramatically. On one occasion, Starrett's Special Branch contact told him that he would not allow his asset to be polygraphed, and Starrett said, "No polygraph, no money." The man was tested and failed.

In Chau Doc, I came upon a theme (or, more accurately, a threat) to use in getting young male subjects to make admissions. Many of those we tested were draft dodgers. They were too poor to buy their way out of the military, had families to support, and were terrified of being conscripted.

One young man I tested could not have been more than twenty-one years old, yet he had an identification card that said he was forty-six. Testing clearly indicated that the information he was providing was fabricated. When I confronted him, he denied any fabrications. "You are a draft dodger," I said. "If you tell me the truth, I will not report you to the ARVN. If we don't resolve this issue, we [the Chau Doc office] will have to turn you over to the ARVN." The threat was enough. The young man admitted that he had made up the information. I felt sorry for that young man, as well as several others in the same boat, and am pleased that none was ever turned over to the ARVN.

My next stop was Ben Tre. The Porter picked me up at the Chau Doc airstrip. The high-pitched whine of the Porter's engine was a sound that I would come to know and love during the next four years. Twenty minutes later, "Ric Delgado" met me at the Ben Tre airstrip. He was sitting in the passenger seat of a jeep and carrying an M-16. In most provinces, depending on how far the landing strip was from the CIA compound, a driver and one of the staffers (armed) met the plane.

Of all the places in Vietnam to which I traveled, Ben Tre was one of the more vulnerable and gave me the most concern. The road from the airstrip into Ben Tre was lined on both sides with thick vegetation and trees. I always felt uneasy along that road because it was an ideal location for an ambush.

On one occasion, the POIC in Ben Tre left me at the airstrip to wait for the Porter. Not another soul was in sight. I was sitting on the box and musing on the vagaries of life in Vietnam when a loud explosion suddenly went off behind me. I turned to see some ARVN soldiers loading a shell into a 105-mm howitzer. I had not seen them when we pulled up in the jeep and had no idea what their target could be. They fired four more shells and then stopped.

After Ben Tre, my next stop was My Tho, where I tested a Vietnamese who was being hired as an interpreter. The test went well, and I was finished late that afternoon. "Mike Hearn," who had been the MR/4 coordinator in Saigon, took a second tour in Vietnam and became the POIC in My Tho. A David Niven look-alike, Hearn was a well-dressed man in his early forties, of slender build, with salt-and-pepper hair, and a pencil-thin mustache. He spoke with a slight New England accent, was married, and was the father of seven or eight children. "John Galway," the POIC in Bac Lieu, once commented, and not in a negative way, "Mike missed his calling. He would make a great salesman in a classy men's store."

During Hearn's reign as the POIC in My Tho, life seemed a little more chic than in the other provinces. As nice as it was, however, the ambience, in my opinion, tended to distract us from the mission. One time when I went down there to do a polygraph test, we sat down for lunch before the test and, surprisingly, the subject ate with us. I did not project a hostile or negative visage to my test subjects, but I liked to maintain some distance in order to preserve my objectivity. Hearn appeared to be sandbagging me, and I resented it. This was the only time I had any problem with Hearn, and overall, we had a good relationship.

My next stop after My Tho was Rach Gia, a small fishing village near the Gulf of Thailand and one of the more isolated sites in which I worked. During my tenure, I traveled there many times, and on one occasion, I brought Lee with me. While I conducted a test, the deputy POIC took Lee to a restaurant for some great seafood. In order to land in Rach Gia, vehicular traffic had to be stopped because the landing strip was Rach Gia's main street.

On this, my first trip, "Charley Moses" was the POIC, and he was waiting for me. Moses was a straight arrow and very intense. He was a true believer who thought that he could run good operations against the VC. My first test for him went well, but it was the last one that did. When I was finished, the Porter picked me up for my trip back to Can Tho. I summarized the tests for the C/OPS and then took my first helicopter ride to Saigon.

After three weeks in Vietnam, I had spent a week in MR/1 and a week in MR/4, worked at the NIC, and tested an agent in Saigon. By then, I felt that I had a pretty good handle on what the future held for me. My first trip to the Delta gave me a good sense of the operations down there and also a sense of what it was like to travel around the provinces. During those three weeks, I developed some reservations about the quality of the operations we were running but had few concerns about my safety. My only real worry was the amount of flying I would be doing. If I went down in a plane, it would most likely happen in a VC-controlled area, but I forced myself not to dwell on that possibility. The relaxed and almost complacent attitude of our POICs was infectious. I concluded that if anything were to happen to me, it would be the result of an accident or misadventure as opposed to any direct action against me.

Mel Heath had suffered a detached retina while I was in MR/4 and had departed for the States before I returned to Saigon. Without warning, I was on my own. There was more than enough work for two examiners, and handling the workload was going to be a challenge. Gordon more or less left it up to me how I would handle requests for polygraph support. Juggling and prioritizing these requests was one of the more difficult aspects of being on my own. I have a real problem saying no, and during those early days in Vietnam, I overextended myself, doing tests day or night—whenever it was convenient for the case officer. During one burst, I worked eighty straight days. I did not do a test every day, but I was in the office writing reports, answering cables, or discussing future cases with operations people when I was not in the provinces or Cambodia.

One Sunday in early June, I was in the office when a car parked outside the Norodom Complex was firebombed. A Vietnamese on a motorbike with a passenger on the back rode by, and the passenger threw some kind of bomb at the car. The car was completely destroyed, and the Vietnamese policeman on duty was unable to, or did not want to, get a shot off at the bomber. Firebombings of U.S. cars had been going on for a few weeks, but this was the first attack near the embassy. I think Ambassador Bunker complained, because the next day, President Thieu ordered the police to "shoot to kill" car bombers. The attacks stopped.

The following Sunday, I was in the office when a marine guard came into the office and told Gordon that a man was having a seizure on the street in front of Norodom (Thong Nhut Street). Gordon took off like a rocket and found a man in the throes of an epileptic seizure. He used a pencil to make sure that the man did not swallow his tongue and received a serious bite on the finger for his efforts.

In mid-June, "Peter Crone," an examiner assigned to Okinawa, came to Saigon to help me out for a week. I had never met Peter, but Jon Kirk (IRD training officer) was a good friend of Peter's and often talked about him. Kirk told me that Peter was a Sinophile and had never failed a Chinese on a polygraph test. When I met Peter at Tan Son Nhut, he made it clear that he was there only to do the highest-priority cases and would not be running around Vietnam. Personality was not Peter's strong suit, and I did not question his reluctance to travel outside of Saigon. I gave him cases to be done in Saigon and stayed out of his way.

After Peter left, headquarters sent "Sean Singer" to give me a hand. I had worked with Sean at headquarters and had had one of my more memorable trips with him: We were going to Miami to do some work, and because of the threat of being hijacked to Cuba, we took the train. After dinner, Sean was in his cups and started rambling about agents he had tested. He leaned across the table and said in a very loud voice, "John, how many of us has had an agent commit suicide? I have!" He then stood up and began to sing the Greek national anthem. I had no idea that Sean had a drinking problem and was at a loss as to what to do. I just wanted to get the hell out of there, but I knew that I should stick around and try to make sure that Sean was all right. After one verse he sat down, and I was able to talk him into shutting it down for the night.

During that trip, we had a car accident that was Sean's fault. I suggested that he call "Colin King," the CIA special agent in charge in Miami, who would later become director of the Office of Security. Sean refused. When the police arrived, Sean approached one of the officers and said, "We're from the CIA on official business." When the officer asked for some CIA identification, Sean could not produce any, and he ended up getting a ticket as well as looking foolish.

Afterward, back in headquarters, Osborne's first words to me were, "All I want to know is, was he drunk when the accident happened?" I told him no, and he responded by chewing me out for not reporting the accident to King.

Gordon made it clear that he expected me to keep an eye on Sean in Saigon, but I felt uncomfortable doing that and passed. Fortunately, the one test Sean did, he did very well. Unfortunately, on Sean's third night in Saigon, he went to a party at the U.S. Army's Explosive Ordnance Demolition house. While Sean was there, a noncommissioned officer pulled the pin on a hand grenade, put the grenade between his legs, and blew himself up. Sean became slightly unglued, as would anyone.

Three incidents occurred during this period that would impact my tour in Saigon. The first took place in MR/4. I was scheduled to do some tests in one of the provinces and arrived to find the POIC, "Gregory Lanza," drunk and disheveled. He was unshaven and seemingly unwashed, and he was wandering around the compound with his young, female Vietnamese playmate draped all over him.

"Paul Heroux," his assistant, was both a fine person and a fine case officer. He told me that Lanza was in bad shape. Heroux said that the U.S. Army colonel in charge of the province had personally complained to ROIC "Bob Elliot" and asked him to get Lanza out of the province because he was not only an embarrassment to the U.S. government but also a danger to himself. Elliot took no action.

After doing a test for Heroux that night, I returned to the compound to find Lanza on the living room couch with his paramour of the moment. The next morning, I was writing up notes in Lanza's office when the Vietnamese compound manager came in and opened Lanza's safe. I could not believe that a local employee had the combination. By the time I left for Saigon, Lanza had not made an appearance.

The room where I stayed was the armory for the compound and contained two M-16s, an M-79 grenade launcher, several cases of hand grenades, a flak vest, a helmet, and, on the night table, a Browning 9-mm pistol. Alcohol and weapons are a bad combination, and I was concerned. When I arrived in Saigon, I told Gordon and Dorne what I had seen.

Gordon's response was, "John, you don't drink. You have Lee here and don't understand the pressures these men are under. You really shouldn't judge them."

I told Gordon that Lanza was a danger to himself and should be taken out of there. He politely brushed me off. Two weeks later, Lanza was medevaced with delirium tremens. Heroux had to carry him to the Porter.

The second incident occurred in MR/2. I had gone there to test members of one of the Cambodian reconnaissance teams. "Rob Fox," a former Dade County, Florida, detective, was preparing to send a team over the border and wanted me to test each team member. I tested all five of them and concluded that one was a "no-goodnik" (i.e., he might be working for the Khmer Rouge). Fox was not pleased and told me that he would "get it out of him," since he could not launch the team until this issue was resolved.

Three days later, Fox called me in Saigon to ask if I would retest the team member who had failed. I said that I was willing to try and, against my better judgment,[1] agreed to do the test Sunday morning in Saigon. I ran the test and let Fox talk me into calling the results inconclusive rather than deceptive. He launched the team, and it never came back. That was the last time I let a case officer influence one of my calls.

The third incident was much more personal and had a more long-lasting impact. Before June 21, 1971, war in Vietnam was the sound of outgoing mortars, the noise of an occasional explosion, or the sight of a wounded Vietnamese veteran who was panhandling. I had seen a destroyer shelling VC positions outside of Da Nang, F-4 Phantoms roaring off into battle, and a Spectre gunship doing its thing. To someone who, prior to coming to Vietnam, had never heard a shot fired in anger, this was exciting but rather impersonal. On June 21, 1971, the war became a little more personal.

On the afternoon of June 20, Gordon called me into his office to tell me that my services were needed immediately in Quang Ngai. Paul Daly's PRU team had talked to a woman who claimed that she had seen a red-headed American deserter. At that time, there were rumors in MR/1 of a redheaded deserter who was helping the VC ambush Americans. This was a hot case. Daly's PRUs were going to bring her into the compound in Quang Ngai, where, after she was debriefed, I would polygraph

1. Once an examiner concludes that a subject has been deceptive, no additional testing should be done until the subject provides an explanation for his reactions to the questions on which he was deemed deceptive.

her. The three top priorities in terms of the information we collected were (1) information about an imminent attack, (2) information about prisoners of war (POWs), and (3) information about VC plans and policies.

The next morning, an army major, an interpreter, and I flew to Da Nang, where we switched to a Porter that took us to Quang Ngai. The major was with us because if the story turned out to be true, an operation to find the deserter had to be organized.

Quang Ngai is not far from My Lai, the site of the 1968 massacre. During four or five trips there, I never saw any smiling Vietnamese. The peasants were sullen and definitely not glad to see Americans. "Chris Terry" was the POIC in Quang Ngai, and from my contacts with him, I judged him to be a good officer. Unfortunately, he was out of country, and "Franklin Squire" was acting POIC. Squire was grossly overweight, a profligate, and certainly not in the "forward-leaning" mode espoused by Shackley. Terry had expressed concern about Squire because their escape route, in the event they had to evacuate, would require them to climb over a couple of roofs. "There's no way Frank would ever make it. He's just too fat," Terry had said.

When we arrived, Daly had already left with his PRUs to pick up the woman who had reported the sighting. While waiting for them to return, we sat around and discussed the upcoming debriefing. When the major took a bathroom break, Squire said that if we got any good information from the woman, we should treat it as "our" case and not clue the major in until we had passed the information to Saigon.

"Frank, this is a military case. It is theirs and should be, period. Let's not get in a pissing contest. We will only look bad," I said.

I never did the test. Daly stepped on a mine before he and his PRUs could pick up the woman. He was blown to pieces and died instantly. Mark Verity had to make the arrangements to get what was left of Daly back to the States. A few weeks after Daly was killed, Verity received a letter from Daly's sister, who asked about Daly's missing Rolex watch. Verity told me, "I didn't find his arm, let alone his watch."

Daly's death did not shock me as much as it saddened me. He had been a soldier, and death happens to soldiers. But he was too young, too full of life, and too full of promise to be snuffed out in such a cruel way. I felt closer to him than to any of the other five men killed in Vietnam I had known.

Daly's death was the low point of my first three months in Vietnam, but those ninety days, more or less on my own, had also been a trial by fire. In that time, I had worked in each of the MRs and Cambodia, conducted a variety of tests, managed to catch some liars and fabricators, and established some credibility not only with the case officers but also with station management. It was a hectic time, but those experiences prepared me well for the next three and a half years.

7

· · · · · · · · · · · · · · · · ·

RESPITE AND REALITY

With the arrival of Amos Spitz in August, the pace slowed, my travel diminished, and Lee and I were able to work out a routine. Over the next six months, life was much less hectic and, on occasion, bordered on idyllic. There were times, however, when the reality of Vietnam intruded, and by the end of our first year there, I had concluded that we were in a no-win situation.

When I was in Saigon, we would usually get up at around 6:30, eat breakfast in the Duc restaurant, and catch the Duc car to the embassy. The two-hour lunch break allowed me to get a good workout. There was a small track across from the Duc, and I began running every day. I got up to about three miles a day and would finish off with a swim in the Duc pool. We would get off work at about 5:00, have dinner in the Duc restaurant, and go to the nightly movie in the Duc theater. Four or five times a month, we would attend dinner parties or some other social function, and it was a comfortable routine.

On most weekends, I was in Saigon. My trips to the provinces and Cambodia were set up so that I would return on Friday afternoon. On a few occasions when I had to be away from Saigon on weekends, I took Lee with me.

This routine might sound boring to some, but for us, it worked. When Lee and I were married the previous August, we had known each other for only eight months, and most of that time had been spent apart. We had a lot to learn about each other, and Vietnam was proving to be a great place to do that.

Life in Saigon was pretty good, and then along came VIOLET/2 and the reality of our relationship with the Special Branch.[1] Of the hundreds of polygraph tests I did on operational assets in Vietnam, I saw no better example of how the Special Branch[2] foisted bad operations on us than in the VIOLET operation. VIOLET/2 was an asset brought to us by a Special Branch officer who claimed that she was a VC security cadre in Kien Hoa province. Her brother, VIOLET/1, was also used in the operation.

In late 1970, a "Captain Dinh" of the Kien Hoa province Special Branch told his CIA liaison contact, "Paul Mathis," that he had recruited a woman who was a district security cadre for the VC. Mathis thought that VIOLET was the best thing since sliced bread. Bypassing the MR/4 C/OPS and the ROIC, he went straight to Shackley with the news that he had a potentially great operation in the offing. Shackley not only gave his seal of approval to the operation but took a hands-on interest in it. From that point on, the VIOLET operation was above criticism. As part of Shackley's authentication process, VIOLET/2 was polygraphed by Bo and, according to him, passed with flying colors.

During the running of the operation, VIOLET/2 produced information that resulted in 209 disseminated reports. In terms of production, VIOLET/2 was second only to FIREBALL, Saigon Station's number-one asset. Producing reports was what the CIA in Vietnam was all about, and VIOLET/2 made a lot of people happy.

When Mathis rotated back to the States, "Benjamin Gruber," a case officer with extensive European experience, replaced him. Gruber was not a Boy Scout, nor was he one of my favorite case officers, but he knew a thing or two about running operations. From the minute that he took over the VIOLET operation, Gruber questioned its validity. He did not

1. VIOLET/2 was the agent Bo Mooney had mentioned to me on our way in from Tan Son Nhut the day we arrived in Vietnam. See chapter 5.

2. The Special Branch was the element of the South Vietnamese National Police specifically targeted against the VC.

win any points with the powers that be in MR/4, but he pushed hard for
another polygraph test of VIOLET/2, and in late July 1971, Gruber was
granted his wish.

At that time, I was the only polygraph examiner in-country, and we
had to request help from Okinawa. "Ron Romanowski" answered the
call. I had worked with Ron back at headquarters. A physically imposing
man, he could be overbearing and a pain in the ass, but he was a good
examiner. I had wanted to do the test on VIOLET/2 myself, but at the
time, I was involved in a lengthy case at the NIC.

On the day of the test, Ron was waiting in my office when I returned
from the NIC, and he was more than a little excited. "How did it go?" I
asked.

Ron told me that he had concluded that the woman was under hostile
control. No examiner ever makes such a call frivolously, and Ron was no
exception. In looking at the questions he had asked and at the charts
from the test, I was in complete agreement with him.

I am not sure why, but Ron had not interrogated VIOLET/2, and no
admission or acknowledgment that she was under hostile control had
been obtained during the interview. Admission or not, Ron submitted
his report stating that VIOLET/2 was under hostile control. When the
report reached headquarters, the reaction was immediate. The next day,
a cable came from headquarters that asked, "What do we do with the 209
disseminated reports VIOLET/2 has provided?"

Shackley had been in Washington for consultations when Ron tested
VIOLET/2, but when he returned to Saigon, he passed down the word
that he wanted the VIOLET issue resolved: Is she a VC security cadre?
Is she under control by either the VC or the Special Branch? Is she fabricating her reports?

This time, I had a chance to test her. I thought it curious that I did
not meet with Gruber before the test, but I had a good idea what I wanted
to ask VIOLET/2. "Greg Collins," one of the best interpreters in Saigon,
would work with me, and that was a real plus.

In addition to testing VIOLET/2, I was asked to test her brother, VIO-
LET/1. Neither VIOLET nor their Special Branch case officer, Captain
Dinh, was told about the tests. Captain Dinh was told that we wanted to
give the VIOLETs some training.

Because I had no faith in Bo and the test he had done on VIOLET/2,
and because VIOLET/2 had failed Ron's test, I was more anxious than

usual about the tests. I had been in-country just a little over four months, but I already knew that the chances of the Special Branch running a good operation ranged from slim to none. I also knew that VIOLET/2 had Shackley's stamp of approval. If I called her bad, I had to get the admission to go along with the call.

Both VIOLETs were brought to a safe house in Saigon, and VIOLET/2 was told to go shopping while her brother was given training. Greg and I arrived at the safe house where VIOLET/1 was waiting. He was a peasant, approximately thirty years old, who appeared bright and quite pleasant. During my conversation with him before the test, I asked him some questions about VIOLET/2. Apparently, neither Mathis nor anyone else had asked VIOLET/2 whether she was married. When I asked VIOLET/1, he said, "Sure." I asked to whom she was married, and he said, "Captain Dinh."

This information was not part of any file or biographical data we had on VIOLET/2. If true, it meant that a captain in the Special Branch had a wife who was a district-level security cadre in the VC. The odds of that happening were minuscule. When I asked VIOLET/1 how he knew that they were married, he looked surprised and said, "I was at the wedding." I tested him and verified that VIOLET/2 and Captain Dinh were married.

As Greg and I were talking with VIOLET/1 after his test, VIOLET/2 showed up. I found her to be an unsophisticated but attractive woman in her mid-twenties. She wore a white blouse, black trousers, and a *non,* the conical straw hat worn by Vietnamese peasants. When she saw us, she seemed surprised.

"Your brother has been telling us some very interesting things about you," I said.

Reacting rather dramatically, she almost screamed, "What have you told them?"

VIOLET/1 recoiled with an "Oh, shit, what have I done?" look on his face. He squirmed on the sofa and looked truly frightened as VIOLET/2 glared at him.

"He told us that you and Captain Dinh are married," I said before he could answer.

VIOLET/2 then lost control. She yelled at her brother and vehemently insisted that she was not Captain Dinh's wife.

I suggested that there was an easy way to resolve the issue. "I just tested your brother on the polygraph. He was telling the truth. I can test you just as easily."

Enraged, VIOLET/2 said, "You have insulted me, and I will not take your test."

My next offer was one that I thought she could not refuse. "It's either take the test or go to jail. You have admitted to being a VC. If you don't take the test, I will have you arrested, right now!"

"I've been in jail before. Go ahead," she said.

I did, and VIOLET/2 was taken off to jail. Within twenty-four hours, she was back in Ben Tre, where she went up to Gruber and laughed in his face. Her husband was promoted to major, and Gruber was transferred out of Kien Hoa province. That Captain Dinh had not even told VIOLET/1 not to tell us that VIOLET/2 was his wife spoke volumes about the Special Branch's disdain for us.

Back at the office, we heard nothing from management about the case. I did not expect Shackley to thank me for ending what had been a productive VC operation, but neither did I anticipate a complete lack of acknowledgment for having resolved the case. In my naiveté, I had expected Shackley to take the Special Branch to task for such a blatant scam. By not doing so, he gave the Special Branch tacit approval to continue foisting fabricated operations on us.

Part of the reason for this could have been that the VIOLET operation was one in which Shackley had taken a personal interest, and the fact that it was phony reflected badly on him. He had touted it as an example of a good operation, and brave was the soul who told him otherwise.

It was my contention that Captain Dinh could not have run this scam without the approval of his superiors. When I broached this with Chris Hanlon, he disagreed, saying that some of the Special Branch officers had enough autonomy to carry off such a scam. I had my doubts, mainly because Dinh had VIOLET/2 out of jail so soon. No captain could pull that off without high-level support. I do not know how much we were paying Dinh for the VIOLET operation, but whatever the amount, I am sure that Dinh's superiors were getting their share.

The VIOLET operation highlighted the CIA's inability to verify even the most basic information about its sources and established that the Special Branch's bad operations were by design, not happenstance. CIA people were gullible, uninformed, and ripe for the plucking. The Special Branch was venal and corrupt, and its people knew that no one, not even they, could run operations against the VC. Just as Shackley pressured ROICs and POICs to recruit and refused to take no for an answer, so, too, our officers pressured the Special Branch with the promise of rewards for recruitments. Shackley used the stick on case officers, and the CIA's Special Branch advisers used the carrot. Neither method had much success in producing VC recruitments.

Prior to VIOLET/2, I had tested Special Branch assets and determined that they were fabricating, but I did not see those fabrications as operations necessarily directed against us by the Special Branch. VIOLET/2 changed my perspective on the Special Branch and South Vietnam's commitment to winning the war.

Approximately 90 percent of the CIA's operational empire in Vietnam was built on leads provided by the Special Branch. CIA's Special Branch liaison officers oversaw operations targeted against the VC by the Special Branch and, at least in theory, guided them in these operations. This was a case of the blind leading the unwilling. I do not know of any CIA Special Branch advisers with whom I worked in Vietnam who had the experience or qualifications to carry out that assignment. I know of two advisers whose previous jobs had been as schoolteachers; neither had any relevant experience with the VC or intelligence collection.

When the CIA began running joint operations with the Special Branch, the Special Branch had been operating against the VC for more than ten years, and to my knowledge, had had no success in penetrating the VC infrastructure. Special Branch officers knew better than we that doing so was almost impossible.

An opinion shared by almost every case officer I met in Vietnam was that the Special Branch was the most incompetent and corrupt entity with which the CIA worked. Perhaps the Special Branch had some good officers, but during my four years in Vietnam, I never had the pleasure of meeting one. After six months in Vietnam, I understood why not a word about the Special Branch had been mentioned in the VNO course—there was nothing positive to say. CIA instructors could not tell the truth about the Special Branch and then expect assignees to go to Vietnam in the "forward-leaning" posture that Shackley demanded. In retrospect, I get goose bumps when I think of a VNO instructor telling us, "Ladies and gentlemen, the main source of our leads in Vietnam works harder running bad operations on us than it does trying to neutralize the VC."

In many cases, a Special Branch officer "ran" (controlled) his CIA case liaison officer. He would tell his CIA contact that he had a lead, or even perhaps an agent, within the VC. The Special Branch case officer might provide some biographical data, some supposed VC documents, and other information to establish his alleged source's bona fides. Unfortunately, we had no way to verify the information the Special Branch officer provided.

Of the inanities that constituted our operations in Vietnam, none was more unrealistic than the idea that our case officers could engage in clandestine operations against the VC and actually recruit them. It was not only the lack of language capability that inhibited our efforts to penetrate the VC, although that was a factor, but also our lack of cultural awareness and physical resemblance to the Vietnamese.

In Saigon, one of our officers might have been able to have a clandestine meeting with a Vietnamese, but that was never going to happen in the provinces. For most of our officers in Vietnam, the transition from such places as Berlin, Buenos Aires, and San Jose to Rach Gia, Da Lat, and Quang Ngai was traumatic. Special Branch officers were the only ones who could "work the streets," and our case officers were in the position of having to sit back and wait for a Special Branch case officer to bring in a lead or an agent.

Some CIA case officers knew from the start that recruiting VC was a figment of Shackley's imagination, and they faked it. Others, less cynical, actually tried to get with the program and ended up disillusioned.

Shackley recognized that regardless of how corrupt or inept the Special Branch was, the CIA could not run operations without it. He was unreceptive to any criticism that our case officers and Special Branch advisers had about the Special Branch. This was not a marriage made in heaven. The Special Branch ran its operations through multiple cutouts whose salaries we paid, and it was rare for one of our case officers to meet face-to-face with a source.

Another example of the extent to which the Special Branch would go to foist a bad operation on us was a test I did on a woman in MR/4 who told me (through an interpreter) that she had been yanked off the street by a Special Branch officer and told that she was going to take a lie detector test conducted by an American. The Special Branch officer who brought her in had briefed her as best he could and told her that he would pay her if the American believed that she was a VC. He was not in the room when I tested her, and it took only about five minutes for her to admit that she had no idea what was going on. She was afraid of the Special Branch officer, and I covered for her by telling him that she was too nervous to be tested.

I thought that the POIC would raise hell with the Special Branch officer, but it did not happen. "John," the POIC said, "we have to live with these assholes, and when the shit finally hits the fan, we may need them. It's easier to look the other way."

Between July 1971 and January 1972, I tested five people who admitted being part of phony operations concocted by the Special Branch. One of them, a seventeen-year-old boy, claimed to have been a VC. Actually, he had lived in a district controlled by the VC and had undergone some training, but then he ran away. On a whim, I handed him an AK-47 and told him to fieldstrip it. He took that weapon apart and put it back together in less time than it would take me to lace a jungle boot. I often used this ploy during the next three years. If someone claiming to be a VC could fieldstrip an AK-47, it did not prove that he was a VC, but if he was unable to do it, the odds were that he was not a VC.

Knowledge about the VC was another matter. The boy did not know anything that a VC should have known. When I tested him, it became clear that he had given us information that he knew was untrue. Ultimately, he admitted that his Special Branch case officer had tried to "coach" him on what to tell us. The Special Branch officer had actually given him a list, which he had with him, of VC terminology to memorize.

In my naiveté, I wrote a memorandum to "Art Korn," chief of Saigon Station's Liaison Branch, in which I identified phony cases the Special Branch had tried to foist on us. I never received a reply. As time went on, I realized that the problem was not that Korn did not care that the Special Branch was conning us but that he could not do anything about it. If we were going to operate against the VC, we had to work with the Special Branch.

One of our Special Branch advisers in MR/2 told me that many of the "suspected VC" the Special Branch arrested were not VC at all but targets for extortion. "They arrest these people and let their relatives buy them out of jail. What a sorry bunch of bastards they are," he said.

It was disturbing, to say the least, to know that our allies were conning us, but even more disturbing was the fact that we never tested any of the Special Branch officers who were doing the conning. With our suspicions that the VC had penetrated the Special Branch, I strongly felt that we should have tested the Special Branch officers working with us to determine whether they were in collusion with the VC. In most cases, Special Branch officers acted as principal agents, that is, agents who ran or controlled one or more other agents in a net. In other countries where we used principal agents, we tested them.

Was there collusion between some Special Branch officers and the VC to keep our case officers preoccupied with operations that went nowhere? Or were these phony operations just another venality of the Special Branch that was directed from the highest levels? My guess would be the latter. I found this very frustrating and occasionally felt a need to get away from the madness.

In September, Lee and I took a trip to Hong Kong. The military ran free R&R flights to Hong Kong, and we had a great week there. Even better, however, was our trip to Kathmandu, Nepal, in October. Ambassador Bunker's wife, Carol Laise, was the consul general in Kathmandu, and when she visited Saigon, there would be room available on her return flight. Lee and I managed to get a couple of seats and had a wonderful week there. The scenery was breathtaking, the atmosphere was restful, and it was like a second honeymoon.

Jack Gordon hosted a Thanksgiving dinner for the office, and except for it being over ninety degrees and no football to watch, it was great.

Just after Thanksgiving 1971, an interpreter and I were driving in MR/2 when we came upon a young Regional Force soldier walking down the road. His arms and face were blistered, and he was clearly in pain. I told the interpreter to ask the soldier if he needed a ride.

"Yes," said the soldier, and we drove him to a small village.

During the ride, he told us that he could not go to the medic unless he paid his captain a bribe. My thought on hearing that was, "Troops are not going to fight for officers who treat them that way."

In December 1971, "Donald Stohl," chief of the CIA's Military Security Service (MSS) Liaison Branch, asked me to test a Chieu Hoi who was suspected of having been re-recruited by the VC. He had rallied to the ARVN sometime in 1970 and had been working with the MSS as an informant and source.

During the pretest, the man claimed that his last contact with the VC had been just before he rallied, and he was adamant that he had had no contact with the VC since then. Testing did not support that claim.

When I confronted him, he suddenly admitted, without any duress, that the VC had contacted him about four months ago and that he had been feeding them information ever since. He was arrested on the spot.

What made the incident so memorable was that just before his arrest, the man made a point of speaking directly to me. "I want you to understand. I like the Americans; it is the Vietnamese government I hate. They lie; they steal. I hate them." Here was a man in his mid-twenties who had been a VC for eight years when he rallied. He told me that he had rallied because his only future as a VC was being killed in a B-52 strike or on a barbed-wire fence outside an ARVN base. Yet he was willing to go back to the VC and face those possibilities rather than work for the government of South Vietnam. As he was being led downstairs to be taken to the NIC, he suddenly stopped and came running back up the stairs. He asked me, "Do I still get my last month's salary?"

The holy grail for CIA polygraphers is catching a double agent. This man was the first of seven that I would catch over the next twenty-eight years, and although I experienced an emotional high at having done so, the man's fervor was disquieting.

Christmas and New Year were quiet, and Lee and I ended the year thinking that we had made the right decision in coming to Vietnam. The good life we were leading continued into January, but during that month, I had a firsthand encounter with a VC that reinforced the idea that we were in a no-win situation.

In January 1972, I was on an army Huey chopper in MR/3 when we received a radio call to pick up a VC who had just been captured. We landed in a mangrove swamp where a blindfolded man with his hands tied behind his back was turned over to us for transportation to the Joint Interrogation Center (JIC) in Bien Hoa. The man, bleeding from shrapnel wounds and crying in pain, was barefoot and dressed in ragged remnants of black pajamas. He was gaunt to the point of emaciation. About five feet, seven inches tall, he could not have weighed 100 pounds.

The contrast between him and his captors was striking. One of the GIs was a little over six feet tall, weighed about 170 pounds, glowed with health, and wore sunglasses. The other GI was several inches shorter than his companion, seemed a bit stocky, and looked Latino. They wore camouflage fatigues caked with dust and floppy hats, and both carried M-16s. Not a word was said during the exchange.

My immediate thought on seeing my first live VC was, "This is who we have been fighting all these years?" If this battered and bleeding man and his fellow VC had fought the U.S. military and its South Vietnamese allies to a standstill, it did not bode well for us.

One sidelight to this event occurred when we landed in Bien Hoa. I found a cigarette lighter on the seat and asked the crew if it belonged to any of them. When none of the three crewmen claimed it, they became a little nervous. Perhaps the prisoner, tied though he was, had left it as some kind of booby trap. Luckily, it was not.

In February 1972, I was in Nha Trang when I received an emergency call from Lee. Her brother Eddie had just called to tell her that their father had died of a stroke. "Cecil Conn," the ROIC, ordered a plane for me, and I was on my way back to Saigon within an hour. By the time I arrived, Lee had already made arrangements for us to fly to Laredo, Texas.

Before we left, Jack Gordon called me into his office to tell me that I would have to check in with IRD and make Bill Osborne aware of Bo Mooney's incompetence. "We can't have him running around the world doing polygraph tests," was the way he put it.

We arrived in Laredo two days before the funeral. It was good to see the family after being away for ten months, even on this sad occasion. Alvaro Tijerina, Lee's father, had been drafted during World War II. Leaving his wife and five children, he went off to war, and while fighting in the battle of Huertgen Forest (known as the "Green Hell") in November 1944, he was captured by the Germans. He ended up a POW in Stalag IV-B near Dresden. Although he came back to the States in one piece in June 1945, he had been traumatized and never regained his prewar health. He was only fifty-seven when he died. After the funeral, Lee stayed in Laredo while I went to headquarters.

First on my list of things to do was to fill in Bill Osborne about Bo. Then I had to check in with Harry West in OS, and finally with VNO. Osborne, who had overridden Kirk's decision not to certify Bo, was unmoved by my report on him. "Jesus H. Christ, when 'Cliff Deal' [the regional security officer] comes through Saigon, you better tell him," he said.

I went to see Harry West and was surprised that he remembered me. He asked how it was going in Vietnam, and when I told him about being shot at coming out of Moc Hoa, he laughed and assured me that being shot at was par for the course. Then he said, "John, I hate to rush, but I have a meeting. You're doing a great job out there. Have a great trip back." No "How's Lee doing?" or "Is there anything we can help you with?"

I was off to VNO. In my vanity, I honestly thought that I might have something to offer at a VNO course. I had been in each of the MRs and most of the provinces, met many of the case officers, and had a pretty good sense of the operational climate, as well as the living conditions, in both Saigon and the provinces. I called VNO as directed by EA Personnel and asked if there was any interest in having me speak to a VNO class. "Not really," was the answer.

During the flights to and from the States, I thought about where our people were headed in Vietnam. Based on what I had seen during my first ten months there, I was certain that the South Vietnamese military would never be able to make up for the loss of American troops. During those ten months, the number of U.S. troops in Vietnam had dropped from about 220,000 to approximately 70,000, and the drawdown was still going on.[3]

It occurred to me that I could not recall one ROIC, POIC, or case officer giving a positive prognosis for the outcome of the war. Bill Buckley[4] had told me that, during General Westmoreland's visit to Saigon in 1971, he had told Westmoreland, "There is no way the ARVN can do it without our army." That was after Westmoreland had said that he would be proud to lead any ARVN unit into combat.

Operations, such as they were, were of abysmal quality. I had not tested anyone who had even come close to penetrating the VC, and most of the case officers were frustrated. From what I had seen, there was little support among the South Vietnamese for Thieu or his government, nor did I see any possibility of the South Vietnamese becoming communists. They were the ultimate capitalists and always would be.

I thought that the NVA would wait until all the American troops were gone before engaging in any major attacks. But on March 30, 1972, the NVA launched a massive offensive and showed me how wrong I was. Perhaps emboldened by their success in driving the ARVN out of Laos during Lam Son 719 and encouraged by the continuing withdrawal of

3. George Donelson Moss, *Vietnam, an American Ordeal* (Upper Saddle River, N.J.: Prentice-Hall, 1990), p. 446.
4. Bill Buckley was the COS in Beirut who was kidnapped and executed by Hezbollah.

American troops, the NVA launched a three-pronged major offensive with attacks on Quang Tri in MR/1, Kontum in MR/2, and An Loc in MR/3. These attacks are identified in history books as the Easter Offensive. The North Vietnamese referred to the action as the Nguyen Hue Offensive. At that time, only about 70,000 U.S. troops remained in Vietnam, 6,000 of which were combat troops,[5] and the numbers were declining each month. By comparison, there had been 450,000 more U.S. troops in Vietnam when the NVA launched the Tet Offensive of 1968. To the North Vietnamese, the timing of the 1972 Easter Offensive seemed right. The bombing halt called by President Johnson in October 1968 was still in effect, and the continuing withdrawal of U.S. troops left the South Vietnamese in a vulnerable position.

Of the three attacks launched by the North Vietnamese, the April 7 attack on An Loc turned out to be the most significant battle of the offensive. President Thieu made a public declaration in which he stated that An Loc would be held at all costs. An Loc became the biggest battle since Tet of 1968, and it received extensive press coverage. I was the CIA duty officer in the embassy when I received a radio message from one of the American advisers at An Loc that said, in effect, "We can't hold out any longer and will probably be overrun either tonight or tomorrow morning."

They were not overrun. Some of the soldiers who were there told me later that the B-52s inflicted massive casualties on the NVA. A U.S. Army adviser said that the NVA had not left the ARVN an escape route, which, according to him, was a tactical error. The ARVN troops, with nowhere to run, had no choice but to fight, and they fought well.

An NVA prisoner revealed that NVA soldiers hid in the craters created by previous B-52 strikes because they thought the Americans would not bomb an area a second time. Maj. Gen. James Hollingsworth ordered strikes on previously bombed areas, however, and those attacks were devastating to the NVA.

I was in MR/3 in May 1972, conducting a test, when the house began to shake and plaster fell from the ceiling. I had experienced two earthquakes in Latin America and thought I was experiencing another one. "B-52 strike, Mr. John," my interpreter told me. We were more than ten

5. Stanley Karnow, *Vietnam, a History* (New York: Penguin Books, 1991), p. 657.

miles away from the target, and I thought, at the time, how terrifying
these attacks must be for the people in their paths.

Two VC I tested said that there was nothing more terrifying than
being in an underground tunnel during a B-52 strike. "We sit there in
the dark, feeling the earth shake, and wonder if we are going to suffo-
cate," one said. Another VC told me that the craters created by the
bombs were dangerous, especially during the rainy season. "The holes
fill up with rain, and when we run at night, we sometimes fall in. Com-
rades have drowned in these holes."

The siege of An Loc lasted ninety-five days, and in my opinion, its
failure signaled to the North Vietnamese that as long as American air-
power and advisers were on the scene, they could not militarily defeat
South Vietnam.

The Easter Offensive actually lasted until September, when South
Vietnamese marines drove the NVA out of Quang Tri.[6] By then, according to author John Pimlott, "the NVA had lost about half its committed
force—an estimated 100,000 men—against a South Vietnamese casualty
figure half that size."[7] George Donelson Moss claims that the NVA committed 122,000 troops to the offensive and notes that "North Vietnam
lost over 100,000 troops killed in battle, most of their tanks and much of
their artillery in three months."[8] Although there may be some question
about the exact number of casualties the NVA sustained, there is little
doubt that the Nguyen Hue Offensive was the worst defeat of the war for
the NVA.

Flying around Vietnam during the Easter Offensive was as close as I
ever came to the actual war. But throughout my time in Vietnam and
Cambodia, I caught glimpses that gave me a feel for the war that few
noncombatants had.

On my first trip to Da Nang in April 1971, Bo drove me out to the end
of a runway at Da Nang Air Base to watch F-4 Phantoms, with bombs
under their wings, take off and fly north. They flew about fifty feet over
our jeep, and the noise was deafening. The lack of antiaircraft defenses
was noticeable. Throughout the war, North Vietnam did not deploy its
planes south of Hanoi or Haiphong but used them only in an air defense

6. Moss, *Vietnam, an American Ordeal*, p. 386.
7. John Pimlott, *Vietnam, the Decisive Battles* (New York: Macmillan, 1990), p. 171.
8. Moss, *Vietnam, an American Ordeal*, pp. 377, 386.

capacity. U.S. and allied forces, as well as the ARVN and South Vietnamese civilians, did not have to worry about air attacks. When one considers how large a role air power played in the American prosecution of the war, it is amazing that the NVA forces won without utilizing it.

I have a more poignant memory of a July morning in Pleiku, in MR/2. I was sitting in the doorway of an army Huey helicopter talking with a crewman. He was a young E-4 from the Upper Peninsula of Michigan, and we were discussing Michigan State football when we heard the *"mot, hai, ba"* (one, two, three) of ARVN troops marching across the tarmac toward some waiting helicopters. As one column passed, an ARVN soldier broke ranks, ran over to our helicopter, and tried to take the fifty-round magazine out of the M-16 that was leaning against the door. That magazine was not the usual load for an M-16 and had to be specially made. Obviously, the ARVN soldier wanted more firepower, but the American crewman had other ideas. He grabbed the M-16 before the Vietnamese could disengage the magazine and said, "Sorry, buddy, I need it as much as you do." The ARVN soldier probably did not understand what the GI was saying, but he knew that he was not going to get the magazine and took off to join his column. "Those guys are always trying to get our equipment, and I feel for them, but these big magazines are hard to come by," the E-4 said.

In June 1972, I was flying in the right-hand seat of a Porter when the pilot nudged me. "Look at that," he said. He then pointed to his left. Way off, and high in the distance, a B-52 was dropping bombs. The sun was glinting off the B-52, and there was no sense of motion. We were too far away to hear the roar of the plane or the whistling of the falling bombs, but we did see the huge geysers of dust and debris as the bombs impacted. The pilot told me that Air America was usually informed where B-52 strikes would be taking place, but in this case, that had not been done.

On an Air America flight from Nha Trang to Saigon, I took a picture of a young Vietnamese girl who had been burned by napalm. The resignation on the face of the little girl's mother seemed to say to me, "Why?" When I showed the picture to Amos Spitz, he said, "Someone should get ahold of that girl right now and tell her that if it weren't for the communists, she would not have been burned." I found his comment to be out of place.

I will never forget two young boys who were begging near our compound in Da Nang. Between them, they had one functioning leg and three arms. I saw a dead VC on a street in Qui Nhon, another reminder that people die in war. Thankfully, I never saw a dead GI. Such sights and sounds let me know that there was a war going on, but I was never directly involved in the fighting. During my four years in Vietnam, I was a passenger in two planes that came under enemy fire. I came under "friendly fire" on one occasion and rocket barrages on two occasions. Those events were as close to the war as I wanted to get. I have never fired a weapon in anger or had any kind of fire directed at me, personally. Thirty years later, I am glad that that's the way it was.

Between its withdrawal from An Loc in June 1972 and the signing of the Paris Peace Accords on January 27, 1973, the NVA licked its wounds and tried to consolidate what gains it had made during the Easter Offensive. With the retaking of Quang Tri came a lull in the fighting. Losses inflicted on the NVA during the offensive seemed to arouse some intransigence at the Paris peace talks. As a result, on December 14, the American delegation walked out, and Nixon ordered a resumption of air attacks against North Vietnam. In conjunction with the massive casualties suffered by the NVA during the Easter Offensive, the air attacks seemed to give the communist forces reason to reassess their strategy, as well as to convince the North Vietnamese delegation to cooperate at the peace talks.

During December 1972, while the Christmas bombings (or Linebacker II, as the operation was known) were being carried out, Lee and I attended the last Bob Hope Christmas show. Redd Foxx and Lola Falana were the headliners, and we enjoyed the show at Tan Son Nhut, which played to a large and appreciative audience.

Our tour was due to end in April 1973, but Lee and I were both enjoying our work and decided to ask for a second tour. Keith Barry, who had replaced Jack Gordon as my boss, supported my request, and the Office of Security concurred. Although not optimistic about the outcome of the war, I felt no sense of personal danger and was looking forward to a second tour.

8

SAIGON STATION

Saigon Station was the theater in which most of the experiences I describe were played out. It consisted of four military regions and Saigon/Gia Dinh, which was sometimes referred to as MR/5.[1] During my first tour, I worked extensively in each of the military regions, traveled to almost all the provinces, and acquired a pretty good feel for the country. The variety of personalities I dealt with, the geographic locations of the military regions, and the tests I conducted during these travels defined for me the "personalilty" of each military region, and each one was different.

Having worked in more than forty CIA stations, I can attest to the fact that Saigon Station was unparalleled in the amount of support it provided to CIA personnel who served in Vietnam. Our housing was excellent, and we did not have to so much as change a lightbulb. It was easy to become spoiled, and many of us did.

1. The U.S. military referred to the military regions as corps. For example, MR/1 was I Corps, MR/2 was II Corps, and so forth.

Staff members had three choices regarding family arrangements: (1) if they brought their spouses, the tour lasted for two years; (2) if an employee opted to leave his or her family in the States and come to Vietnam on an unaccompanied tour, the tour lasted for eighteen months, and the employee was allowed one paid round-trip visit back to the States; or (3) families could be safe-havened in Taipei, Taiwan, and the employee could visit the family every six weeks at CIA expense. One result of this was that at all times at least one-third of Saigon Station was traveling. Supporting that travel was no small task, and the office that handled the station's travel had more employees than some other countries' entire intelligence services.

In 1971, a GS-13 earned between $13,760 and $22,000 a year, depending on his or her step in the pay scale. There was also a 25 percent bonus for being in Vietnam. One of our GS-13s in Saigon had a wife and ten children safe-havened in Taipei. Because of the size of his family, he needed two houses. Counting salary, housing, schooling, and travel from the States to Taipei and back, as well as travel every six weeks for family visits, this employee was costing American taxpayers more than $150,000 a year.

A mail clerk (GS-5) and his wife were assigned a five-bedroom house and a car. In addition, they had two maids and a cook. Compared with their lifestyle back in the States, they lived quite well.

CIA officers overseas are assigned rent-free housing. The chief of station is usually provided with a car and sometimes a chauffeur. Furniture is not usually provided, and officers bring their own cars. Unless there is a post exchange nearby, food is bought at local markets. Medical care can be a problem, but regional medical officers periodically visit CIA stations.

In Saigon during the early 1970s, however, the situation was different. The housing provided for our people was excellent, and some of it bordered on elegant. All furniture, glassware, flatware, and utensils were provided. Most staffers were given cars, and no one brought his or her own car to Vietnam; gas and servicing were free. GS-15s and above were assigned chauffeurs. One of the more memorable sights in Saigon was of Vietnamese chauffeurs sitting across the street from the embassy weaving multicolored baskets made of telephone wires. These baskets, a cottage industry for the chauffeurs, are souvenirs unique to Vietnam.

Partying hearty was another reality of Saigon, and keeping up with

Saigon's social life was a challenge. Lee and I saved a lot of our party invitations in a wire basket and counted them before leaving Vietnam. We had 204.

Two physicians were assigned to Saigon Station. Although some CIA people complained about the quality of the care, Lee and I (and later our son John) were well served by them. One of the doctors, "Don Kildare," was young, handsome, and the most eligible bachelor in the station. When he married a Vietnamese woman, he broke a lot of hearts.

As good as the living was in Saigon, I missed American magazines and periodicals. I loved the *New York Times* and *Sports Illustrated* and had been accustomed to reading the *Washington Post* every day. Lee and I had been avid followers of TV news as well, and the lack of it contributed to a sense of isolation. I had depended on the news media to help me formulate positions on current issues relating to the war and politics and, in general, to keep me informed.

Life in three of the four regional capitals was scaled down from that in Saigon. But Bien Hoa, being only twelve miles from Saigon, basked in its social life, and several staff employees assigned to Bien Hoa lived in Saigon. Nha Trang was the most aesthetically pleasing of the other three regional capitals. No significant operations were going on there, and life was good. Da Nang, the second largest city in Vietnam, offered much in the way of nightlife and recreation, but the housing was better in Saigon and Nha Trang. Can Tho, the ugliest of the regional capitals, was also the busiest in terms of operational activity. Large numbers of Americans, including State Department employees, military personnel, and construction workers, lived in the regional capitals. Consequently, the sense of isolation was diminished.

In the provinces, as in Saigon, free housing was provided, along with household staffs, and the amenities were more than adequate. I recall one such amenity in the house of the POIC in Vinh Long: a Limoges china commode that he took with him when he rotated back to the States.

The two primary differences between life in Saigon and life in the provinces were the danger and the social life. I am unaware of any NVA or VC attacks on American residences in the provinces, but the potential was always there. Social life in the provinces was limited. No CIA women were assigned to the provincial offices, although many female staffers visited the provinces at least once during their tours. Occasionally, provincial officers brought their spouses in-country for a visit. Nightlife in the provinces, as compared with Saigon's, was practically nonexistent. The primary social activity was happy hour with U.S. military, USAID, and State Department personnel. My most memorable night out in the provinces occurred in Chau Doc (MR/4). Armed with an Armalite survival rifle, the POIC and I went out to a huge trash dump and shot rats.

During my time in Vietnam, I visited every CIA province office and sometimes experienced minor discomforts, such as a power outage or sleeping next to a noisy generator. One night in Chau Doc, I slept in a room that had a big hole in the wall where an air conditioner had been. Mosquitoes swarmed in and had a feast. I ended up sleeping on the living room couch.

A slower pace and less pressure from management were upsides to the less sybaritic life in the provinces. Officers who wanted to save money were also in a much better position to do so in the provinces. Provincial officers were pretty much on their own, however, and this turned out to be a problem for some of them. A number of those who were unhappy about being in Vietnam, and in many cases even less happy about being in a province, turned to alcohol or women for solace. Officers who liked working independently or who had an aversion to bureaucracy were much more comfortable away from Saigon.

Regardless of where they served, most CIA officers in Vietnam realized that they had a good deal. It was de rigueur and politically correct to trumpet the hardships, but most of the CIA people I know recall their experiences in Vietnam favorably.

MR/1

The province of Quang Tri bordered North Vietnam, and Quang Ngai was the southernmost province in MR/1. Our regional headquarters was in Da Nang, located in Quang Nam province. Subordinate to Da Nang were provincial offices in Hue, Tam Ky, and Quang Ngai, each with a POIC and two or three case officers. The regional headquarters were miniversions of Saigon Station, with an ROIC, a deputy, a C/OPS, a reports officer, a support officer, an air ops officer to coordinate Air America flights, a communications technician, case officers, and secretaries. There were two offices in Da Nang—one in our compound and another at the consulate downtown.

Hue, the old imperial capital of Vietnam, was the site of horrific fighting, as well as an NVA massacre of civilians during the Tet Offensive of

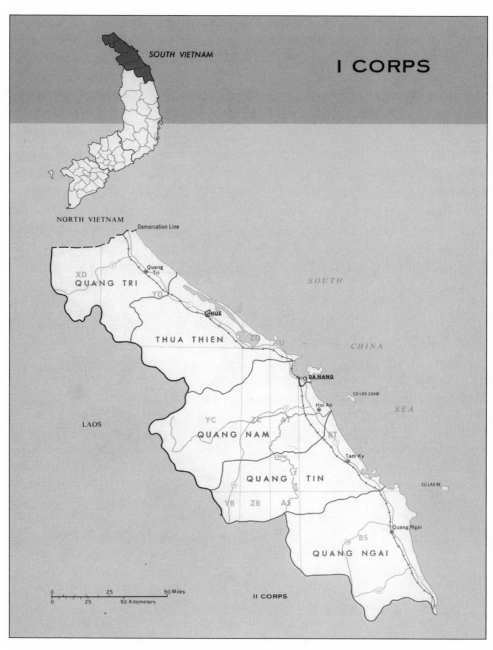

MR/1, consisting of five provinces on the North China Sea, was the northernmost
military region in South Vietnam.

1968. It was also one of my favorite places to visit. Situated on the Hue River and full of old French colonial villas, Hue is a photographer's paradise. I took more pictures there than in any other area of Vietnam.

It was always assumed by the military that the big push by the NVA would come through MR/1. As a result, much of the focus for case officers in the region was getting information on the military situation, such as the deployment and disposition of North Vietnamese forces.

No one ever shot at me in MR/1, but on one of my visits to Da Nang, I did encounter a potentially life-threatening situation. During a lunch break, "Denise Bennett," an office secretary, offered me a ride from the consulate back to our compound. She was driving an old, dilapidated Datsun from the car pool, and as we drove through Da Nang, I heard something rattling in the trunk. When we arrived at the compound, I opened the trunk and saw two M-26 grenades in a pool of gasoline. A five-gallon gasoline can, with its top open, was lying on its side. I did not dwell on what might have happened had we been rear-ended during that brief ride.

"Mike Rogers" was the ROIC in MR/1, "Sam Wallace" the deputy ROIC, and "Dave Ritter" the C/OPS when I arrived in Vietnam. "Sue Wayne," whom I knew from my trips to Latin America, was the reports officer. During my tour, I worked with four ROICs in MR/1. Most of them appeared to have given up the idea of trying to penetrate the VC.

"Stan Amott," Rogers's successor, impressed me as a good officer, and I enjoyed working with him. His attitude toward his assignment appeared to be, Don't let anything bad happen on my watch. The atmosphere in Da Nang was pretty relaxed during Amott's reign, and the morale was good.

During Amott's tour, I tested a VC sapper whom our marines had caught sneaking onto the Da Nang Air Base. He had a satchel charge strapped to his back, and plausible denial was out of the question. How the CIA obtained custody of him is still unclear, but it was hoped that he would identify some of the other VC in his cell.

I worked on this case with "Vern Morgan," a case officer who had previously served a tour in MR/1 as a marine. John Long, MR/1's best Vietnamese interpreter, worked with us on the case, and our plan was to tell the VC that we would not turn him over to the South Vietnamese if he cooperated with us.

What I remember most about this particular VC was how clean-cut and soft he looked. He was about seventeen years old and seemed more like a schoolboy than a VC. His skin and hands were soft, and he obviously had not spent much time in a rice paddy or behind a team of water buffalo.

I yelled, I cajoled, I raged, and I threatened him. He cried. Morgan, the ex-marine, cried too, and said, "You don't have to be so mean to him," but all my yelling was to no avail. The sapper said only that his mission had been to throw the explosives under one of the barracks. He did not know the name of the VC who had given him the satchel. Morgan turned him over to the South Vietnamese MSS.

"Pedro Torres," Amott's replacement, was the most colorful of the ROICs who ran MR/1. Awarded a Distinguished Service Cross during World War II, Torres had spent much of his youth at West Point, where his father had been the Master of the Sword (physical training instructor). Full of Latin machismo, Torres was short, overweight, and bald and wore glasses; he had grown children and was separated from his wife.

Denise Bennett told me a story that more or less demonstrated Torres's thinking. "Last Saturday," she said, "Pedro and a bunch of us went swimming on one of the deserted beaches. Pedro and Steve [an MR/1 logistics officer] were wandering around off the beach and came upon a hut hidden in some bushes. Pedro and Steve took out their guns and charged the hut with guns blazing."

Paul Theroux describes meeting an individual in Da Nang who identified himself as "the head spook around here."[2] Based on the physical description of the "spook" and the timing of the meeting, he appears to be describing Torres. It is not a flattering description. Theroux's characterization of this individual is that of a drunken and dissipated lecher, but I never saw Torres drunk or looking seedy. I did, however, have some problems with him. He was an empire builder, and he ran MR/1 like a fiefdom.

Torres had been Lee's boss in Latin America, and despite my reservations, we actually had a pretty good relationship with him. Lee joined me in MR/1 for a weekend as Torres's guests, and we had a good time. Nowhere, outside of Saigon, was social life more robust than in Da Nang during Torres's reign. He arranged what he pompously called "cultural weekends" in Da Nang and invited the single women in Saigon to join

2. Paul Theroux, *The Great Railway Bazaar* (Boston: Houghton Mifflin, 1975), p. 263.

in the fun. One of our secretaries went to a cultural weekend and came back incensed. "We were expected to sleep with those guys up there. Who the hell do they think they are?" she said.

Two incidents, or situations, occurred during Torres's tenure that demonstrated that there was a price to pay for the lifestyle he fostered in Da Nang. The first was tragic, the second, pathetic.

"Harry Land," an administrative officer in MR/1, had a wife and two young children. In my contacts with him, he impressed me as being a nice guy—mild mannered, unassuming, and always helpful. He fell in love with a young, attractive Vietnamese woman who worked in our compound. Land was so taken by her that he decided to divorce his wife and marry his newfound love. Land went to Taipei, where his family was safe-havened, and told his wife that he wanted a divorce. When he returned to Da Nang, he found that his paramour had run off with an American GI. Having lost what he thought was the love of his life and having burned bridges with his wife, Land shot and killed himself. In the suicide note he left, Land apologized to his wife for not having done the taxes.

My most poignant memory of that incident was a conversation I had with "Kenneth Little," the personnel officer who had to break the news to Land's family. Little told me that he had helped the family make arrangements to return to the States. When he was taking the family to the airport, Land's young son had asked him, "Who's going to play football with me now?"

The second incident involved "Graham Ford," a C/OPS in MR/1 during Torres's reign. He had inherited the house and mistress of his predecessor, but unfortunately, his mistress was a bit of a dragon lady—corrupt and mean. She found maids and other types of household servants for CIA employees and, as was the custom, took kickbacks from them.

"Bruce Green," a bright young officer, was one of Ford's subordinates. A Special Branch adviser, he was a pleasure to work with and was one of the few case officers who spoke Vietnamese. His wife was with him in Da Nang, and they were a great young couple.

On one of my trips to Da Nang, I was working with Green, and he related the first of many stories about the "Dragon Lady." He had gone home for lunch one day and found a young Vietnamese refugee waiting in front of his house. She was crying and claimed that the Dragon Lady had taken her identification (ID) card and would not give it back unless she "worked" for her. Green wrote a note to the Dragon Lady and told her that if she did not return the ID card within two hours, he would go directly to Saigon and bring her and Ford's affair to the attention of the chief of station. Within the hour, the girl had her ID card back, and Green became a permanent member of Ford's "shit list." The Dragon Lady made some threats, and Green went to Torres and told him that if anything happened to his wife he would personally kill the Dragon Lady.

Before returning to Saigon, I told Torres that the Dragon Lady was bad news, that she had been in the house when I conducted a test, and that she had operated the Special Branch radio net while Ford was passed out drunk. "Pedro, this is a bad situation that is not going to get any better," I said. "Graham is an alcoholic, and the Dragon Lady is just that. You should do something before something really bad happens."

Torres said that he knew the Dragon Lady was no Girl Scout. "If I take her away from him [Ford], it would destroy him," he added. "She keeps him going." Then he said that if she exacted retribution in any way, he would take action.

"Are you going to wait until someone gets hurt before you do anything?" I asked.

He blew me off and said that nothing would happen. He also sent a message to Keith Barry, my boss, expressing his concern that, in my fit of moral indignation, I might do something rash. He referred to me as a "loose cannon." Barry told me that I might be blowing the situation out of proportion and suggested that I not pursue it.

Moral indignation, my ass! The Dragon Lady was bad and, as far as I was concerned, a security risk. I had asked Torres to let me polygraph her, but he declined. It had not been my intention to go to Polgar or anyone else, because I felt that Green could handle the situation. However, I was irritated at Torres for his laissez-faire attitude about the Dragon Lady and for having sent the letter to Barry.

Another and far more egregious aspect of the Dragon Lady saga was that she tried to extort money from one of Green's assets. Green had recruited a politician in Da Nang who was a member of Thieu's party. He spoke some English, and they met at Green's house under the guise of Green taking Vietnamese lessons. Through the servant network, the Dragon Lady became aware of these meetings. She approached Green's agent and told him that unless he paid her off, she would report him to the police. The agent told Green about the attempted extortion. He said that if the Dragon Lady reported him, at the very least, he would have to pay the police off. Also, he was afraid that he would be arrested and exposed. Green reported this to the OS in Saigon, and nothing was done.[3] I know nothing was done because the Dragon Lady and Ford were together until the end of Ford's tour, almost a year after the incident. Green also told me that he continued his clandestine relationship with the agent and suspected that he was paying the Dragon Lady off.[4]

Torres was also vindictive. Green had incurred Torres's wrath over the Dragon Lady situation. To assuage his need for retribution, Torres wrote a back-channel memorandum to headquarters in which he questioned Green's character and competence and suggested that Green was unfit to be a case officer. One of the results of Torres's character assassination was that Green resigned from the CIA and became a very successful lawyer.

Torres's replacement, "Bob Beal," was in sharp contrast to Torres. Beal brought his wife, "Monica," with him, and the sexual liaisons that had been so common among our staffers during Torres's tenure were considerably toned down.

Beal was an experienced officer with considerable East Asia experience. My initial contact with him left me feeling that he had little, if any, use for polygraph testing and even less for polygraph examiners. He and I did not exchange fifty words from that initial contact until I left Vietnam.

The Beals had brought an impressive collection of Chinese artifacts to Da Nang, and one of the logistics people told me that Beal had a light installed in one of the closets to prevent Monica's fur coat from getting mildewed. The Beals had to abandon all their artifacts when they fled Da Nang.

Overall, MR/1 was a fun place to visit. Not much happened there, and I was never overworked.

MR/2

Kontum was the northernmost province in MR/2, and Binh Thuan the southernmost. Our regional headquarters was at Nha Trang in Khanh Hoa province, and there were provincial offices in the cities and

3. Bruce Green, e-mail, June 11, 2000.
4. Bruce Green, e-mail, August 6, 2000.

towns of Ban Me Thuot, Da Lat, Phan Thiet, Pleiku, Qui Nhon, and Tuy Hoa. In terms of area, MR/2 was the largest military region in Vietnam, but it was also the least populated.

Flying into Nha Trang was one of the more aesthetically pleasing experiences of my time in Vietnam. Da Lat, in some ways, reminded me of southern Germany. Although the mountains were not as high as the Alps, it could get cold up there. Many of the houses resembled chalets. The POIC's house in Da Lat was a beautiful mountain retreat that I enjoyed visiting.

There were three ROICs in MR/2 during my time in Vietnam. "Tito Cortez" was the ROIC at the time we arrived in Vietnam and was one of the more colorful characters I met. He had served with Shackley in Miami and Laos prior to coming to Vietnam and was an established member of the Shackley team.

My most substantive contact with Cortez took place one night in the recreation room in Nha Trang. I was playing pool with an officer friend when Cortez came in with another officer. To me, Cortez resembled an enlarged version of the Latin movie star Cesar Romero—wavy, silver-streaked hair; small but elegant mustache; well spoken with a slight southwestern-Latin accent, and a diamond-in-the-rough charm.

Cortez and his friend were a little drunk and asked us if they could play. I was the only gringo among us, but I joined in when they began speaking Spanish. This seemed to loosen Cortez up, and he talked pretty openly for the next hour or so. When I told him that this was my first experience working with Shackley, Cortez said, "Ted and I go back a long way. I've known him since he was a shavetail [lieutenant] in Berlin, and I pulled his ass out of a fire." He did not elaborate, and I did not push him.

I do not remember the context in which it came up, but at one point during the evening, Cortez made the statement that he and Pedro Torres had offered to kill Philip Agee.[5] Cortez claimed that he and Torres had made the offer to Thomas H. Karamessines, the deputy director for plans (1967–1973), and Cortez added, laughingly, "Karamessines threw both of us out of his office." On a visit to Da Nang, Torres volunteered the same story.

5. Agee, a disgruntled former CIA case officer, identified agents he had recruited in his book *Inside the Company: CIA Diary*. Agee, who now lives in Hamburg, Germany, has an Internet site on which he promotes tourist trips to Cuba.

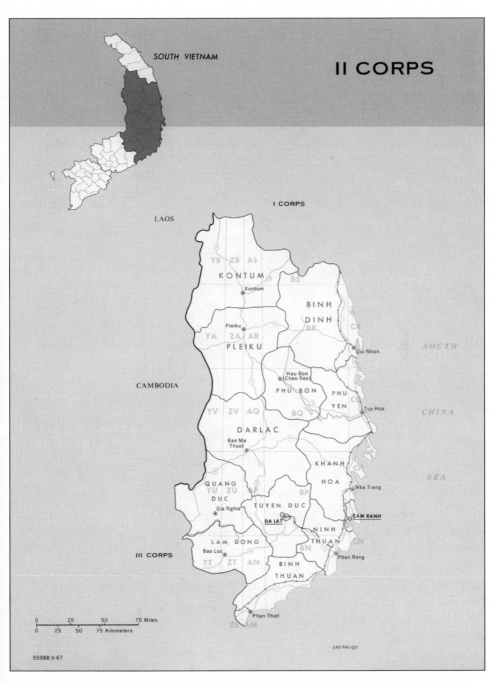

II CORPS

I CORPS

LAOS

KONTUM

Kontum

BINH
DINH

Pleiku

PLEIKU

Qui Nhon

SOUTH

CAMBODIA

Hau Bon
(Cheo Reo)

PHU BON

PHU
YEN

Tuy Hoa

CHINA

DARLAC

Ban Me
Thuot

KHANH
HOA

Nha Trang

SEA

QUANG
DUC

TUYEN DUC

BP

Gia Nghia

DA LAT

CAM RANH

NINH
THUAN

LAM DONG

Bao Loc

Phan Rang

III CORPS

BINH
THUAN

Phan Thiet

0   25   50   75 Miles
0   25   50   75 Kilometers

DAO PHU QUI

55988 9-67

MR/2 consisted of twelve provinces and covered primarily the Vietnamese highlands.

Cortez was always friendly when we met, but on a couple of occasions I heard him ream out some of his subordinates. He reminded me of one of my drill sergeants in basic training. That behavior did not go over well in Nha Trang, and my impression was that morale was pretty low.

Cecil Conn replaced Cortez in Nha Trang. He had been deputy ROIC in MR/3 when we arrived, and he had asked me to test his mistress, because he wanted to hire her as an office manager. During the test, I developed information that precluded her from being hired, but Conn never seemed to have any hard feelings toward me, and we got along very well.

Morale in MR/2 definitely improved under Conn, with one notable exception. He had a finance officer, "Bill Webb," who had a drinking problem and was incompetent. I was present when Cortez's deputy, "Dick Parsons," chewed Webb out as harshly as I have ever heard it done. "Webb, you are the biggest fuck-up since the Edsel. I can't wait to get you out of here," Parsons screamed at him.

Webb, who had been with the CIA for more than twenty years, silently took the abuse. For whatever reason, Webb saw me as a shoulder to cry on, and when I was in Nha Trang, he would seek me out and tell me about his problems with Conn and Parsons. "John, this job is just too much for me," he would say. "At the end of my career, I shouldn't have to work like this. Conn and Parsons are pricks, and I hate them as much as they hate me." This was the tenor of most of the conversations I had with him.

In December 1972, Webb overnighted at the Duc on his way back to the States for Christmas leave. I was doing laps in the pool when Webb asked if he could speak with me. "John, you saw how they treated me up there. Now it's my turn." Webb then proceeded to tell me how he had documented many instances of malfeasance by Conn. Most incriminating were photocopies of vouchers that Conn had submitted for operational expenses that were not legitimate. "What those assholes don't know is that my wife used to be [DCI William] Colby's secretary, and she has set up an appointment for me with him," Webb bragged.

Apparently, Webb got his appointment with Colby, because within two weeks, Bill Evans was put in charge of an investigation of allegations of malfeasance on the part of Conn. Evans's investigation supported Webb's claims. When Conn returned from Christmas leave, he was given the option of retiring or facing prosecution. He paid approximately $8,000 in restitution and retired.

Both Frank Snepp and Arnold R. Isaacs allude to this malfeasance in their books and cite it as a reason for the failure to develop intelligence in MR/2. But from what I saw, no amount of money could have improved the operational climate in MR/2.

"Claude Shin" replaced Conn and was the last ROIC in MR/2. An ethnic Chinese, Shin was an experienced officer and had an excellent reputation in EA Division. Shin came across as professional, competent, and supportive in my contacts with him. The operational climate in MR/2 made it difficult for any ROIC to look good, but Shin looked much better than his two predecessors.

An event that colored my perspective on MR/2 was a trip I made to Pleiku in October 1971. The POIC was on leave, and "Jack Craig" was in charge. He was the worst of the "ugly Americans" I encountered in Vietnam. Craig was a former schoolteacher who had decided that he needed a change of scenery.

When the Porter dropped me off at the military airstrip in Pleiku, no one was there to meet me. I waited for an hour and then went to the U.S. Army operations center, where I radioed the office in Saigon, which in turn contacted Nha Trang. Someone there called Craig and told him to get to the airstrip and pick me up. "Jesus, we didn't know you were coming. Sorry!" were Craig's first words.

I had already visited several province compounds and, for the most part, had found them well maintained and fairly clean. Pleiku was not. Empty beer cans were everywhere; C-ration cans and dirty clothes were strewn about. Craig had picked me up at about 4:30 P.M., and when I arrived at the compound, happy hour was about to begin. Case officer "Rob Young" was there. Much younger than Craig, Young was not only a good guy but also a good officer. He had two of the better recruits I would test in Vietnam.

The three of us sat around and traded war stories until dinner. Craig told me that his Special Branch contact had a couple of assets he wanted tested and that he would set up the tests the next day. That night, some U.S. Army officers came over, and we all watched a movie. After the movie, I told Craig that I was going to turn in, and he asked me if I wanted a girl. "No, thanks, I have my wife here with me," I said.

"Well, if you have your own cunt, then you don't need any of mine," he said.

"What a classy guy," I thought. The fact that he had a sexually trans-mitted disease of the throat only solidified my low opinion of him.

Craig had his Vietnamese girlfriend (and, subsequently, mother of his children) with him, and she was very pleasant. For the three days I was there, Craig did not leave the compound. He wandered around unshaven and disheveled. The Special Branch officer brought his assets to be tested, and both failed. Craig seemed unconcerned.

My thought on leaving Pleiku on that occasion was that Craig was not the kind of guy I wanted representing the CIA in Vietnam, or anywhere else. He had no relevant experience to bring to the table, was a slob, and did not seem to care.

MR/2, in terms of operations, recruitments, and polygraph, was a wasteland. There were Special Branch operations in the larger cities of Nha Trang, Pleiku, and Qui Nhon, but much of our effort was directed at getting information on NVA troop movements by using Cambodian and Montagnard reconnaissance teams.

In the summer of 1972, I was in MR/2 to test one of the Cambodian reconnaissance teams. These teams had been recruited to report on the NVA military buildup along the South Vietnamese–Cambodian border. I had tested a lot of road-watch teams in Laos, and I saw many similarities between them and the Cambodian teams I tested in Vietnam. The team members ranged in age from teenagers to septuagenarians. They were rather unsophisticated people, and I remember the look of awe on the face of one man after his first flight in a Porter.

One aspect of testing them did not amuse me. Many of the Cambodi-ans had serious health problems, and malaria, hepatitis, and tuberculosis were prevalent. Having a person with active tuberculosis cough in my face was not an experience I relished. One team member had an advanced case of syphilis, with running sores on his face and arms. Their sense of personal hygiene also left something to be desired.

Those problems aside, these teams were fun to test. They were doing what we asked of them and giving us good information. The members were enthusiastic, simplistic, and, as far as I could tell, honest. One of the team leaders, a bright seventeen-year-old, was full of life. He was the oldest member of his team and stood about five feet tall. During the de-briefing prior to the test, he offered detailed, precise information without any obvious embellishment.

"Does anyone in your village know what you are doing?" I asked him.

He told me about a Khmer Rouge sympathizer in his village who had said that he knew the team was working for the Americans and was going to tell on its members.

"We took him away from the village and warned him, if he told, we would kill him," the boy said.

"If you let me go, I will tell," the sympathizer told the boy.

"So we killed him with our knives," the boy said.

To the team leader, this was a simple way to resolve the problem, and he showed no remorse. The team had seen the sympathizer as a threat and eliminated him. I tested all four team members and confirmed that they had, in fact, killed their fellow villager.

When I returned to Saigon, I wrote up my reports and briefed the MR/2 coordinator, "Dan Horan." He had apparently received word of the killing and was engaging in spin control. "That guy they killed was a tyrant and the whole village hated him," was the way that Horan put it.

Although I did not specifically address the question, my impression from talking to the team members was that the person they had killed was in their age group. None of them made any mention of tyrannical behavior.

Apparently, the Special Forces case in Nha Trang (see chapter 4) was still fresh in many people's minds, and such incidents could raise embarrassing questions. As far as I know, my reports of those cases never left Saigon. To my knowledge, neither I nor any of my colleagues tested another Cambodian reconnaissance team.

In February 1972, I was in Ban Me Thuot, sitting in the White Rat Bar with case officers "Lee Best" and "Del Foley" and watching French plantation owners pay protection money to VC bagmen. Best was a tall, lanky southerner and an alumnus of the Virginia Military Institute. I had worked with him in Europe. He was articulate and soft-spoken, and he reminded me of Gregory Peck in *To Kill a Mockingbird*. Foley was an unknown quantity, but he seemed to be a good guy. As the night wore on, I began to regale them with tales of polygraph derring-do. At one point during the festivities, Best suggested that I should write a book. "I'm going to, and I'm going to call it *Of Spies and Lies*," was my spontaneous response.

The next night, I did a test on one of Foley's assets. It did not go well, and Foley began screaming at the man. "The polygraph can't be wrong! If it says you are lying, you are!" he yelled.

Foley's reaction took me completely by surprise. As much as I appreciated his endorsement, it was a little more than I wanted. I was not as adamant about the reliability of polygraph testing as he seemed to be.

Another memory of MR/2 is my first night in Da Lat. The province house in Da Lat was the most elegant and beautiful one in Vietnam. "Paul Wynn," the POIC, had invited me to stay there. After dinner, he had to go to a meeting, and I was in the house alone, or so I thought. I opened the door to what I thought was my room and found a man sitting at a desk with his back to me, reading a book.

"Excuse me. Paul told me this was my room."

On hearing my voice, the man let out a yell, threw the book in the air, and came out of the chair like a scalded cat. "Jesus, you scared me!" he said when he turned around. "I didn't know anyone was in the house. Paul didn't tell me you were coming." My new acquaintance was "Jeff Mellon," a case officer assigned to Da Lat.

An interesting but gruesome experience took place in Qui Nhon, in Binh Dinh province, and reminded me that there was a war going on. I was walking around the marketplace when some South Vietnamese Regional Forces came down the street with a body strung up like game on a pole. They dumped the body in the street and just kept walking.

"What was that?" I asked one of the locals, who fortunately spoke some English.

"They just kill VC and leave body in street," he said.

The dead man was dressed in black pajama trousers and a gray shirt. He had taken several rounds in the body and at least one in the head. Gray matter was running down the side of his face.

"Bob Vale," the POIC in Tuy Hoa, was probably the brightest CIA officer I met in Vietnam. A bit iconoclastic, he seemed to have a realistic attitude about the CIA's operations in Vietnam. "Shackley and his numbers! If he wants numbers, I can give them to him. I just make three or four reports out of one debriefing," he explained.

Vale also offered me his opinion of the Republic of Korea (ROK) troops. He did not have much use for our South Korean allies. "An ROK deuce and a half [two-and-a-half ton truck] ran off the road up here," he said. "It was loaded with cigarettes and booze. They [the South Koreans] run the black market in Vietnam."

MR/2 was the primary area of operation for the ROK troops, and their brutality was the subject of many war stories. "Yeah, they're brutal," Vale said. "I was in a chopper one day when we got a message saying that the ROKs had just killed eleven VC. We went over to check it out and found eleven dead Vietnamese in a rice paddy. Not one of them had a weapon. Those bastards just killed eleven farmers."

Just before I left Vietnam, the Vietnamese police tried to arrest an ROK major at the South Korean embassy after a Vietnamese woman had accused the major of raping her. One of the ROK guards, without hesitation, shot and killed one of the Vietnamese policemen when he tried to take the ROK officer into custody.

As brutal and omnipotent as the Koreans were alleged to be, they occasionally had their noses bloodied. During the 1972 Easter Offensive, the NVA launched a massive attack on and around Kontum. The ROK forces were caught in the wringer but reported no casualties, which our reports officer in Nha Trang thought strange. A U.S. Army major subsequently told us that the ROK commander had asked for 356 coffins. The ROK troops were brutal and tough, but not invincible.

Another memory of MR/2 was a reminder that just being in Vietnam could be dangerous. "Sam Warner," formerly with the Office of Security, had switched to the Directorate of Plans and was assigned to Tuy Hoa as a case officer. One morning, he opened an ammunition can being used as a toolbox, and a rigged grenade exploded and killed him.

Claude Shin ordered a full-scale investigation. Two weeks later, he concluded that Warner had not been the target. A disgruntled South Vietnamese employee had booby-trapped the ammunition box in an attempt to get revenge on the compound manager, who had fired him.

Rabies was almost as big a threat in Vietnam as the NVA, and we had a scare in our compound in Tuy Hoa. Everyone had to be vaccinated, and it took two men to hold down the cook's five-year-old son when he received his shot. I was there when he had to get his second shot. He ran over to the dining room table, jumped up on it, pulled up his shirt, and laughed as the army medic gave him the shot.

★　★　★

I developed a great deal of respect and admiration for "Al Hanes," one of the POICs in Pleiku. Another Virginia Military Institute alumnus, he was a straight arrow, and he turned the Pleiku compound into a well-run facility, making it a pleasure to work there.

Hanes was a chain smoker and seemed to have the shakes. He was also rather introspective, and I had some of my best conversations in Vietnam with him. One of my favorite souvenirs of Vietnam is a gift from Hanes. One night, after I did a case for him, he gave me a beautiful, handmade Loveless boot knife, which I still have.

Operationally and militarily, not much was going on in MR/2. The nearest I ever came to any action while in MR/2 occurred when I was driving outside of Nha Trang. After passing an ARVN artillery battery, I had gone about two miles when I heard the *zzzzziiiippp* of incoming artillery. A round hit about 100 yards to my left and shot up a geyser of sand that fell on the jeep. It scared the hell out of me, and I could think of nothing else to do but keep going. Another round hit on my right, then another on my left, and a final round on my left. The explosions seemed to follow me down the road, and I could not figure out what was going on. I knew it was the ARVN that was firing, and I wondered what they were firing at and why.

Another time, while driving from Pleiku to Ben Cat, I was startled to see a naked woman running right down the middle of the road. The interpreter with me said that she was a Montagnard whose husband had probably caught her with another man. Four hours later on our way back to Pleiku, we passed her, still naked and curled up in the middle of the road.

One of our officers assigned to Qui Nhon, "Fred Curry," had a close call. He was driving outside of Qui Nhon when a VC stepped into the road and started firing an AK-47 at him. The VC blew out one of Fred's rear tires, and he drove the rest of the way on three tires.

A real problem in MR/2 was that the hatred between the South Vietnamese and montagnard tribes seriously impeded joint operations. Tony Batastogne (see chapter 1) told me of an incident in which he saw a "Yard" (montagnard) wrap his arm around the neck of an ARVN sergeant and empty a Thompson submachine gun into him, almost cutting him in half.

★   ★   ★

Two of the best case officers I worked with in Vietnam, "Dave Carson" and Rob Young, were in sharp contrast to the worst POIC I encountered in Vietnam. All of them worked in MR/2.

"Jerry Morse" was the POIC in Binh Dinh province, which, in terms of security, ranked forty-fourth out of forty-four provinces. Morse had spent most of his CIA career in Europe as a gofer. He rented safe houses, picked up mail, and performed other menial tasks, but he was not a case officer before he came to Vietnam. He was seriously overweight and had a drinking problem. During the two years that I knew him, I do not think I ever saw him completely sober.

Morse's subordinates worried about him because he did outrageous things. Rob Young met me at the airfield in Qui Nhon one day, and on our drive to the compound he told me that Morse was really over the line. That morning, he and Morse had gone out to the airfield to meet a plane, and Morse had parked right on the runway. When the VNAF air traffic controller sent someone down to ask him to move, Morse turned to the control tower and screamed at the top of his voice that he was an American and would park wherever he damn well pleased. He then screamed at the air traffic controller to go fuck himself and gave him the finger. Young was really concerned and summed up his comments by saying that Morse did not know how close he had come to getting hurt that morning.

Each time Morse left Vietnam for a family visitation at Taipei, an incident occurred at Tan Son Nhut. Unfortunately, he had the same name as a Canadian on a watch list (most airports have lists of people who are to be detained if they pass through), and the South Vietnamese immigration authorities stopped him and questioned him extensively. On each occasion, Morse went crazy and cursed out the Vietnamese. On several occasions, OS got calls from Tan Son Nhut, and Bill Evans had to go out there to keep Morse from getting into serious trouble.

One Sunday night, Lee and I were having dinner in the Duc when Morse, clearly in his cups, approached. He cursed me out, telling me that I had fucked up by failing one of his agents that he knew was good. Then, uninvited, he sat down at our table and harangued me to set up another test.

Morse had absolutely no sense of security. I was in the compound one morning with Rob Young when Morse, hung over and disheveled, walked into the courtyard and screamed at the top of his voice, "John Jones, where the hell are you?"

"John Jones" was the CIA pseudonym Young used in official communications. English-speaking Vietnamese were in the compound at the time, and I thought that Morse had committed a breach of security. When I mentioned it to Morse, he shrugged it off by saying that no one really gave a shit.

During another conversation with Morse, he told me that when he took his pre-Vietnam physical, the medic told him that he was at least twenty-five pounds overweight. "Does that I mean I don't have to go," Morse asked the medic. "He told me, 'You're not that fat,'" said Morse. "Jesus, John, they have to be pretty hard up to send me here." He was right.

Many Americans in Vietnam knew that corruption on the part of the South Vietnamese government was one of the main reasons we were losing the war. We also knew that we could not do a thing about it. Rob Young showed me a Saigon directive specifically telling him that reports on corruption were not welcome because they were "old hat."

"Goddamn it, John, this is one of the main reasons we are losing this war, and they don't want to hear it," he said.

Young had recruited a good agent who was a captain in the South Vietnamese National Police (known as "White Mice" because of their gray and white uniforms). The captain had given Young a detailed report about serious corruption on the part of a National Police colonel in his district. Young sent the report to Nha Trang for review and possible dissemination. The following week at a conference of district police officers, "Fred Ayres," MR/2 C/OPS at the time, approached Young's agent and said, "Captain Hung, why are you telling such lies about my good friend Colonel Binh?" Captain Hung was stunned. On his return to Qui Nhon, he told Young that he would never get another piece of information from him.

Young had also recruited an ARVN major who had been giving him excellent information. This source, WHISPER, probably saved Young's life when, in March 1975, he tipped him off that the ARVN was abandoning the highlands.

In MR/2, as was the case in all the regions, local women were given jobs in exchange for sexual favors. One such young woman, "Trin," was a payroll clerk in Nha Trang. In an investigation, after the fact, it came out that Trin had vowed to exact revenge on the person who had hired her.

In what could be seen as poetic justice, Trin took us to the cleaners. She was responsible for submitting time and attendance cards for our local employees. Trin had been working for us for more than a year, and all seemed to be going well until "Iola Roush" came on the scene. Iola was a finance officer who took her job seriously. In reviewing Trin's payroll records, Iola noticed some discrepancies; specifically, the same handwriting appeared on receipts signed in the names of different employees, and there were too many people with the same name. Iola suggested that something was seriously amiss, and she and another finance officer went to Nha Trang with Amos Spitz to interview and polygraph Trin. About midway through the interview, Trin asked to be excused to go to lunch. She never returned. It was later determined that Trin had siphoned off more than $50,000, and the story among the local employees was that she fled to France.

Corruption and malfeasance were one thing, extortion another. One of the more egregious examples of extortion about which I had firsthand knowledge took place in Phan Thiet. A young U.S. Army lieutenant, who was an adviser to an ARVN infantry unit, told me that three days earlier his unit had come under attack, and three of his men had been wounded. They radioed the VNAF unit supporting them and asked for a helicopter to come in and pick up the wounded. Before he would agree, the helicopter pilot asked, "How much will you pay me to pick them up?" When told that they had no money, the pilot asked, "What do you have?" According to the lieutenant, the ARVN unit scrounged up some chickens for the pilot.

MR/2 was the Wild West of Vietnam. It was a beautiful and nice place to visit but was not fertile ground for intelligence collection.

MR/3

With three provinces right on the Cambodian border, MR/3 was the "hottest" region in Vietnam throughout the war. Regional headquarters was in Bien Hoa, twelve miles from Saigon, with provincial offices in Hau Nghia, Tay Ninh, and Vung Tau. While I was in Vietnam, there was more military activity in MR/3 than in any other region.

Bien Hoa was an easy drive from Saigon, and I frequently traveled

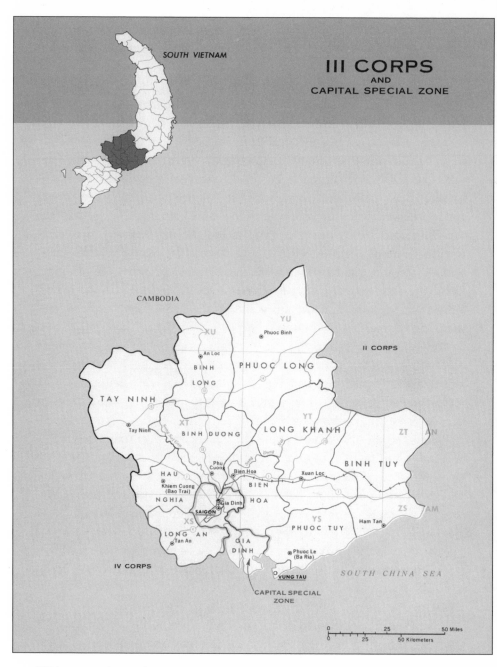

III CORPS
AND
CAPITAL SPECIAL ZONE

CAMBODIA

YU

XU

Phuoc Binh

An Loc

II CORPS

BINH

LONG

PHUOC LONG

TAY NINH

XT

Tay Ninh

BINH DUONG

YT

LONG KHANH

ZT   AN

Phu
Cuong   Bien Hoa

BINH TUY

HAU

Khiem Cuong
(Bao Trai)

NGHIA

Xuan Loc

BIEN

Gia Dinh   HOA

SAIGON

LONG AN

Tan An

XS

GIA

DINH

YS

PHUOC TUY

Ham Tan

ZS   AM

Phuoc Le
(Ba Ria)

IV CORPS

VUNG TAU

SOUTH CHINA SEA

CAPITAL SPECIAL
ZONE

0   25   50 Miles
0   25   50 Kilometers

MR/3 was made up of nine provinces west and north of Saigon.

there by car. On one occasion, the Duc driver became lost, and we ended up in the boondocks. That was one of the more nerve-racking situations I encountered in Vietnam.

As indicated in chapter 3, Don Gregg, the ROIC in MR/3, was the best ROIC I worked with in Vietnam. Gregg was from Colorado, the son of a Methodist minister, and an alumnus of Williams College in Massachusetts. He had success written all over him and inspired loyalty in his staff.

Orrin DeForest, who ran the Joint Interrogation Center (JIC) in Bien Hoa, provided my polygraph colleagues and me with a fair amount of work. In his book *Slow Burn*, DeForest portrays his JIC as an effective tool in neutralizing the VC. Debriefings and interrogations conducted in the JIC did provide a lot of data, but the CIA had no mechanism in place for full utilization of the information. DeForest's basic idea was a good one, but it was developed too late to make a difference.

"Ed Ballard," Gregg's successor, had devoted much of his previous CIA career to Africa. In his mid to late fifties, he spoke with a clipped, distinctly British accent and ran MR/3 well. Ballard projected a dapper and distinguished image in the safari, or "Jerry JUSPAO" (Joint United States Public Affairs Office), outfits he wore, and morale was good under his watch. On my visits to Bien Hoa, he treated me well. Ballard did not appear to have much faith in polygraph testing, but I never faulted him, or any case officer, for that reason.

"Steve Jolly" replaced Ballard in Bien Hoa, and if there is one thing Jolly was not, it was jolly. In my contacts with him, Jolly came on very strong with what I perceived as a false sense of bonhomie and an effort to "play" me. His crocodile smiles never reached his eyes, and he was known among his staff to have a mean temper. Jolly's most notable trait was his cheating at every type of game he played. It was somewhat of a joke in the compound.

"John Pierce," one of our more talented young case officers and an excellent tennis player, and his lovely Scandinavian wife, Anna, were assigned to Bien Hoa. I was having dinner with them one night when Anna mentioned Jolly's cheating. "John, why do you let him cheat?" she asked her husband. "He is so obvious."

"He's never going to beat me, so why make a big deal over it?" Pierce replied.

On another occasion, I was in the recreation room while Jolly, "Louis Clef" (a reports officer), and "Bill Mangone" (the C/OPS) were playing pool. DeForest, in a highly inebriated state, came in. Noticing his condition, Jolly suggested that Clef team up with DeForest and play him and Mangone. Clef was amenable, and when DeForest agreed, Jolly suggested that they play for $20. Drunk or not, DeForest ran the table. Jolly, absolutely pissed, threw down his cue and stomped out.

Jolly closed down the JIC and was pretty harsh on some of the officers who had been assigned to work there. Morale in MR/3 was very low during Jolly's reign.

"Gil Mayer," a pleasant change, replaced Jolly. Without the JIC, however, the polygraph examiners did not have much business in MR/3. I had less contact with Mayer than with any of the other ROICs in that region and recall little about him.

One of my memories of MR/3 is taxiing down the runway at the Bien Hoa airfield in a Porter when, on either side of the runway, there were tremendous explosions. Army engineers had detonated the minefields around the entire airfield. I was sitting in the cockpit and watching as huge clouds of dust rose around us and debris hit the plane. Neither the pilot nor I knew what was going on. "Uh-oh, this doesn't look good," the pilot said. But then we saw men walking around the other planes as though nothing was happening.

Any attack on Saigon would have to come through MR/3, and most of the VC infiltration-exfiltration routes ran through MR/3. Also, the NVA and the VC stockpiled much of their ammunition and fuel in MR/3. Locating these caches was a priority for our assets in the region, and many of the caches were located and neutralized.

Most of the CIA people with whom I served in Vietnam have retired or passed on. Only rarely do I run into a Vietnam colleague. During my four years in Vietnam, I met and worked with more than 2,000 CIA employees. Some of them made good impressions, some made bad impressions, and others made no impression. One who made a strong impression on me was Felix Rodriguez, the PRU (provincial reconnaissance unit) adviser in MR/3, who worked out of Bien Hoa.

The PRUs were part of the notorious Phoenix program, a joint CIA, MACV, and South Vietnamese Central Intelligence Organization effort to identify and neutralize members of the VC infrastructure. The PRUs took the war to the VC and, from what I saw, were very effective.

By the time I arrived in Vietnam, PRU operations had been significantly reduced, and there were no Agency PRU advisers (at least that I saw) in MR/2 or MR/4. Prior to Shackley's ordering a cutback in PRU operations, Stonewall Forrest's PRU had been one of the best-run units in Vietnam. I remember Stonewall telling me that one of his scariest moments in Vietnam occurred when he received the order to disband and disarm his PRU. "John, I really didn't know what to expect, but it went okay."

In 1972, to counter its effectiveness, the North Vietnamese launched a massive propaganda offensive against Phoenix and called it an assassination program.[6] The North Vietnamese were successful in their efforts, in that the propaganda ultimately led to the total phasing out of the PRUs. In postwar interviews, several NVA and VC leaders acknowledged their fear of the Phoenix program, as well as its effectiveness.

Among my colleagues, PRU advisers were the ones who went to war. One night in Da Nang, "Larry Patton," the PRU adviser there, came in from a mission. He had an M-16 and held it out to me. The M-16 had taken an AK-47 round that went right down the barrel and split it. An inch or two up or to the left, and Patton would have taken a round in the chest.

Felix's PRU was the most effective and efficiently operated unit still functioning in Vietnam. Nguyen Van Ai, the team leader of Felix's unit, spent ten years in reeducation camps after the war. Now in the States, he is in poor health and destitute. Felix and "Rudy Emmons," Felix's supervisor, are trying to get the CIA to do something for Ai, but they have not been successful to date.

Prior to my tour in Vietnam, when I worked extensively in Latin America and in Miami, I had often heard Felix's name. Felix was somewhat of a legend. He had been with revolutionary leader Ernesto ("Che") Guevara in Bolivia when he was executed in 1967. Some of the "white-collar" managers in the Latin America Division considered Felix to be a loose cannon and too outspoken, but I never heard anyone question his courage or his commitment.

Many of the people I worked with in Miami were Cuban refugees fleeing Fidel Castro's Cuba. I had also debriefed Cuban refugees when I was

6. Harry G. Summers, Jr., *Vietnam War Almanac* (New York: Facts on File, 1985), p. 167.

in the army and developed a strong liking for them. They were dynamic, enthusiastic, and totally sincere in their loathing of communism.

When Lee and I first moved into our apartment at the Duc in Saigon, Felix was our neighbor. For the first few weeks, we spoke in passing, but our contact was peripheral. Felix was well known at the Duc and well liked. Shortly before our arrival, someone had challenged him to swim three lengths of the Duc pool underwater. He did it and was trying to go for four when he passed out.

Before I actually became friends with Felix, I met Rudy Emmons, the senior PRU adviser for MR/3. Emmons was married to a Vietnamese woman and lived in Saigon. Occasionally, he gave me a ride to Saigon from Bien Hoa. On one trip, we discovered that we had met in 1949. Emmons had been working on a boat docked in my hometown, and I had taken him to one of my high school team's football practices.

On another occasion, Emmons told me that he had to "ground" Felix because he was taking too many chances. My impression was that he admired Felix but was worried about his being killed.

My friendship with Felix began when he offered me a ride to Saigon from Bien Hoa. We discovered that we had several mutual friends, one of whom, like himself, was a Bay of Pigs veteran, as well as some acquaintances for whom we had similar disdain.

Knowing the "legend" of Felix Rodriguez, I was surprised to find that, at least with me, the word "I" was not a large part of his vocabulary. One of his trademarks was his strong Cuban accent. I never had trouble understanding Felix, but other people did, and some of them even interpreted his less-than-perfect English as a sign of intellectual inferiority.

One of the most memorable incidents involving Felix occurred in Bien Hoa. I was at the helicopter pad when Felix landed. I noticed several bullet holes running along the chopper's fuselage. "Felix, what happened?" I asked.

"John, we were a few miles out, starting to descend, when I saw a VC silhouetting himself behind a tree to hide. I told the pilot to turn around and go down lower. When he realized we had seen him, he started shooting at us with his AK. John, you don't know what it's like to be sitting in the door of a helicopter, shooting at someone while he's shooting at you. He hit the helicopter, but I got him."

On the way back to Saigon from Bien Hoa, we sometimes stopped at the U.S. Army Aviation Battalion stationed in Long Binh. Many PRU operations had to be coordinated with the battalion, and Felix had great entree. The army chopper pilots seemed more than willing to accede to his expertise, and there was camaraderie between Felix and his military colleagues that appeared to be missing in his interactions with CIA people.

Maj. Gen. James Hollingsworth, the American military commander in MR/3, called Felix "Chi Chi" (like the golf professional "Chi Chi" Rodriguez), and they got along very well. During the time that Emmons's "grounding" of Felix was in effect, a large search-and-destroy mission was scheduled. General Hollingsworth insisted that Felix fly in the lead helicopter, or the operation was a "no go."

On another occasion, I was in Bien Hoa when Don Gregg needed some additional helicopter support and told the C/OPS, "Get Felix to call the army. He can get us whatever we need from them."

Felix had taught himself how to fly helicopters, and he flew a LOCH (light observation chopper) on missions. With his Cuban accent, his "Roger that" came out "Royer that" during radio transmissions. That idiosyncrasy was copied by several army and Air America pilots—not in derision, but out of respect.

One of Felix's sadder experiences occurred while he was coming in for a landing at Bien Hoa. He had radioed ahead and asked case officer "Dave Kemp" to mark the landing zone with a smoke grenade. Kemp set off a white phosphorus grenade instead of a smoke grenade and was horribly burned. He was medevaced to Tokyo and, from there, to the Brooke Burn Center in San Antonio, Texas, where he died.

As we drove back and forth between Saigon and Bien Hoa, I heard Felix's story of being with Che Guevara when he died. As Felix told it, he had thought that good propaganda use could be made of Che and had appealed to the Bolivian high command to spare him. He was waiting to hear from the Bolivians when a schoolteacher who was translating Che's diary told Felix that the news of Che's death was already in the newspapers. Upon hearing that, Felix told Che that there would be no reprieve. Che gave Felix his pipe as a souvenir, they embraced, and Felix ordered the Bolivians to carry out the execution. He could not actually watch the execution and walked off until it was over. A member of the firing squad had taken Che's Rolex, and Felix exchanged his Rolex for the Rolex the Bolivian had taken from Che.

Felix was involved in two helicopter crashes—one during a mission with his PRUs, and another while on a mission into Cambodia with U.S. military advisers. During the latter mission, the helicopter took enemy fire and was forced to land a few miles inside Cambodia. The army major on board insisted that they start walking east toward Vietnam. Felix was adamant that they go west, because whoever had shot them down (VC, Khmer Rouge, or NVA) would expect them to go east and be waiting for them. The argument turned into a pissing contest, but Felix finally started walking west. The others followed him. They had gone down around 8 A.M. and were picked up by an army chopper around 4:30 P.M.

My most vivid memory of MR/3 is a helicopter trip with a U.S. Army Air Cavalry unit. I had been in Tay Ninh and was looking for a ride back to Saigon. The army air ops said that an air cavalry squadron was going back to Saigon, and I could probably catch a ride. He pointed out the squadron commander, and I asked him for a ride.

"Sure, but we have a mission to do before going back to Saigon," the commander said. "We have to check out the Michelin Rubber plantation before going back. We think the NVA is hiding armor in there."

There were five helicopters in the squadron, and I flew in the lead chopper with the pilot who had offered me the ride. We had been flying for about fifteen minutes when it got a little exciting. I was more or less dozing off when I heard what sounded like firecrackers going off. "We're taking fire!" the pilot or copilot yelled.

One of the crew dropped a smoke grenade, and then we began to turn. The chopper seemed to go in a circle and decrease its altitude. Looking out the side doors, I could see only trees and grass. Sweat was running down my back. As we picked up speed, the air started to rush through the helicopter, and my shirt became clammy. I felt a "this is it" apprehension and what I assume was an adrenaline rush.

We were skimming along at about treetop level, and I thought that we were chasing someone. I had read about an activity in which a helicopter would pursue fleeing VC at almost ground level and "skid" them (hit them with the skid of the chopper). Perhaps that was happening now, I thought. The "chase" lasted no more than a minute. If we were chasing anyone, he got away. The pilot took the chopper up, and we landed at Tan Son Nhut about forty-five minutes later.

On another occasion, I was riding from Bien Hoa to Saigon with a PRU adviser, and we stopped at the Long Binh officers' club. The PRU adviser began talking with some helicopter pilots about an operation planned for the following Tuesday. He was specific in mentioning the time and place of the operation, and the conversation occurred in the presence of an English-speaking barmaid. On Tuesday, when the PRUs arrived at the target hamlet, it was empty.

Another of the more interesting people I met in Vietnam was John Stockwell. Stockwell replaced Dave Carey as POIC in Tay Ninh after Carey committed suicide. I was at the Tay Ninh airstrip when Stockwell arrived on the Porter that was to take me back to Saigon. On first glance, he fit my idea of what the lead character in an adventure story should look like—tall and well built with thick, wavy brown hair and wearing a half-unbuttoned white shirt, khaki pants, boots, and a cross on a thick chain around his neck. I introduced myself, and during the next few minutes, we played "Who do you know that I know?" It so happened that we did know some of the same people, and we traded some war stories.

One memorable comment that Stockwell made was in reference to corruption. He said, "Sure there is corruption here, but you haven't seen corruption until you have served in Africa. The difference between African corruption and Vietnamese corruption is that with the Vietnamese, you get competent corruption. You pay them off to do something, and they do it well."

When it was time to board the Porter, I felt that I had met someone I was going to enjoy working with. A former Marine Corps officer and an alumnus of the University of Texas, Stockwell had been raised in Africa. He seemed right at home in the heat, dust, and excitement of Vietnam. As I came to know him better, I found him a bit messianic in his zeal to protect the Vietnamese, and I admired him for it. Occasionally, in my travels, I shared a plane ride with him and a lovely Vietnamese woman who was always at his side.

When the war began to fall apart, Mayer ordered Stockwell out of Tay Ninh. Mayer was concerned that in his zeal to help his employees in Tay Ninh, Stockwell might do something irrational. Mayer was probably right, but I know Stockwell left feeling that the CIA had not done enough to ensure the evacuation of his people.

★   ★   ★

One of the more titillating incidents I experienced in Vietnam occurred in Vung Tau. I had gone there to conduct a test for "Bob Price," the POIC and a classmate from the VNO course.

When he picked me up at the airstrip, he was accompanied by a tall, beautiful woman whom he introduced as Am, who turned out to be his live-in mistress. A well-educated Cambodian, she spoke Cambodian, Vietnamese, French, and English. She appeared to be cultured and gracious.

Price drove us to the compound, where we set up the case schedule and had lunch. That evening, after the test, I went to bed as soon as Price and I returned to the house. During the night, the sound of rain woke me up, and I was about to get up and close the window when the door opened. Am, naked, crossed the room and closed the window. In the grand scheme of things, that incident had no significance, but in reflecting on Vietnam, it is one I remember.

My work in MR/3 was closer to the action than in any of the other military regions. I always felt that the potential for uncovering good information during my polygraph examinations was greatest there, but it just did not happen.

MR/4

As the most heavily populated military region in Vietnam, MR/4 had more agents and assets (at least on paper) and more disseminated reports than all the other military regions combined. When Shackley held meetings with the ROICs to inspire them to greater efforts, he held up MR/4 up as the exemplar for other regions to emulate.[7]

Can Tho was the regional headquarters for MR/4, and provincial offices were located in Bac Lieu, Ben Tre, Chau Doc, My Tho, Rach Gia, Soc Trang, and Vinh Long. The CIA also had an unmanned office in Ca Mau, which was near the U-Minh Forest, a huge VC sanctuary in An Xuyen province. It was too dangerous to keep anyone there on a permanent basis. During four years in Vietnam, I went to Ca Mau only once. I flew there with the Soc Trang POIC to do a test. What I remember most were the huge potholes we had to negotiate during the drive into Ca Mau from the airstrip, and that a case officer assigned to cover Ca Mau, "Den-

---

7. David Corn, *Blond Ghost* (New York: Simon and Schuster, 1994), p. 188.

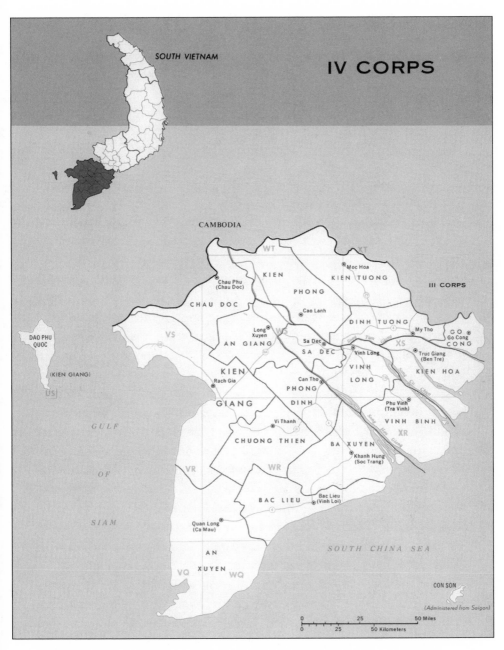

MR/4, the Delta, consisted of sixteen provinces from Go Cong, south of Saigon, to An Xuyen, the southernmost province in South Vietnam.

nis Allen," had a wooden horse built so that he could practice his polo strokes.

On my first trip to MR/4, the C/OPS said, "We have 441 carded assets and 11 authenticated penetrations of the VC." By carded, I assumed he meant assets who had been authenticated as well as those who were in the various stages of the authentication process. When I left Vietnam in 1975, the only four assets remaining on MR/4's books had not been polygraphed.

With so many provinces to service in MR/4, my fellow examiners and I spent more time there than in any of the other regions. We also uncovered more fabricated operations in MR/4 than anywhere else. One result of our efforts was that our trips were often referred to as "visits from the Grim Reaper."

Can Tho was always busy, and it provided a sense of excitement that was lacking in the other regions. In retrospect, I look back on all the work we did there as a waste of time and effort. At the time, however, I believed that I was a toiler in the vineyards of truth and justice and was probably naive in thinking that I was doing something not only important but also of historical significance.

On one of my trips to Can Tho, I was sitting next to an army officer with a lieutenant colonel's silver oak leaves on his collar. When I saw "DONLON" on his name tape and the blue ribbon with white stars under his Combat Infantry Badge, I had an idea that he was Lt. Col. Roger Donlon. I asked, and he confirmed it, and I found myself talking to the first person to win the Medal of Honor in Vietnam. Donlon, who was then assigned to the Military Advisory Assistance Group (MAAG) working out of Thailand, was on an inspection tour. Most of my heroes are military types, and spending almost an hour in conversation with Colonel Donlon was one of my most memorable MR/4 moments.

"Dan Mauer" was just finishing his tour as ROIC in MR/4 when I arrived in-country, and I never worked with him. My only remembrance of him is at his going-away party in Can Tho. After the party, he was walking out of the restaurant with the local police chief when two local bandits rode by on a motorcycle and the passenger snatched Mauer's Rolex off his wrist. This was a loss of face for the police chief, and he launched a hunt for the thieves. It took him almost a month, but he caught the thieves, as well as the Indian fence to whom they had sold the watch. After a tête-à-tête with the fence, he got the watch back and returned it to Mauer.

Mauer's successor, Bob Elliot, was a Shackley favorite because of the numbers that MR/4 produced. Elliot and his wife were both nice people and always treated me well on my visits to Can Tho. He ruled over a house of cards, however, and did not seem to know it.

Elliot finished his stint in MR/4 in the summer of 1972. Subsequently, during a tour of Asian stations, he made it a point to mention at each station how many penetrations of the VC he had managed in MR/4. A year after leaving Vietnam, Elliot returned on a TDY to try to determine why so many of the supposed penetrations of the VC and other good operations were going up in smoke and the roster of agents and assets was shrinking.

I was in Bac Lieu when Elliot was there to give the officers a pep talk and to find out what was going on. Dick Mills took issue with Elliot's use of "good" in characterizing MR/4 operations. "Mr. Elliot, I don't think those operations were any good to begin with," Mills commented. As right as he was, Mills was not promoted while he was in Vietnam.

Early in my tour, an incident that occurred in MR/4 reminded me that the enemy was not the only source of danger in Vietnam. On a Sunday afternoon in My Tho, POIC "Jon Broom" and some of the other officers went out to fire some captured AK-47s and ammunition. Broom had fired about half a magazine when the weapon exploded in his hands. The top of the receiver flew straight back and hit him in the middle of the forehead. It knocked him out and left a large gash. An Air America plane medevaced Broom to Saigon, and he survived with nothing more serious than a few stitches and a bad headache. He later told me that the ammunition they had been using was part of a VC cache that our GIs had "doctored" so that it would explode when the VC used it.

A more serious incident occurred on another Sunday afternoon when "Gene Holman" drowned. I had known Holman in Latin America, and Lee had worked with him. When I saw him in Saigon, he did not appear to be healthy. Our doctor concluded that a heart attack had precipitated Holman's drowning. His estranged wife in the States was able to collect double on his life insurance.

In the summer of 1972, "Ed Stark" replaced Elliot. Shortly after arriving, he called me in for a one-on-one conversation and asked for input on the quality of MR/4 operations. Stark, a retired Marine Corps officer in his late forties, was very straightforward, and during my four years in Vietnam, he was the only ROIC who asked my opinion about CIA operations in Vietnam. Stark was a true bon vivant. He could sing, dance, play the piano, and tell a great story. That was his way of adjusting to Vietnam. The operational empire he had inherited from his predecessors was built of flimsy material, and he could not help looking less than good as it came tumbling down.

During Stark's tenure, Sundays were fun days in Can Tho. One Sunday, some staffers went waterskiing on the Mekong River. Stark was in the boat that was towing "Eli Rich" when a VC popped up on the shoreline and took some shots at Rich. A bullet hit him in the face—going in one cheek and out the other without so much as hitting a tooth. It was a scary moment and spoiled the outing for everyone. Rich was medevaced to Saigon, and he fully recovered. Waterskiing was curtailed, and I never accepted another offer to take a ride on any Vietnamese river.

One of the reasons for the large number of "carded" assets in MR/4 was that many of them had not been polygraphed. This was particularly true in Chau Doc, the most productive province in MR/4. Another reason was that little combat was taking place in MR/4. Until the last few months of the war, no main-force NVA units were in the Delta, and case officers could easily travel around the region to make contacts leading to recruitments.

Of the ROICs I worked with in MR/4, "Jim Warren," Stark's successor, was the most memorable. He was a redheaded, in-your-face Irishman, and his personality was so strong that I initially found it abrasive. In my first contact with him, in early 1973, his lack of faith in polygraph testing was obvious. As time went on, however, my respect for him far outweighed any defensiveness I had about his disdain for polygraph testing and his somewhat pugnacious attitude. Leaders take care of their people, and Warren certainly did that. Jim Parker told me that during the evacuation, Warren was instrumental in getting CIA people out of Vietnam and actually disregarded COS Polgar's directives. According to Parker, had he not done so, some of our people would have been left behind.

The Delta is one of the most fertile areas in the world. Flying across those miles and miles of rice paddies was inspiring. When USAID people introduced "miracle rice" to the Delta farmers, the VC tried hard to discredit it as a propaganda trick. When the farmers began harvesting an extra crop a year after planting the miracle rice, however, the Vietnamese became real believers in American agricultural know-how.

The miracle rice had been developed at Michigan State University. When I was there in graduate school, we referred to the agricultural students as being from the "Udder School" or "Moo U." Three years after leaving Michigan, I was rethinking my position and viewed those "aggies" as having done far more than I could ever do to make the world a better place.

Saigon and Gia Dinh

Few CIA people referred to Saigon as MR/5, but on some of the maps, the city of Saigon and Gia Dinh province were delineated as a separate military region. Officers assigned to work in MR/5 referred to it as Saigon Operational Base (SOB), and their primary target was the North Vietnamese intelligence service known as the Cuc Nghien Cuu/COSVN (Research Department/Central Office for South Vietnam, or the Military Intelligence Department). These officers were in a better position to run classic intelligence operations than our regional and provincial officers were. My fellow examiners and I got a lot of work from SOB, without the need to travel, and those cases were some of the more interesting ones we had.

Saigon Station was an immense bureaucracy. I recall one of the officers describing it as a paper pusher's paradise. Redundancy was rampant in the way the CIA conducted its business, and the reasons why we were there were often lost in the shuffling of papers.

Each military region had an operations officer stationed in Saigon to coordinate its activities. If a case officer in MR/1, for instance, required an asset to be polygraphed, to be seen by a medic, or to get some training, he advised the operations chief in Da Nang, who in turn made the request to his coordinator in Saigon; the coordinator then made the necessary arrangements. I thought that this was pretty redundant, but that is how CIA empires are built. At times, conflicts arose. If, for example, MR/1 and MR/3 submitted simultaneous requests for polygraph tests, C/OPS, Saigon, decided on the order of priority.

A major requirement of any large bureaucracy is secretarial and clerical help. In that regard, too, Saigon was like no other place I had previously worked. Approximately 20 percent of the CIA's employees in Vietnam were female. The majority of the women assigned to Saigon Sta-

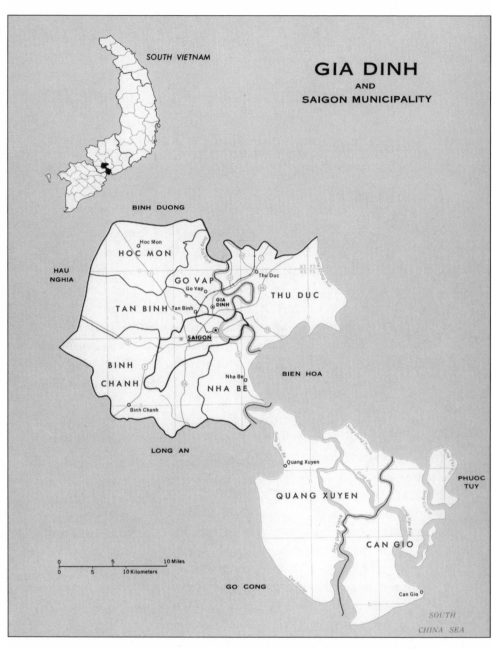

The city of Saigon and Gia Dinh province were sometimes referred to as MR/5, but the officers assigned to work there called it Saigon Operational Base (SOB).

tion were secretaries and clerks, but there were some reports officers, at least one regional coordinator, and a few analysts in the mix.

One of the more surprising aspects of Saigon Station, compared with other foreign stations, was that the CIA women assigned there did not date the local men. In every other country I had previously served, the female employees did not confine their dating to other Americans and were vigorously pursued by the locals. During four years in Vietnam, I knew of only one female staffer dating a Vietnamese man and knew of no situation in which a Vietnamese man pursued an American woman. Saigon Station, in terms of romance, was a difficult place for single women who were looking for serious relationships. Most of the men were married, and the majority of the single men seemed to be more interested in the local women. Regardless of the poor social life and stressful working conditions, our distaffers performed above and beyond the call and were a tremendous asset.

Saigon Station also had more contract employees than any other station I had previously visited. The demands for manpower were such that CIA divisions could not meet Saigon Station's requirements. Two programs, Builder and Jeweler, were created for the purpose of recruiting people to go to Vietnam. Most of the candidates were former military types who had served in Vietnam, and there was no guarantee that they would be retained by the CIA after serving in Vietnam.

People from every division of the Directorate of Plans were assigned to Saigon Station. The different perspectives they brought to Saigon made for some very interesting discussions. My experiences working with them gave me insights into the workings of the various divisions and afforded me opportunities to network, which served me well for the rest of my career.

Another characteristic of Saigon Station that made it different from other stations was the need for and use of interpreters. I had never been in a station where so few of the officers spoke the native language, and most offices had a native Vietnamese to act as a go-between to conduct business. In the operational arena, the need for interpreters was more pressing. Case officers in Vietnam had to use interpreters when dealing with agents, and I never met a staffer above the grade of GS-10 who spoke fluent Vietnamese or any of the Montagnard dialects. In Cambodia, I did meet two staffers who spoke a smattering of Cambodian, but neither could read the language.

Fortunately, in Vietnam we had two excellent interpreters. Shortly after arriving, I met Greg Collins and "Lynn Bell." Both were Americans who had initially learned Vietnamese while in the U.S. Air Force. Later on their own, they perfected their fluency to the point where they spoke Vietnamese like natives. Greg was white and Lynn was African American; they were the "salt-and-pepper" duet.

Greg had been polygraphed when he began to work with the CIA and was due for retesting when I arrived in Vietnam. My first substantive contact with him occurred when I polygraphed him, and I took an immediate liking to him. He was straightforward, with a wry sense of humor, and was very knowledgeable regarding the situation in Vietnam.

My impression was that Greg was the interpreter of choice for the most important cases. He interpreted for the FIREBALL case, as well as for some of the more sensitive unilateral cases in Saigon. For me, he was the perfect interpreter. He translated questions as I wanted them, used the same intonations I used, and offered me advice but never tried to take over an interview. He captured not only the letter of what I was trying to get across but also the spirit.

Greg was the consummate family man, totally devoted to Catherine, his Vietnamese wife, and their three sons. As such, he was not a social lion on the Saigon party circuit. To me, Catherine represented the best of what Vietnam had to offer; she was gracious, genteel, lovely, and a devoted mother.

After enlisting in the U.S. Air Force in the mid-1950s, Greg studied Vietnamese. He had flunked the air force's aptitude test for Chinese but was given his pick of other language schools. Greg selected Vietnamese (not knowing precisely where the country was) because he wanted to learn an Asian language, and Vietnamese was the only other course open at the time. Thanks to that single decision, he gained a wife and a lifetime career.

Greg met Catherine through his Vietnamese teacher in Washington, who introduced him to her as a pen pal. Greg visited Catherine in Saigon several times before he left the military in 1960. They were married in Saigon a year later and stayed to raise a family. Greg taught English for a living and was totally immersed in the Vietnamese milieu for many years. He had little contact with other Americans, and he joked that the only time he spoke English in those days was for money. After he offered his services to Saigon Station, he was paid for both languages. Greg's linguistic ability led to his being utilized as an operational interpreter, and he helped case officers, most of whom knew little of Vietnamese customs, handle their local agents. These activities led to a wealth of varied operational experiences before he ended more than a decade in Vietnam and moved his family Stateside.

Ferreting out fabricated documents was a significant aspect of Greg's expertise. Many of the CIA's assets in Vietnam tried to establish their bona fides with what they claimed were VC documents. The ability of Greg and Lynn to identify the fakes was of great value in helping us weed out fabricators. The best thing that a polygraph examiner can have going into a test is a known lie (i.e., if the examiner can ask a question he knows the person will lie about, the examiner can use the reaction or nonreaction as a basis of comparison). If there is no reaction when the person being tested is known to be lying, the test is invalid.

My introduction to Lynn Bell was somewhat different. The Special Branch liaison officer in Norodom had an asset he wanted tested and said that Lynn would be my interpreter. I went to Lynn's office to introduce myself and to make arrangements for the test. The first thing I noticed on entering his office was that there were 8½-by-11-inch sheets of paper filled with Chinese characters all over the office walls. Vietnamese and Chinese newspapers, books, and dictionaries were everywhere. Lynn was sitting at his desk reading a Vietnamese newspaper.

Physically, Lynn was impressive. He was about six feet two inches tall and did not weigh more than 170 pounds, with not an ounce of fat on him. He appeared to be the prototype wide receiver or defensive back. As I was to learn later, Lynn was one of the most nonathletic people I have known, and his physique was attributed to the fact that he just did not eat very much. He wore glasses, had short-cropped hair, and spoke with a high-pitched voice. That first day, Lynn was wearing a white shortsleeved shirt, dark trousers, and Hush Puppies. Except for his wedding, which Lee and I attended, I cannot remember seeing him in any other attire. Although simple, his clothing was impeccable, and his dark skin, in contrast with his white shirt, created a striking picture. Lynn was friendly, but not effusive, and we quickly got down to business. We arranged to do the case two nights later. Our first case set the stage for our future cases together.

The man to be tested was supposedly a former VC who had agreed to be an informant for the Special Branch. Lynn drove me to the safe house, and we were waiting in the living room when the Special Branch liaison officer came in with the subject. We had worked out a set of questions to ask during the test, but before we actually started, Lynn said, "John, let me talk to him for a few minutes." Lynn sat next to the man on the sofa and began talking with him in a low voice. After about ten minutes, Lynn turned to me and said, "He just told me he has never been a VC and basically is here because he heard he could make some money by providing information about the VC."

That was the first of several occasions on which Lynn would obtain admissions before I conducted a polygraph test. One of the factors that helped Lynn was that the Vietnamese subjects were astounded by his fluency and identified with him to the extent that they forgot he was an American. He never raised his voice or in any way demeaned them.

As I came to know Lynn, I found out that he was from Arizona and had come to Vietnam as an air force enlisted man. He became fascinated with Vietnam, moved in with a Vietnamese family, bought a set of elementary school textbooks, and totally immersed himself in the Vietnamese culture. After completing his air force tour, Lynn stayed on and was hired by the CIA.

I worked with Lynn more than with any other interpreter, and I came to the conclusion that, with the exception of Greg Collins, Lynn probably knew more about Vietnam than all the other CIA people combined. Unfortunately, he had a tendency to be pedantic, and that turned off a lot of people, particularly some of his supervisors. Lynn wrote treatises on the VC, the political situation, what we had to do to win the war, what we were doing to lose the war, and other such topics. He gave many of them to me, and they were useful in my debriefings of VC. Lynn railed against the corruption of the South Vietnamese, seemed to extol the virtue of the VC, and implied that we were doing it all wrong. At one point, his boss sent him a memo, which he showed me, enjoining him from these activities.

Besides coming across as pedantic, Lynn also projected an image of infallibility in preaching about the VC. My perception was that some of our people had an attitude of "who the hell does he think he is?" and wanted to cut him down to size.

Lynn held four specific positions: (1) if the NVA won, there would be no bloodbath; (2) the VC were not involved in drug trafficking; (3) after the Paris Peace Accords, no American POWs were being held in Vietnam against their will; and (4) neither the VC nor the NVA targeted women against the Americans. "The VC are too moral to do that," he said about the last point. Lynn also told me that he had read an article put out by the VC, which stated that when the Americans were driven out of Vietnam and South Vietnam President Nguyen Van Thieu was overthrown, the prostitutes would be rounded up and marched to the countryside to be purified.

As prevalent as liaisons between American men and Vietnamese women were, I found it hard to believe that the VC and NVA did not make use of them. In my military intelligence training at Fort Holabird, a lot of emphasis had been placed on warning us against "Mata Haris" who would use their feminine wiles to compromise us. CIA regulations require that continuous or ongoing contact with foreign nationals be reported. Our people in Vietnam completely disregarded this requirement.

In my four years in Vietnam, I saw no evidence that any of the women with whom our people were involved were VC. I know of no case in which any of our men were "pitched" or entrapped. One case officer apparently impregnated his Vietnamese paramour, who in turn wrote a letter to his wife telling her of the pregnancy, but there did not seem to be any counterintelligence implications in the incident.

When I asked Greg Collins about this, he seemed to support Lynn's position. He did say, however, that in the early 1960s, VC women would flirt with ARVN soldiers in order to get supplies for the VC. Greg also commented that the VC had used women to seduce the French and that the French had "doubled" most of them back against the VC. Greg rejected the idea that the VC would use women to get information from Americans.

One constant in working with Lynn was his frugality. Jesus might have saved, but Lynn invested. On our trips, he told me about putting his money into U.S. certificates of deposit and kept me posted on the changes in interest rates. In the provinces where we had to pay for our food, Lynn would ask the Vietnamese cooks to make him gruel rather than pay for real food. I thought that this was a bit much, but it was his way. Also, Lynn received overtime pay, and he requested that I schedule tests at night and on weekends so that he would qualify for it. I was being paid well, but I did not get overtime, and at times, I resented being asked to give up my free time.

Lynn was a straight arrow. He had a bumper sticker with the words

"Tin Lanh" (Protestant) on his car. Lynn and I spent a lot of time together. I never saw him take a drink, never heard him utter a word of profanity, never saw him at the Duc or any social function, and never saw him use his language capability to secure the favors of the local women.

Much of whatever success I had in Vietnam was due in large part to the professionalism of Greg Collins and Lynn Bell, and in the years after Vietnam, I have never worked with better interpreters.

My promotion ceremony in 1966. M. Sgt. Art Lee (left) and Lt. Col. Don Mattson (right) made the presentation.

A new "spook" at CIA head-quarters, September 1968.

A Hmong tribesman smoking opium, Long Tieng, Laos, June 1969.

Lee and I on our wedding day, August 29, 1970.

Lee and I in Vietnam, November 1971.

"The box," a Stoelting three-channel polygraph instrument, typical of those I used in Vietnam. Respiration is measured by a pneumo tube, the accordion-like rubber tube shown in the picture. Heart rate is measured with a blood pressure cuff, the gray cuff shown in the picture. The cuff is inflated by pumping air into it by squeezing the rubber ball. Electrodermal activity is measured by attaching the two finger clips shown in the picture to two fingers of the subject's hands. In newer analog instruments (noncomputerized), there is an additional pneumo tube. Also, these newer instruments have been electronically enhanced to compensate for people whose physiology makes getting good cardiogram tracings difficult (obese people, in particular). Without electronic enhancement, the cuff would have to be inflated beyond the point of discomfort.

A Pilatus Porter, workhorse of Air America's fleet in Vietnam.

An F-4 Phantom rolling toward the runway of Da Nang.

Do Lap Palace, President Nguyen Van Thieu's residence.

The U.S. embassy in Saigon.

The Duc Hotel swimming pool (or "Bay of Pigs," as some called it) on a Sunday afternoon.

Co Thu (in white blouse) was the cook and Co Ba the laundress at our compound in Chau Doc (MR/4), May 1971.

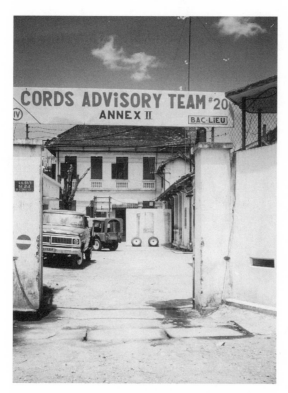

Province house, Bac Lieu
(MR/4).

Province house, Rach Gia (MR/4).

Province house, Ben Tre (MR/4).

The guest house in Siem Reab, Cambodia, where I spent the longest night of my four-year tour.

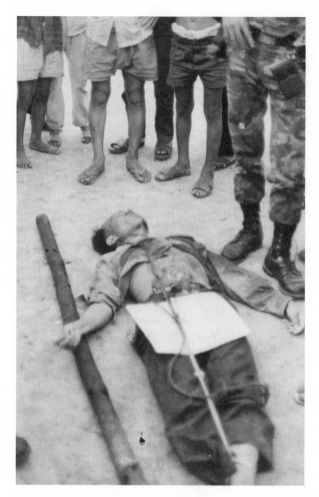

A dead Vietcong who was shot by Regional Force
soldiers in Qui Nhon (MR/2) and left in the street.

Vietnamese woman and her young daughter with napalm burns on her legs and arms, on an Air America flight from Nha Trang (MR/2), June 1972.

Two young boys who used to beg near the consulate in Da Nang (MR/1), June 1972. Victims of the war, they had one good leg and three arms between them.

Lee and I (far right) at Bob Hope's last overseas show, December 1972.

Our son John's christening at Queen of Peace Church in January 1974, with Sean Dolan and Donna Beard.

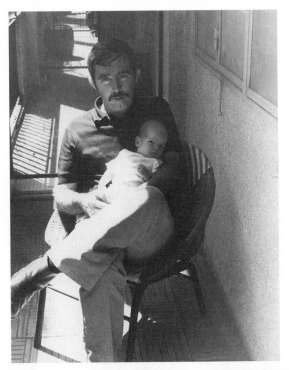

John and I in March 1974.

John, Lee, and I in the Duc garden, May 1974.

Lee with CIA Chief of Station Tom Polgar.

Lee with Keith Barry.

Lee with Pedro Torres.

General Timmes and Chris Hanlon (both far right) at Tito Cortez's farewell party.

Art O'Leary at Keith Barry's farewell party.

Our household staff at the TDY quarters in Phnom Penh.

Cambodian "soldier" I photographed at Pochentong airport, February 1975.

T-28s taking off from Pochentong, February 1975.

John and Lee waiting in Tan Son Nhut for their flight home, April 3, 1975.

John bidding farewell to the Duc's maids, April 3, 1975.

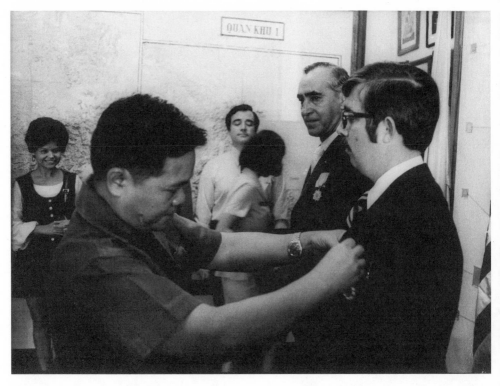

At my award ceremony, Brig. Gen. Pham Huu Nhon pins a medal to my lapel.

9

CAMBODIA

I made my first trip to Cambodia in mid-May 1971. The flight from Tan Son Nhut to Phnom Penh took less than an hour, and I made the trip about a hundred times during my four years in Vietnam. Phnom Penh Station was a bureaucratic replication of Saigon Station, with a COS, deputy COS, C/OPS, and support personnel. I also worked in Pursat, Batdambang, Siem Reab, and Svay Rieng, where we had officers stationed. The biggest difference between Saigon and Phnom Penh, in terms of operations, was targeting. Saigon was focusing on the penetration of VC infrastructure, whereas in Cambodia, the focus was on order of battle information for the communist Khmer Rouge.

My first test in Cambodia was a strange one. The test subject was a Cambodian who spoke only Cambodian, and the case officer spoke only English. Since there was no English-Cambodian interpreter, we needed two interpreters—one to translate from English to French, and another to translate from French to Cambodian. It was quite awkward, and I could not get a valid test from him.

That situation pointed out one of the real weaknesses of our programs

Although not an integral part of Saigon Station, Cambodia received much of its operational and logistical support from Saigon.

in Southeast Asia—lack of language capability. Only two CIA officers I met in Cambodia spoke any Cambodian at all. One was "Jerry North," a case officer who had "gone native," and the other was "Charles Buono-conte," a former finance officer who had switched to the Directorate of Plans and was one of the most gifted natural linguists I ever encountered. Once, in a gift shop in Phnom Penh, I heard two foreigners speaking Cambodian to the gift shop proprietor and German to each other. I asked them, "Woher kommen Sie aus in Deutschland?" (Where in Germany do you come from?) When one answered, "Dresden" and the other, "Leip-zig," I knew that I was talking to two East Germans. That is as far as our conversation went, but I thought it interesting that two East Germans spoke fluent Cambodian.

I found working with Cambodians to be different from working with Vietnamese. They were rather simplistic but, compared with the Viet-namese, not very good polygraph subjects. My sense was that most of the Cambodians did not understand the purpose of the test or the process itself. Also, at least percentagewise, the agents in Phnom Penh were of much poorer quality. There was no Special Branch or, for that matter, an infrastructure to coordinate contact with potential assets.

Two tests that I did in Phnom Penh dramatically demonstrated the poor quality of our Cambodian operations and the desperation of our case officers. "Gary Barth" was the case officer for both of these so-called agents. The first one was very old and infirm, appeared to be senile, and did not know his age. He had been "recruited" because he occasionally traveled into a Khmer Rouge–controlled area. I could not believe that Barth was thinking of recruiting this man. Before the test, I said to Barth, "Even if I could get a good test out of him and he passed it with flying colors, you would be putting him in real danger by using him in an oper-ation."

Barth became a little irritated and told me that I was there to test, not to assess; that was his job. My thought when Barth said this was, "Are we really that hard up?" My answer was yes. The test was inconclusive, and Barth used the old man.

Barth's second offering was also in need of geriatric rehabilitation and had no idea what he was getting into. He appeared to be absolutely terri-fied. Again, I tried to dissuade Barth from using this poor old man, but to no avail.

As bad as the Cambodian operations were, there were some bright spots. The administrative officer, "Anne Geraghty," was one of the sharpest CIA officers I met. She ran a tight ship and did so without stepping on toes. Unfortunately, after Cambodia, she took early retirement to care for a terminally ill brother.

My other bright spot was "Delta Rissolli," the reports officer in Phnom Penh. In her early thirties, she was outstanding in her job. She was fluent in French and one of the best reports officers I ever worked with. In the "it's a small world" category, it turned out that a friend and army buddy of mine had been a classmate of Delta's at Brown University. On occasion, Delta interpreted for me. On one of those occasions, a case officer was trying to put his girlfriend of the moment on the payroll. It was almost comical, but Delta elicited from the girl that she would never engage in any type of intelligence activity. "Henri is my good friend, and I will tell him things if he asks, but that is it," she said.

Delta was also the Pearl Mesta (the renowned Washington hostess) of Phnom Penh and a required guest at any social function. This occasionally aroused some jealousy. One time when I was in Phnom Penh, Delta was invited to a diplomatic reception on a Sunday morning. She asked COS "Walter Enger" if she could attend. Enger told her that she could go if, after the reception, she came into work to make up the time. Enger had not been invited to the reception.

In May 1972, I came down with pneumonia while I was working in Cambodia. During a flight from Saigon to Phnom Penh, a case of Campbell's soup had come loose from a stack of supplies and hit me in the back. There was no real pain, and I was not particularly concerned, but during the lunch hour, I took a twenty-minute walk that absolutely exhausted me. I had to sit down and rest before going back to the embassy. By the time I returned to Saigon that afternoon, I felt as weak as I had ever felt and was having trouble breathing. My initial thought was that I had a cracked rib, and I went right to the dispensary. Dr. Frank Shore had me X-rayed. He said, "You don't have a cracked rib; you have pneumonia." That put me down for a few days, which, for me, was a novel experience. Until that day, I had not spent twenty-four hours in bed since a knee operation in 1958.

Compared with the terrain of other countries in Southeast Asia where I traveled, Cambodia's was the least attractive. There was a lot of military action all around, but it was rarely close enough to scare me. During two actions, however, I heard the combatants scream as they were hit. One

battle occurred in Siem Reab when I had flown up to test a captured
Khmer Rouge for case officers "Brad Corey" and "Mike Baron." I had
known Corey, a big, forceful presence, in Vietnam. He was a University
of Michigan graduate, a former marine, and the son of a University of
Michigan All-American football player, and he seemed to be serious
about his job.

That evening, Corey and Baron took me to the local police station,
where I was to conduct the test. It was pitch-black, and the Khmer Rouge
were making probing attacks all around the city. When we arrived at the
police station, the subject and interpreter were waiting. I set up the box
and was ready to go when the lights went out. A Cambodian military
officer said that he thought the Khmer Rouge had probably hit the power
station, and he did not know how long we would be without power. A
gas-powered generator was on hand, and one of the Cambodians hooked
it up so that I could continue the test. The noise was deafening and the
atmosphere eerie among the shadows cast by the candlelight and flash-
lights. These were not the best conditions under which to conduct a
polygraph examination. After about ten minutes of testing, I could see
that my subject was too nervous to go on, and I recommended that we
stop. Everyone agreed, and we terminated the test.

I assumed that I would be going back to our compound with Corey
and Baron, but such was not to be. A few minutes after leaving the police
station, Corey pulled into the courtyard of what appeared to be a large,
one-story building. "This is the guest house where Charles de Gaulle
stayed when he visited Angkor Wat. So did Jackie Kennedy when she
visited," Corey announced. "Find an empty room and sack out. We'll
pick you up in the morning."

Without another word, they took off and left me in total darkness. In
the distance, I could hear the crump of mortars and a lot of automatic
weapons fire, but at that point, I was not particularly concerned. In some
ways, I found the darkness more ominous. There were no streetlights or
other lights, just inky blackness at the windows. In the woods on a camp-
ing trip or away from inhabited areas, darkness does not seem as ominous. In an inhabited area, however, it borders on the eerie.

I assumed that someone would be in the building, but on inspection,
I found it empty. There was no electricity or running water; I discovered
some bed frames with mattresses, but no sheets or pillows. Still not concerned, I lay down on a mattress and tried to go to sleep, but it was only

about 8:30. Not being tired, I could not sleep, and with no light, I could not read the book I had with me.

At about 9:30, the shooting seemed to intensify, and I began to get concerned. Several questions popped into my head. What happens if the Khmer Rouge break through and I have to get out of here? Where do I go? Would Corey and Baron try to get me? I had no idea how to get to our compound. I did not know one word of Cambodian and was unarmed—not that having a gun would have done me much good. As the shooting intensified, I heard screams after each burst of fire. I had no idea how close the fighting actually was, but it was closer than I wanted it to be. Fear started to set in. I had a wife and a six-month-old son waiting for me in Saigon, and I began to wonder if I would ever see them again.

To anyone who has never been in such a situation, my reactions might sound melodramatic. Looking back, however, I know that this event evoked the most intense physical fear I have ever experienced. I was never at the point where I made bargains with God to get me out of it, but the thought occurred to me. When I played high school football, the fear of getting hurt was always there, but I was more afraid of screwing up than of getting hurt. That type of fear is fleeting, but there was nothing transitory about what I felt in Cambodia that night.

With sleep out of the question, I wandered around the building. Occasionally, I would see flashes of gunfire, but the noise was pretty constant. Of one thing I was certain—if anything did happen, I did not want to be asleep. I crawled under one of the beds, folded my arms behind my head, and lay there to wait for whatever was to come. So many thoughts ran through my mind. Would I be safer outside than inside? Would hiding in a tree be better? How about hiding on the roof? If the Khmer Rouge came near the building, would they throw grenades inside before entering? Would I be safer from shrapnel under a bed? Would they even look under the beds? I eventually decided that it did not make much difference and stayed where I was.

I spent the night in meditation, but my musings were pretty banal. What a waste to get "greased" while participating in a war that had no chance of being won. In all probability, if I did die, it would be as a noncombatant, unknown and devoid of any heroic gesture. What a legacy for our son.

Growing up on heroic stories, I had often thought about what I would do in a dangerous situation. Jan DeHaartog, one of my favorite authors, said that there are two choices when faced with danger: stick your head in the sand like an ostrich and do nothing, or take action. I thought about DeHaartog's words, and it seemed like a plan, but in Siem Reab that night, what possible action could I take? Crawling under a bed might have been lame, but it was all I could think of.

More than dying, I was afraid of being captured. To be alive and unable to see or take care of my family would be more than I could bear. I was also scared witless at the thought of being tortured. I remembered that movie star Errol Flynn's son, Sean, had disappeared in Cambodia, never to be heard from again. If I were captured, I would probably face the same fate.

The adrenaline, the gunfire, and the screams kept me awake all night. At about 4 A.M., everything outside stopped. Was this good or bad? I lay under the bed for another hour to see if anything else would happen. As the sun came up, I went around the building and looked out the windows. There was not a soul in sight, and it appeared that another lovely day in Cambodia was about to begin.

At about 7:00, Corey showed up in front of the guest house. As we drove back to the compound, I told him that I had had some doubts about making it through the night, but I was too embarrassed to tell him that I had spent the night under the bed. I did take a picture of the guest house before we left; even then, I knew that night had been one to remember.

To Corey's credit, he did not laugh at me or make fun of me, but he assured me that I had been in no real danger. "The Khmer Rouge probe the city's defenses every night but really aren't strong enough to break through. We never would have left you there if we thought you were in danger," he said.

I wished that he had told me that the night before. I did not think, however, that Corey, Baron, or anyone else with the CIA had a grasp of the military situation. It was so fluid that anything could have happened. To this day, I have no idea why they left me there. Sleeping on someone's living room couch or on the floor would have been better than where they put me up.

For some reason or other, the Khmer Rouge I was supposed to test was no longer available, and I flew back to Saigon.

A few months later, I ran into a similar situation in Svay Rieng. I was staying in Jerry North's house, and he had a radio so that he could keep in touch with the Cambodian forces engaging the Khmer Rouge. Throughout the night, I could hear the same sounds of gunfire exchanges, screams, and mortar and grenade explosions that I had heard in Siem Reab. Having someone in the house with me made all the difference in the world. Those two incidents were as close as I ever came to ground combat.

As a vineyard for intelligence collection, Cambodia did not yield much of a harvest. The CIA was even more out of touch in Cambodia than it was in Vietnam. The station summoned case officers from other parts of Southeast Asia on TDYs to supplement the permanent staff. This diminished the continuity of operations, such as they were, and was a stopgap measure. One piece of intelligence that did result from our activities in Cambodia was that the CIA had been wrong about how North Vietnam was getting supplies into South Vietnam. For years, army intelligence had claimed that huge quantities of supplies were coming in through Sihanoukville, Cambodia's main seaport. The CIA position was to reject the army claim and to maintain that the great majority of North Vietnamese supplies was coming down the Ho Chi Minh Trail through Laos. One of our assets, a truck driver, claimed that he was driving huge quantities of supplies from Sihanoukville to the Cambodia–South Vietnam border area. We polygraphed him three times, and he passed all three tests. CIA analysts could not accept the fact that army intelligence, at least in this case, had been right and they had been wrong.

Cambodia and Laos were pretty much on the back burner and received neither the attention nor the support that Vietnam did. Initially, I had some optimism about Vietnam, but from day one in Cambodia, I felt as though we were using garden hoses to put out the great Chicago fire of 1871.

By the end of February 1975, only one question remained as to when Cambodia would fall to the Khmer Rouge: would it be days or weeks? Our case officers in Cambodia were focused on trying to recruit some stay-behinds,[1] and I went to Phnom Penh on February 26, to test some of them. Khmer Rouge forces were within shelling distance of the airport. While waiting to be picked up and taken to the embassy, I watched Cambodian government T-28s take off with bombs under their wings, return less than ten minutes later, load up with more bombs, and take off on another sortie.

---

1. Assets recruited to remain in place after the enemy takes over a territory.

Of the many photographs I took during my tours, the best is one from my last trip to Cambodia in February 1975. While waiting to be picked up at the airport in Phnom Penh, I saw an army truck parked nearby. About ten young boys, none of whom could have been more than fifteen years old, were sitting in the back of the truck. Dressed in tattered fatigues and carrying well-worn M-16s, they had just returned from the front. I thought, "My God, these kids shouldn't be here." Two of the child soldiers were glassy-eyed and appeared to be in a state of shock.

There was a pall over Phnom Penh but no panic. At the embassy, it was a foregone conclusion that the Khmer Rouge would win. Over the next couple of days, I tested two supposed stay-behinds. As soon as they were told that they would be expected to stay in Cambodia, neither wanted any part of the deal.

On February 28, at about 9:30 A.M., I was in the embassy to wait for my ride to the airport. I heard what I thought was a door slamming. One of the case officers said, "What the hell was that?" Then the sirens went off. Someone said, "Rocket attack! Get away from the windows!" I heard a couple more rockets hit, and then they seemed to stop.

Huey, the Cambodian who was to take me to the airport, said, "Mr. John, if we're going to go, we better do it now."

I grabbed the box, and we were off to the airport. On the way, I saw a rocket hit a Volkswagen Beetle. What was left of that car would have fit in a suitcase.

At the airport, the C-46 was revving its motor, and I boarded immediately. I had no sooner sat down when a rocket hit the airfield. Shrapnel rained down on the plane, sirens went off, and the Air America pilot told us that we would have to get off the plane. Another rocket hit and sprinkled shrapnel all around me as I left the plane. I crouched under the wing and managed to collect a couple of pieces of shrapnel. Two more rockets hit while I was under the plane, and one of them smashed a small shed about fifty yards away.

When I saw an arm flying through the air, I asked myself, "What in hell am I doing here?" Seeing that unattached arm is a memory I will never forget. Also, I recall thinking, "Bill Mauldin [a famous World War II cartoonist] was right." In 1966, I had attended the U.S. Army Europe Intelligence School in Oberammergau, Germany. Cartoon murals on the wall in the dining room depicted Joe and Willy, Mauldin's famous GI characters. One of them showed Joe hitting the deck, face down in a mud hole, with Willy explaining, "Sorry, Joe, I just zipped my field jacket." I can verify that incoming rockets make the same sound as a field jacket being zipped.

During the flight back to Saigon, I thought to myself, "This is the last time I will be visiting Cambodia. This war is over." When I arrived in Saigon, I suggested to Art O'Leary that if Phnom Penh called for more polygraph help, we should respectfully decline. "There is absolutely nothing there of any operational interest, and it is getting dangerous."

O'Leary replied that we had to be "forward leaning" and support our people there in any way we could. I countered by inviting him to come with me the next time I had to go. That was a cheap shot, and in retrospect, I feel bad about it. O'Leary had paid his dues in World War II, and I had no right to talk to him that way. I also felt, however, that he had no idea how bad the situation was. To my knowledge, he had not been out of Saigon since his arrival, and he was going along with Polgar's "all is well" program. Rob Creed did make one more trip to Cambodia to test purported stay-behinds, and again, when they found out that they were supposed to stay in Cambodia after the Americans left, their reaction was not only "No" but "Hell, no!" Rob told me that one of his subjects was on the plane with him when he returned to Saigon.

I still have the shrapnel and a Cambodian flag I picked up in Phnom Penh, as well as a bit of a guilty conscience. My impression was that the Cambodian government put its absolute, blind faith in us Americans, and we let them down even more so than we did the Vietnamese.

During the late 1970s, I saw a debate on television between political commentator William F. Buckley, Jr., and some of the Chicago Seven, a group of antiwar radicals. Buckley asked one of them, in words to the effect, "Knowing what happened in Cambodia, do you think we made a mistake in leaving?"

One of them answered, "No one could be aware of what happened there and not feel a sense of guilt." On that, the radical and I definitely agree.

From my impressions of the Cambodians, I believed the government to be politically unsophisticated, the people simplistic, and their faith in America naive. Opinions varied as to whether there would be a bloodbath in Vietnam, but among CIA people in Cambodia, no one had any doubt what would happen when communist strongman Pol Pot, the Khmer Rouge leader, took over.

Call it a lack of sophistication or just plain barbarism, but as late as 1975, Cambodian combatants were cutting out the hearts of enemy soldiers they had killed. Pol Pot was a barbarian, and the Cambodians I spoke with had no illusions about what would happen when the Khmer Rouge won the war.

The Khmer Rouge, though communists, operated independently and were subject to no one's control. KGB defector Stan Levchenko told me, when I polygraphed him, that the Soviet ambassador to Cambodia in 1975 had been given the Order of Lenin for keeping Soviet codebooks and other classified material from the Khmer Rouge. No one I spoke with in Phnom Penh ever mentioned the term *negotiated settlement*. My impression was that the Cambodians were fatalistic and resigned to their fate.

Our abandonment of Vietnam occurred concomitantly with our abandonment of Laos and Cambodia. We managed to evacuate thousands of Vietnamese and a significant number of Laotians but seem to have more or less ignored the Cambodians. On April 12, 1975, U.S. Ambassador John Dean made an offer to Cambodian officials that, if they wanted to leave, we would take them out. Only one official accepted the offer, but 159 Cambodians who had worked for us were evacuated. That same day, a Cambodian official delivered a letter to Ambassador Dean that I found rather moving:

Dear Excellency and friend,

I thank you very sincerely for your letter and for your offer to transport me toward freedom. I cannot, alas, leave in such a cowardly fashion. As for you, and in particular for your great country, I never believed for a moment that you would have this sentiment of abandoning a people that has chosen liberty. You have refused us your protection, and we can do nothing about it.

You leave, and my wish is that you and your country will find happiness under this sky. But, mark it well, that if I shall die here on the spot and in my country that I love, it is too bad, because we are all born and must die one day. I made only one mistake, which was to believe you and to believe the Americans.

Yours most faithfully and cordially,
Sirik Matak[2]

2. Oliver Todd, *Cruel April: The Fall of Saigon* (New York: W. W. Norton, 1990), p. 260.

10

OPERATIONS, VIETNAM STYLE

When Ted Shackley came to Vietnam in December 1968, one of his marching orders from DCI Richard Helms was to cut back on the paramilitary operations, such as the PRU program, and focus on trying to penetrate the VC through traditional clandestine operations.

When I went through operational training in early 1969, the scenarios used as exemplars for recruiting agents seemed to be based on European and other Western models, which bore little resemblance to the operations being run in Vietnam. Part of the problem was that no documented history of running clandestine operations in Vietnam was available to use as a basis for training case officers. I do not recall any of my instructors mentioning having had a tour in Vietnam, nor do I recall any mention of operations in Vietnam. Running operations in Vietnam was an on-the-job-training, learn-as-you-go exercise.

Common sense would suggest that meeting with an agent in an area where one stuck out like basketball star Wilt Chamberlain in a roomful of midgets might impact clandestinity. The inability of case officers to blend, along with a lack of language expertise and cultural knowledge, stacked the deck against them.

More than half the case officers in Vietnam were on rotational assignments from divisions other than Far East Division, which was responsible for conducting all CIA activities in Vietnam. Others were contract officers with no parent division who had been recruited specifically to go to Vietnam. Many of those on rotational assignments had been drafted to meet Directorate of Plans levies and had not volunteered. Most were fish out of water and had difficulty functioning in Vietnam. They were eager to get back to their parent divisions and believed that a tour in Vietnam did nothing to enhance their careers. African Division case officer "Tom Creech" told me that he had shared these thoughts with COS Tom Polgar the day before he left Vietnam. Polgar told him that he should consider another line of work.

Whether a result of the inanity of the situation, the poor morale, or the distractions of Vietnam's good life, the operations I encountered there differed 180 degrees from any others I had been involved in. The biggest difference was the way agents were recruited.

Four steps are usually involved in what is referred to in the CIA as the recruitment cycle. A case officer "spots" (identifies a potential recruitment), "assesses" (decides, often after consulting with superiors, whether the target is worth pursuing), "vets" (runs name checks and tries to find out all he can about the target), and, if the target meets the criteria for recruitment, makes a "pitch" (request to enter into a clandestine relationship). The process usually takes place over an extended period, but that was not how it was done in Vietnam. CIA assets in Vietnam, for the most part, were provided by our liaison services, the Special Branch and the MSS. The recruitment cycle, as I understood it, was almost nonexistent in South Vietnam.

Several examples typify the desperation of our case officers and the quality of the operations we ran in Vietnam. On one of my trips to MR/4, I was scheduled to test a man who claimed to be a VC willing to work for us. He had been recruited by a member of the Special Branch and had a stack of what he claimed were VC documents. When Lynn Bell and I arrived in Rach Gia to do the test, the first thing Lynn did was ask to see the documents that our alleged VC had brought in. After about an hour of reading the documents, Lynn said, "These are fakes."

The POIC became upset and challenged Lynn. "Who says they're fake? What makes you think so?"

"I say so," Lynn said. "I have read over a million real VC documents. I know the format and vocabulary that the VC use. These documents don't use either."

The POIC then made one of those memorable statements that has stuck with me these many years: "So what if they're fake! What difference does it make?"

"You mean to tell me if an agent passes you information that he knows is phony, it doesn't make any difference?" I asked. "How can you say something like that? You're giving him a license to steal."

The situation deteriorated from that point, and I did not do the test. About a week later, the POIC took one of the documents to Saigon. He showed it to one of the American translators in the Vietcong Branch, "Andy Ross" (whose Vietnamese was not very good), and asked him to determine if the document was a fabrication. Ross was not qualified to render such a decision, and his boss told him to have some of the other linguists check the document. To a man, they told Ross, "If Lynn says the document is a fake, it is a fake."

Producing fabricated documents was big business in MR/4. I recall a test in Bac Lieu in which the subject showed me a "VC document" that was a photocopy of a document we already had. There was a crease in the original document, and the same crease showed up on the copy. An operations officer assigned to Can Tho, "Connie Black," told me that most of the fabricated documents were being produced in My Tho, but he did not provide any details.

"Cliff Holmes," a young case officer whose virtues Orrin DeForest extolled in *Slow Burn,* requested that I test an agent he had just recruited. Holmes claimed that the woman was a district-level VC security cadre. Recruiting any VC would have been a great accomplishment, but recruiting a district-level security cadre would have been extraordinary.

For this particular test, I used one of the Vietnamese interpreters in Bien Hoa. He was excellent, and over the years, I came to rely on him. (He is now working at CIA Headquarters.)

During my preliminary discussion with the "agent," the first question I asked was, "How long have you been a VC?"

She looked at me as if I were crazy. "I'm not a VC and never have been," she said.

"Did you ever tell 'Henry' [the name Holmes used with her] that you were a VC?" I asked.

"Never!" was her answer.

At that point, I excused myself and left the office to look for Holmes. I was a bit upset when I confronted him. "What the hell are you thinking?" I asked. "You send me a request to test a district-level security cadre and tell me yourself that's what she is. Did you even ask her? She not only denies being a VC but also says she never told you she was. What kind of crystal ball are you using?"

"Well, I assumed, because she can travel in and out of a VC-controlled area, she would have to be at least a district-level VC," Holmes said.

"I call what you did fabrication. You can't assume," I told him.

When I polygraphed the woman, the test supported her denial of being a VC.

On a trip to Quang Ngai, I ran into a similar situation. "Carl Finney," a longtime EA Division case officer, claimed to have recruited someone with good access to the VC, albeit through the Special Branch. Déjà vu! When I started debriefing the man, he denied having told Finney that he had a close relative who was a VC and that he was in contact with him. I excused myself and went to Finney. "Carl, he says he never told you things that you're telling me he said. What gives?"

"John, he just doesn't remember. Let me go remind him."

Fifteen minutes later, Finney came back and said, "He remembers now. I think the test will go okay."

It did not. When I returned to the testing room, the man affirmed that he did have a close relative who was a VC and that he did have contact with him. My test, however, indicated that he had no VC relatives and that he had no contact with the VC. I confronted him, and he admitted that he had lied. Finney, of course, was quite upset by the turn of events.

Almost every Vietnamese I worked with seemed to have a need to please his or her American boss. Finney was paying the man, and if Finney wanted him to say that he had relatives who were VC, he was willing to say so. This brings up an aspect of testing that I had considered unique to Vietnam but later discovered among many Third World assets I tested. They rarely, if ever, made admissions in front of their case officers because of embarrassment and loss of face. This was one of the reasons that I preferred the case officer not be present during a test. On numerous occasions in Vietnam, I had subjects admit to lying and then say to me, "Please don't tell Mr. Bob or Mr. James [the case officer]."

"John Braxton," a case officer working with the Special Branch in Saigon, was a real down-home Mississippian, a good old boy with a rather good handle on what was going on. Braxton had a cynical (but, unfortunately, justified) attitude as a result of having to work with the Special Branch and came to me with a request to test an asset. "John, this guy is as phony as a $3 bill," he said. "I know he is no fucking good, but the chief of base thinks we have something. Special Branch tells me that the VC sent this guy into Saigon to find a safe house. They gave him the equivalent of about $5 to accomplish this! The Special Branch wants us to put up the rest of the money. They're just running another scam on us. The only reason I am asking you to test him is because I can't get rid of him unless he fails the test. Special Branch will resist testing like hell, but I'm going to insist. Can you help me out?"

"Tell me when and where, and it's a done deal," I said.

It was refreshing to find a case officer who did not think that his agent was the next Oleg Penkovsky. Also, this supposed VC's story did not make sense, and I knew from previous dealings with the Special Branch that in all probability, the operation was a fabrication.

During my months in Saigon, I had often talked with Lynn Bell about the Vietcong, and he had given me a list of questions to ask alleged VC to establish their bona fides, two of which were:

1. What is your party name? (Every VC had a party name.)
2. Who sponsored you into the party? (A potential VC needed two sponsors to vouch for him or her.)

In my preliminary discussion with Braxton's asset, I asked both these questions, and he did not have a clue—strikes one and two. Testing indicated that he was not a VC—strike three.

This case was unique in that the chief of base tried to prove me wrong. That rarely happened—not polygraph examiners being wrong, but case officers trying to prove it. His "proof" was a rusty, malfunctioning AK-47 that the asset had brought in and claimed was his VC weapon. I offered to test the agent to determine where he got the gun, but the chief of base declined my offer. Braxton was delighted with the test results.

★   ★   ★

One of the more interesting aspects of Vietnamese operations was that many polygraph subjects "passed" when responding to questions about the information they were providing but invariably failed on questions about being VC or having direct contact with the VC. Because the authentication process required that sources actually be VC or have direct contact with the VC, Special Branch case officers were telling their informants to claim that they were VC. In many of the provinces, the VC operated pretty openly, and the local people knew what they were doing. Special Branch case officers in many of the provinces knew the identities of local VC and were aware of their activities. However, an accommodation (we won't bother you if you don't bother us) had been reached between the Special Branch and the VC, and no arrests were made. The Special Branch could thus get good thus information on the VC without dealing directly with them, but it could not get the CIA to accept the information. This was a bit of a catch-22 that may have forced good Special Branch officers to fabricate the sources of their information. When they found out how easy it was, a cottage industry was born. If our tests had focused only on the accuracy of the information provided by the people we tested, there would have been a lot more favorable tests.

FIREBALL was the perfect example of an agent who failed a polygraph examination but provided good information. From the time he began reporting to us in 1969 until the fall of Saigon in April 1975, FIREBALL was, in terms of the high-quality information he provided and its timeliness, the best agent we ever had in Vietnam. His information forewarned our military of impending attacks, gave us a heads-up on VC plans and policies, verified information from other sources, and led to the arrests of VC. How could that have happened?

My information on FIREBALL was that he had been recruited through the Special Branch in 1969 because he had a relative who was a high-ranking VC. He himself was not a VC. His uncle, an ARVN officer, had convinced FIREBALL to report on the VC. No one questioned the information FIREBALL provided, because he was right on the money so often.

Every Vietnamese interpreter I worked with in MR/3 (where FIREBALL lived) expressed the opinion that there was something wrong with FIREBALL. As one of them put it, "Mr. John, FIREBALL is never late for a meeting and travels in and out of VC-controlled areas easier than I drive to Saigon. That can't be."

Bill Evans, one of my colleagues in the Office of Security, overheard me discussing FIREBALL and said, "That guy sounds just like an asset we had when I was here in the army. Do you have a picture of him?" When I showed Evans a picture of FIREBALL, he identified him as a source recruited by his military unit during the mid-1960s. If this were true, FIREBALL had concealed from us the fact that he had worked for the Americans before 1969. When I mentioned Evans's comments to John Stockwell, FIREBALL's case officer, he was irritated by my interference with the best agent in Vietnam. He thought that Evans was wrong, but he requested another polygraph test for FIREBALL. Rob Creed polygraphed him, and the test was inconclusive.

Special Branch involvement in the FIREBALL operation was one of my main reasons for doubting its validity. I could not reconcile my experiences involving the Special Branch with any kind of good operation.

Since its inception, the FIREBALL operation had been run jointly with the Special Branch. In 1971, we learned that the South Vietnamese MSS was also running him, apparently without the knowledge of the Special Branch. One of our liaison officers asked the MSS to break off contact with FIREBALL, which it did, but the MSS also indicated that it had been running FIREBALL for years. It seems that FIREBALL had worked for the U.S. Army before he started with the CIA and for the MSS both before and while he was working with us. The people at the MSS did not know that FIREBALL was working with the Special Branch until we told them.

So many people in MR/3 knew about the FIREBALL operation that I felt it highly likely that a VC or VC sympathizer among our staff in Bien Hoa would tip off the VC. In April 1975, we offered to get FIRE-BALL and his family out of Vietnam, but he declined. He must have known that the chance of his being exposed by some of our Vietnamese employees who were not evacuated was very high, and I could not understand his refusal.

Albert, Orrin DeForest's interpreter at the JIC in Bien Hoa, had been Stockwell's last interpreter in Tay Ninh and had probably met face-to-face with FIREBALL. At the end of the war, Albert was in jail for selling phony visas to the South Vietnamese. Knowing Albert, I believe that he would have blown the whistle on FIREBALL in order to curry favor with the North Vietnamese.

Regarding FIREBALL's experiences with polygraph testing, I can say only that good information takes precedence over polygraph test results. There might have been something "wrong" with FIREBALL (i.e., he was not exactly who he said he was), but apparently not with his information. The fact that he was concealing his work with the MSS could have impacted the test results to the point that he failed the test. I left Vietnam with many unanswered questions about FIREBALL.

Among the operations that did not involve liaison was the recruitment of an ARVN officer by Rob Young, a case officer in MR/2. On April 15, 1975, he gave Young a warning about the ARVN's abandonment of Pleiku and probably saved the lives of Young and other CIA employees.

Dave Carson was one of the best case officers I worked with in Vietnam. A thirty-year-old New Englander whose pre-Vietnam experience had been with the European Division, Carson was handling the number-three agent in Vietnam (in terms of production), and one of the reports he turned in ended up going to Henry Kissinger at the Paris peace talks.

In mid-1972, I went to Phan Thiet (MR/2) to test the agent. Before the test began, Dave said to me, "Jesus, John, I hope this guy turns out okay. He seems to be turning in good stuff, and Saigon and headquarters are hot on him."

When I tested the man, I concluded that he was not getting his information from the VC, as he had claimed. For almost two hours, I tried to resolve the issue and got nowhere. If Carson was disappointed, he did not show it. "Okay, John, it's your call. I'll get to the bottom of this." Two days later, I saw Carson in Nha Trang. "You were right, John. The guy was a phony." Carson went on to tell me that the agent had admitted getting his information from newspapers, South Vietnamese military friends, and rumors.

After the Paris Peace Accords were signed in January 1973, Carson recruited a member of the communist delegation to the ICCS. Initially, the man insisted that he would meet only with Carson, but Carson convinced him to take a polygraph test. Carson requested that I do the test, and we arranged to do it in a safe house in Saigon. The man spoke good English, and we would not need an interpreter.

This operation was the closest thing to a "classic" intelligence operation that I encountered in Vietnam. We rode together to the safe house in Cholon, and I entered the house first. As I came through the door, I found myself looking directly into a bedroom. On the bed was a young, naked Vietnamese girl impaling herself on one of our case officers, "Steve Barth." On the wall of the living room, immediately to my left, scrawled in lipstick, were the words, "I love you, Steve." I was in the girl's line of vision, and as soon as she saw me, she let out a shriek. The object of her ministrations said, "Ah shit," shoved her off him, got up, and slammed the bedroom door. By that time, all of us were in the room. Carson was embarrassed and more than just a little angry. The ICCS delegate seemed more confused than anything else. While we were still standing in the living room, Barth came out of the bedroom, seemingly nonplussed, and told us that the girl was embarrassed. He asked us to wait in the bathroom until they left.

Surprisingly, the test went very well. My conclusion was that the delegate had not been ordered or directed to contact us and that he had not told anyone of his contact with Carson. I was pleased, Carson was pleased, and the agent turned out to be productive.

The fact that a safe house set aside for an interview with a very sensitive source was being used as a love nest was a concern, and it did not speak well of the operational security of Saigon Station. In fact, operational security, as I had known and practiced it prior to Vietnam, was nonexistent. On one occasion, I tested an asset in a safe house and called him deceptive. The case officer told me that he wanted to talk to the asset for a while and asked me to leave the safe-house keys with him. I gave him the keys and told him to drop them off in my office. When I got back to the Duc that night, the desk clerk called to me, "Mr. John, man leave these keys here for you." A tag with the address of the safe house was on the key ring. I could not believe the case officer had done that. I brought this up with Barry and O'Leary, both of whom thought it was no big deal.

The quality of the operations in Vietnam was depressing, but on occasion, I found one that evoked a smile. I had gone to MR/3 to test an asset, and a room had been booked in the largest hotel in Vung Tau for the test. The hotel was a "hot sheet" hotel and abounded with prostitutes. "Eddie Rogers," the case officer, had given the asset the room number and told him to be there at 8 P.M. Rogers and I were in the room waiting at 7:30. We waited and waited, and after two hours, we left. The next day, the asset contacted Rogers and told him that he was sorry for not showing up the night before, but one of the lovely ladies in the bar had stopped him on his way to the room, and he had spent the night with her. I have heard a lot of excuses by assets who missed or were late for meetings, but that was a first.

Operations in Vietnam were conceived in chaos and born in confusion. Polygraph examiners were the midwives who told the expectant parents that the fruits of their labors were miscarriages and stillbirths.

11

DIOGENES IN VIETNAM

Diogenes was a fourth century B.C. Greek philosopher and cynic who is often depicted carrying a lantern through the streets of Athens looking for an honest man—whom he never found. I, like Diogenes in Athens, traveled throughout Vietnam, using a polygraph instrument instead of a lantern, on a similar quest. On those infrequent occasions when I managed to find an honest person, my faith in humanity was temporarily restored, and cynicism was rebuffed.

My purpose for being in Vietnam was to do polygraph tests. Although I had conducted about 600 tests before being assigned to Vietnam and was certainly not a novice, I knew that I still had much to learn. Vietnam turned out to be a great place to broaden my education.

Most of the tests that my colleagues and I conducted in Vietnam involved joint operations with the South Vietnamese Special Branch. The purpose of these tests was to determine, if possible, whether the subjects were VC working against us and to verify their access and reporting. Were they who they said they were? Were they doing what we asked them to do? Were they providing accurate information?

The second largest number of tests was conducted for the Directorate General Telecommunications Service, the South Vietnamese version of the U.S. National Security Agency. These were rather basic tests to determine whether its enlisted personnel and junior officers had any involvement with the VC.

We also tested Vietnamese civilians applying for jobs with the CIA such as clerks, chauffeurs, and mechanics. Occasionally, we tested Americans who were applying for jobs with the CIA. Some of them were former military personnel who had stayed in Vietnam, and others were spouses of American civilians working in Vietnam. Tests to solve theft and other types of criminal acts were also part of our repertoire, although we discouraged our clientele from asking us to test theft suspects.

Case officers, ROICs, and POICs also asked us to test their "bed warmers" when they were trying to put them on the payroll as office clerks, interpreters, or office managers. One C/OPS asked me to test his love of the moment to determine whether she had been faithful to him while he was away visiting his family. I refused.

Rounding out this plethora of opportunities to seek the truth were tests given to ralliers and NVA POWs to verify information they had provided. We also tested the occasional "walk-in" who approached us with information on American POWs, Soviet surface-to-air missile (SAM) sightings, or imminent attacks on the embassy.

On one occasion, I tested a drug dealer for the U.S. Bureau of Narcotics and Dangerous Drugs, the forerunner of the Drug Enforcement Administration. He had taken a shot of heroin an hour earlier in an attempt to beat the test, but his efforts were unsuccessful, in that I got him to admit what he had done. I also tested a South Vietnamese working for Air America who was suspected of being involved in drug trafficking. The test indicated that he was trafficking in drugs, but I could not get an admission out of him.

We also tested assets that the Americans recruited on their own, supposedly without the knowledge or cooperation of the local services. These were called unilateral assets. Many of them were South Vietnamese military officers who were recruited to provide us with information on the military situation. We tested the lower-echelon officers but rarely tested any officer above the rank of major.

Before going to Vietnam, while I was there, and after returning home, numerous people told me that polygraph testing does not work on

Asians. Such generalizations bother me. My experience is that it does work on Asians, in the sense that they do react when they lie. Because of communications problems and cultural differences, however, I experienced more inconclusive results with Asians than with people of some other cultures.

One theory about the effectiveness of polygraph testing (or lack thereof) is that the subject reacts when he or she is lying because of feeling guilty. My experience leads me to another conclusion. Fear of detection is the primary factor that makes the lie detector work and is directly proportional to the amount of leverage that can be brought to bear on the person being tested. In Vietnam, most of the people I tested were on our payroll, and the threat of losing their income was enough to create a mind-set conducive to effective testing. For VC, POWs, and those who were not on our payroll, the promise of better treatment was an effective lever if we could convince them that we would make good on our promises. Many Vietnamese subjects were fairly unsophisticated and had no concept of what polygraph testing was all about. They did know, or at least thought they knew, that no good could come from failing a polygraph test.

The Vietnamese were good candidates for polygraph testing and reacted well to test questions. Determining that a person is lying is only one part of an examiner's job. Getting the person to admit to lying is another part. The third and most difficult part of the process is getting a person who has admitted to lying or withholding information to tell the truth. Often, when confronted with the results of their tests, individuals go into fallback positions and come up with new stories, which can result in some very long tests.

Prior to my tour in Vietnam, I had no training in behavioral (verbal and nonverbal) indicators of deception, but the more tests I did in Vietnam, the more aware I became of such indicators. When lying, many Vietnamese engaged in visible, specific behaviors that I came to view as indicators of deception. For example, one man rubbed the inside of his left thigh each time he lied, another turned his head to the left with each lie, and a third pressed his lips together before answering with a lie. In later years, I witnessed similar activities in other cultures and concluded that the people of every culture exhibit some kind of behavioral symptom when they lie.

In Vietnam, just as in the United States or any other place, the most difficult aspect of the polygraph process was determining the answer to the question, "What can I say to make this person tell me the truth?" On one occasion just before Tet, I tested a Cholon Chinese who was clearly lying. I told him that it would be a shame to start the new year with a lie on his conscience. It worked.

The sheer volume and variety of tests I did in Vietnam would have taken me ten years to duplicate at headquarters. I did twice as many tests in Vietnam as I would have done at CIA Headquarters over the same period.

One of my primary concerns on arriving in Vietnam was what kind of polygraph subjects the Vietnamese would be. Previously, my testing of Asians had been limited to some Hmongs and Thais in Laos, a couple of Chinese, one Korean, and one Japanese. Within a month, I was convinced that the Vietnamese were excellent candidates for polygraph testing. For whatever reason, I rarely obtained flat, erratic, or otherwise uninterpretable charts.

With good charts, I had no difficulty making my calls, and therein lay the problem. I was calling assets and agents who had previously passed polygraph tests deceptive. Fortunately, I managed to elicit some admissions from these subjects and was able to establish my bona fides.

The last thing I expected in Vietnam was to get involved in a Soviet operation, but it happened. Our communications technicians intercepted a message from a sophisticated Soviet transmitter and traced it to a French national—a schoolteacher in one of the Saigon high schools. "Timothy LaCroix," chief of base, Saigon, established contact with the Frenchman, and an operation was undertaken to recruit him. Because this operation had Soviet implications, Deputy Director Tom Karamessines was advised. According to Karamessines's instructions, under no circumstances were we to let the Frenchman know that we were aware of the transmissions or on to him. LaCroix had managed to obtain some biographical data on the Frenchman and learned that he had been a radio operator in the French army during World War II. Our recruitment pitch was that we might want him to do some clandestine communications for us. The important question on the test would be, "Since leaving the army, have you done any radio transmissions?"

LaCroix talked the Frenchman into taking a polygraph test, and during the pretest discussion, he denied doing any radio transmissions or working for any other intelligence service. The test indicated that he was lying. My guidelines were not to confront him, but I did want to "probe" and see if I could develop any information. The Frenchman took that decision out of my hands, however. As soon as I finished running the test, he said, "I am sorry, gentlemen, but I have a luncheon engagement and will have to leave. I would be happy to return tomorrow."

The next day, he did return. "Gentlemen, I don't want to do this and don't want to work with you. Please don't contact me again," he said. And with that, he was out the door. That night, the technicians picked up another transmission from the same Soviet transmitter but from a different location.

At the time I did the test, I thought that we were handling the operation incorrectly. I believed that we should have openly, or surreptitiously, broken into his apartment, seized the transmitter, and had him arrested. As it turned out, two CIA officers (LaCroix and myself) were exposed to a Soviet agent, and we did not get the transmitter. Subsequently, we learned that the Frenchman was a Soviet military intelligence (GRU) officer; he was arrested while making contact with another GRU officer in Marseille, France.

Two of the more high-profile and interesting tests I did in Vietnam resulted from a request made by Ambassador Ellsworth Bunker in the fall of 1972. The tests involved cases with important political implications. Nguyen Van Bong, a prominent anti-Thieu figure in Saigon, had been assassinated. Many Vietnamese, as well as Americans, believed that President Thieu had ordered Bong's murder, but Thieu was adamant that he had had nothing to do with it.

That summer, Bong's widow announced that she would go to the United States and embark on a tour of college campuses, where she would preach against the war, in general, and against Thieu, in particular. Supposedly, Ambassador Bunker spoke with Mrs. Bong and tried to dissuade her from making the trip, but to no avail. She was convinced that Thieu had been responsible for the death of her husband, and she planned to exact, as best she could, her pound of flesh.

In September, Thieu's police arrested two men who confessed to assassinating Bong. There was a lot of skepticism in the Saigon community, as well as in the American embassy, about the confessions. People assumed, and rightly so, that the confessions had been made under duress. But were they true? Ambassador Bunker talked with Thieu, who again insisted that he had had nothing to do with Bong's death.

A CIA official recommended that the two men who had confessed be polygraphed. Chief of Security Barry had been a polygraph examiner and broached the idea with me. I had reservations about testing the men because they most certainly had been tortured and might be in poor physical or mental condition. Also, if they were to be returned to Vietnamese control after the tests, they might be more than just a little reluctant to change their stories. Regardless, testing them was the politically correct thing to do, and I ran the tests.

Both tests were conducted in a safe house on the outskirts of Saigon. Having worked at the NIC, I had seen people who had been physically abused, and they shared two commonalties with my prospective subjects: they appeared to have been sandblasted—scoured clean—and they move stiffly and slowly, like very old, infirm people.

The first of the accused assassins I tested appeared to be in his late forties. He was a large, stolid man and was an Asian version of my colleague Amos Spitz. Clearly, he had not read *How to Win Friends and Influence People,* but his hostility was understandable. When I asked him how he had been treated, he said that he had been tortured and told that, if he changed his story, he would be killed. Surprisingly, his polygraph charts were very good and supported his confession.

The other confessed assassin was an ARVN lieutenant who had deserted from Phu Quoc Island. He was much younger than his companion and quite animated. When I asked him if he had been tortured, he denied it. I was a bit surprised and asked him what the police had done to him when they arrested him.

"They stripped me, tied me up, hand and foot, threw me in a mosquito-infested, pitch-black cell, and left me there for four days. But they didn't torture me," he claimed.

His test also indicated that he had been involved in the assassination. The front office was pleased with the results. I do not know if the tests had any effect on Mrs. Bong's decision to cancel her campus tour in the States, but assume it did.

I took more than a little heat from case officers working at the embassy. Some of them claimed that I had sold out and made a bad call. Rarely do polygraph examiners, especially in the world of clandestine operations, receive confirmation of the calls they make. When an agent fails a test and contact is broken off, that is the end of the case for the polygraph examiner. If the test is favorable and there is no occasion for another test, the examiner never knows whether he made the right call. These two cases, however, were different.

In *Gia Phong!* Italian journalist Tisio Terzani documents the liberation of Saigon and cites an interview with one of Bong's assassins, the older of the two men I had tested, in which he admitted his involvement in the assassination of Nguyen Van Bong.[1] On reflection, this man was the most hard-core VC I encountered during my four years in Vietnam. During my session with him, he seethed with hatred for his captors and looked on me with disdain. It was my impression that he confessed to the assassination because he was proud of what he had done, not because of the torture inflicted on him. I had no sense that he was at all afraid or that he felt defeated.

Additional support for my call came from *The Demanding Years*, a compilation of articles about North Vietnamese operations in South Vietnam during the war. One of the articles was entitled "The Successful Effort to Assassinate Nguyen Van Bong."

No one at any level in Saigon suggested or even hinted that it would be a good idea for the test to indicate that the two men in custody had killed Bong. Nor did anyone spell out the implications if I concluded that the men had not killed him.

For polygraph examiners, the holy grail is getting a subject to confess or to admit lying. I have aged years during a three- or four-hour interrogation trying to get an admission from an untruthful subject. Deciding that a person is lying is not nearly as difficult as getting that person to tell the truth, and obtaining an admission from someone who is deliberately trying to evade the truth can be an exhilarating experience. Two tests I did in Vietnam come to mind.

In *Slow Burn*, Orrin DeForest writes that he suspected Albert, his chief interpreter-interrogator, of skimming money and fired him, but the book does not tell the whole story. On one of my trips to Bien Hoa, DeForest pulled me aside and told me that he had given Albert almost $13,000 to buy a VC weapons cache. After a month, Albert had not produced the weapons, and he did not have the money. DeForest asked me to test Albert and find out what had happened to the money.

When I tested Albert, he initially told me some cock-and-bull story

1. Tisio Terzani, *Gia Phong!* (London: Angus and Robertson, 1976), p. 165.

about losing the money. When the test failed to support his claims and I confronted him, he told me that there had never been a weapons cache. He had used the money that DeForest gave him to buy opium and to gamble. DeForest did not fire Albert but passed him on to John Stockwell, the POIC in Tay Ninh.

Albert was a con man, and everyone in Bien Hoa knew it. He was exactly the sort of person (according to those like DeForest, who believe that polygraph testing does not work on Asians) for whom passing a polygraph test should have been a piece of cake. DeForest is entitled to his opinion, but polygraph testing worked with Albert, and he made no mention of Albert's test in his book. When I wrote up the report on Albert's test, Barry read it and advised our Office of Finance that one of the local employees had admitted to stealing $13,000. A finance officer audited Bien Hoa's books and could find no record that Albert had been given that money.

The second of the euphoria-producing tests took place in conjunction with an operation involving a North Vietnamese POW. He was to be sent back to North Vietnam as part of a prisoner exchange and had been recruited to work for us once he was back home. I spent three days with him at the NIC. By noon of the second day, I had concluded that the subject had told someone about his recruitment. I took a break for lunch, conferred with the case officer and the interpreter, and then continued to interrogate him. For three hours, he vehemently denied having told anyone, and I could not shake his story. I decided to break off the test and try again the next day.

The following morning, I returned for one last try. When I arrived at the NIC, all the Vietnamese interpreters and guards were running around like chickens with their heads cut off. Mai, my interpreter, came running up to me and said, "One of the prisoners killed herself last night. She hanged herself with her bra." Mai said that they had found a note in her cell from one of the other VC prisoners that read, "They will break you. Kill yourself." Mai then suggested that we had better go easy on our NVA subject because NIC officials did not want him to kill himself.

Although I was sure that the POW was lying, I was not at all confident that I would ever get him to admit it, but I had to try. After about an hour of rehashing what we had talked about during the previous two sessions, he said, "You Americans are so stupid. You think you can take me off the island [Con Son Island, location of the POW camp], keep me here, and then send me back to the island without my being interrogated?" He then told me that, after being returned to Con Son Island after his first debriefing in Saigon, he had been interrogated for hours by his fellow POWs and had told them everything. He also identified an NVA lieutenant who was in charge of counterintelligence among the POWs. "No one withholds information from him and his people, and I didn't," the POW said. "Every one of us you took out of there has been interrogated, and they [the lieutenant and other POWs] know what you're doing."

My mission was accomplished, and a rather complex, but doomed, operation was put on the shelf. Clearly, polygraph testing worked. The organizers of the operation were not pleased, but that was to be expected.

The success of my test, if it can be called that, was tempered by the suicide of the VC woman. She had killed herself rather than be forced to cooperate with her interrogators. I recalled Frank Celic's story about the VC who had spit the tip of her tongue in the face of an interrogator. Call it fanaticism, or whatever you want, but I never saw that kind of fervor in the South Vietnamese allies I dealt with. President Nixon, in his diary, seemed to capture the essence of the problem when he wrote, "The real problem is that the enemy is willing to sacrifice in order to win, while the South Vietnamese aren't willing to pay that much of a price in order to avoid losing."[2]

The longest test I ever conducted was in Pursat, Cambodia. A Cambodian general told his CIA contact that a farmer in Pursat had seen a Soviet SAM site. We were worried about SAMs, and they were high on the list, along with POW sightings, of things we had to check out. With as much flying as I did, SAMs were a particular concern of mine.

When I arrived in Pursat, the Cambodian general brought the subject to the meeting, but the general wanted a demonstration of how the polygraph worked before he would allow the test to be done. He spoke fair English, and I felt that I could do a good test on him. I wrote the numbers 1 through 10 on a sheet of paper and told the general to circle one of the numbers between 3 and 8, without letting me see which number he circled. I then told him that, during the test, I would ask him if he had circled a particular number. He was to answer each question "no," even when I mentioned the number he had circled. If I failed to identify

2. Quoted in Stanley Karnow, *Vietnam, a History* (New York: Penguin Books, 1991), p. 657.

the number, I would give him 500 riels. While in Vietnam, I did this test ninety-eight times and was beaten only twice. The test worked with the general. He was impressed and allowed me to test the farmer. It took me seventeen hours to get the man to tell me that he had not seen a SAM but had heard someone else say that he thought he had seen a SAM.

Generally, little if any humor is involved in polygraph testing, but I conducted a test in Saigon that bordered on the farcical. I call it my "Captain Queeg" case (à la Humphrey Bogart in *The Caine Mutiny*). Horace Lake had replaced Hugh Berry as chief of support. Lake was a dour, irascible, pompous, and intelligent man who saw himself as the consummate Virginia gentleman. He had a fixation about Virginia ham. On numerous occasions, I heard him decry the poor quality of the ham we were eating in Vietnam and extol the virtues of Virginia ham. At any party he hosted, imported Virginia ham was served. On the morning after a dinner party, Lake checked the leftover ham and concluded that some of it had been stolen. He called Barry and said that he wanted the waitress and waiter who had served the meal to be polygraphed. Barry called me in Bien Hoa and said to get back to Saigon immediately. When I arrived at the office, Barry told me the story of the missing ham. The waiter and the waitress were waiting to be tested at the Duc. An American interpreter was already there. "Are you kidding? You got me back from Bien Hoa to do this?" I asked.

Barry said, "John, he's the chief of support."

After testing them, I determined that Kim, the waitress, had taken four slices of ham from the serving platter of sliced ham (as opposed to cutting slices from the ham), and the waiter had taken none. As far as I was concerned, it was much ado about nothing.

The next day, at the monthly hail and farewell, Barry took some heavy kidding for having me do those tests. In turn, Barry gave me serious grief for having told people about them. In fact, I had not told anyone; Amos Spitz had told case officer Tom Creech, who spread the word. More important, when Barry later requested more polygraph support from headquarters, he was told that if he could afford to use examiners to investigate the theft of a few slices of ham, his need for support could not be all that dire.

In Vietnam, accolades were tossed around to polygraph examiners like manhole covers, and when the COS took time to offer a "Well done!" we appreciated it. I certainly did not receive any compliments for the missing ham case, but I did for another one.

In September 1972, I received a cable asking me to go to Bangkok for a "high-priority" case. The C/OPS in Bangkok, "Ted King," was the case officer for an agent who was a good producer, and King wanted me to determine if the CIA was the only intelligence service with which he was working. I had never worked with King, and I had the impression that he thought I was both too young and too inexperienced to do the test.

Initial testing strongly indicated that the CIA was not the only service the agent was reporting to or being paid by. I told King that, in my opinion, his asset was working for another service and asked him what he wanted me to do.

"John, I want you to find out who he's working for," he replied.

Without having to lean on the agent, I succeeded. I had no doubt, I told him, that he was working for another service. Unless he told me which service, I would have to recommend that we break off all contact with him. After no more than half an hour of denial, he admitted working with another service. I tested him to verify his admission and to ascertain that he had not reported his contact with us to anyone. The test ended on a high note. King was pleased and laudatory.

A few days later in Saigon, while I was giving a message to Polgar's secretary, Polgar looked up from his desk and saw me. "John," he said, "we just got a cable from Bangkok thanking you for your help and the excellent work you did. Congratulations!"

Before I left the States for Vietnam, Henry Kurasaka, the IRD C/OPS, had strongly suggested that I avoid theft tests. "John," he said, "as prevalent as theft, malfeasance, and crime are over there, you could end up spending all your time on those tests, and that isn't what you are there for."

These types of polygraph tests, however, are what most examiners do best. There is usually only one issue to address, and the facts of a case can be used to construct a good test. The reliability of these tests is far higher than that of the screening tests we conducted. Although these tests can convince nonbelievers that polygraph testing works, there is a downside. Employees who are fired as a result of being polygraphed are not happy, and they usually have friends among their former coworkers. Thus, in a fishbowl like Vietnam, the potential for retribution was real.

Testing a waitress to find out that she had stolen four slices of ham was a real waste of time and not worth the risk.

On a more personal note, a hotel maid I had tested and who was subsequently fired for stealing assailed me outside the Duc. I had not wanted to do the test because Lee and I lived in the hotel, and I felt that it was working too close to home. But regardless of how I felt about such cases, I could not refuse to do the tests.

On one occasion, I was again in Bien Hoa when I received an emergency call to return immediately to Saigon. Pat Polgar, wife of the COS, had discovered some money missing from her pocketbook and wanted the household staff polygraphed. Finding the culprit was not difficult. One of the maids "bombed" the test, and I confronted her. Initially, she denied any theft. I then told her, through an American interpreter, that if the matter were not resolved, I would have to turn her over to the police. If she had stolen from me and I reported her, I added, the police would do nothing. "But if Mr. Polgar turns you over to the police," I warned, "you know what's going to happen. It will be a matter of pride to resolve the case." She then wrote out a rather long list of items she had stolen.

When I returned to the office, Art O'Leary was upset that I had threatened the maid and said, "I hope you didn't have to yell at her."

"No, Art, she confessed to me because she liked me."

O'Leary seemed to think that I had been heavy-handed, but he basked in the glow of the Polgars' thanks.

One aspect of Asian culture was that supervisors often took kickbacks from their subordinates. Prior to Tet 1972, I gave money to the head waitress at the Duc to distribute among the rest of the waitresses. Subsequently, I learned that she had not given the other waitresses any of the money. Lee suggested that I not make an issue of it, because "that's the way it is."

Still, the Office of Security sometimes received poison-pen letters accusing Vietnamese supervisors of extorting money from subordinates. One letter was so specific and the charges so egregious that I was ordered to test the supervisor. The test substantiated the allegations. When I confronted him, he denied extorting money but did admit that he allowed his employees to "show their appreciation" for his efforts on their behalf. He was not happy when he was fired, and he gave me some concern. Fortunately, nothing came of his threats, but Vietnamese employees were clearly becoming aware that one of my functions was to test suspected thieves.

Of all the incidents that resulted from my "playing cop," the one that most disturbed me occurred in Qui Nhon at our province compound. The Vietnamese compound manager approached me as I was going out for a run and said, "Mr. John, we're going to kill you before you get out of here."

After my run, I told Rob Young what had happened. "Gee, John," Young said, "I'm surprised. I thought he liked you."

I don't know if Young ever mentioned the incident to the compound manager. During my next two visits to Qui Nhon, however, my contacts with the compound manager were amicable, and I had no problems.

"Rhonda Wilson," one of the secretaries assigned to Saigon and some-one I had worked with in Miami, came into my office on a Saturday morning and asked me to polygraph her maid. Rhonda said that she had left $900 on the kitchen table, and when she returned a short time later, the money was gone.

I told Rhonda that I would do the test and asked her, "What will you do if I find out she took the money?"

Rhonda had not decided what she would do but said that she probably would not fire the maid, because the woman was pregnant.

"Rhonda, you left $900 on a table where a woman who will soon be out of work can see it. That's almost two years' salary for that woman. Not a very smart thing to do," I said.

I tested the maid and determined that her teenage daughter had taken the money. Rhonda did not fire the maid.

On about twenty-five occasions, I had to test Americans. Two of those tests had negative consequences, albeit for different reasons. In one case, a chief of support in another Asian country wanted his college-age de-pendent daughter to work in the station, and in order to do so, she would have to be polygraphed. "Tom Dennis," a colleague assigned to that sta-tion, could not do the test because the girl's father was his boss, and to test her could be a conflict of interest. Dennis cabled Saigon and asked if I could be spared to do the test. Barry saw this as an opportunity to help a colleague and asked me if I would mind going. I agreed to go and told Barry that I would ask the girl the same questions that every applicant was asked.

Prior to the test, the girl's father asked to speak with me privately. He told me that his daughter would not be returning to college and would want to stay on with the CIA when the family returned to the States. He also told me that he had told her to omit some significant (in my opinion) derogatory information from the application she filled out. His rationale was that the information was not so bad and should not be held against her.

As tests go, this one was a piece of cake. The girl was much more straightforward than her father had been, and she made some admissions that would have to be adjudicated at headquarters. She also told me that she would be returning to college in September, which contradicted what her father had said.

"Jim Mullins," the chief of security at the station, was waiting for me when I finished the test. He asked me how it had gone and whether the girl would get the job. Hard-and-fast rules apply to the polygraph testing of Americans overseas. The tests cannot be discussed with anyone, with the exception of the COS, and then only when counterintelligence implications are involved.

"Jim, I really can't discuss the test with you," I said. He then pushed the issue by trying to get me to say that we could hire her. I said that the decision would have to come from headquarters. Mullins then suggested that I cable my test results from the station. As chief of security, he knew better. One of our examiners had previously cabled some derogatory information on an American citizen from the station where the test had been done, and he had been severely chastised. Mullins did not directly order me to tell him the results of the test, but by his tone, facial expression, and body language, he let me know that he was not pleased, and I resented his pressure.

After my conversation with Mullins, the girl's father came into the test room where I was packing up the equipment. He was fawning as he tried to talk me into sending my report from the station. In his position, he had reviewing authority over all cable traffic. He was also Mullins's boss. I left the station without the best wishes of Mullins or the girl's father. They perceived me as being a little too regulations conscious. I never heard whether the girl was hired, but I doubt it. After Vietnam, I ran into her father, and he cut me dead. Jim Mullins never became one of my friends in high places in the Office of Security.

An American I tested in Vietnam brought home a fear that most examiners have: being confronted by someone whose test had not gone well. During the early 1970s, a fair number of former GIs were looking for work with the CIA in Saigon. Some of them had Vietnamese wives and wanted to stay in Vietnam; others just liked the job opportunities. One of the latter had been befriended by some of our logistics people, who convinced him to leave the army and come to work for us. This man, a career soldier, had invested more than eight years in the army.

Before he could come on board, he had to take a polygraph test. I did the test, and it did not go well. He made some admissions that raised questions about his suitability for employment. Additional testing indicated that he was concealing information about his involvement in criminal activities. Subsequently, the situation became a bit acrimonious. I failed to obtain any additional admissions and told him that, as far as I was concerned, he was being deceptive and my report would say that.

The next day, one of his sponsors came into my office and tried to get me to kill the report. That did not happen. The man who asked me to kill my report was Harry Lamont, who had been accused by a Vietnamese logistics employee of stealing a camera and then "cleared" by the director of security without being tested (see chapter 5).

This was a good case, because I was able to provide information that our clearance people could use to make a decision not to hire the man. I felt sorry for him and believed that the people who had offered him a job had led him down the primrose path.

In the grand scheme of things, this case was rather mundane, but it had an aspect that made it a little more noteworthy. If there was one person in Vietnam whom I had tested and did not want to see again, it was this former soldier. But about a month after the test, I walked into an air terminal up-country, and there he was. He had a job with an American construction company and was visiting one of the sites. He recognized me and started toward me, but when I looked up and made eye contact, for some reason he stopped, glared for a minute, and then took a seat in a corner of the terminal.

My first thought was, "Oh, shit!" I did not fear for my life, but I was sure that there would be a confrontation that could get physical. Fortunately, nothing happened, and I boarded the plane with a sigh of relief.

Being disappointed when an asset or agent does not do well on a polygraph test is understandable, but a case officer in Vietnam once misrepresented the results of a test I had conducted to a superior and caused me grief. "Brett Holt," a case officer from MR/3, had a Cambodian asset who was reporting on the military situation in the Parrot's Beak (a section of eastern Cambodia that juts into MR/3), and he asked me to test the asset.

I conducted the test in Bien Hoa and had difficulty getting any kind of readable charts. After about an hour, I took a break and told Holt that it did not look as though I was going to be able to get any conclusive results. Holt asked me to keep trying. After another hour, I decided that it was hopeless and told Holt that the test was inconclusive.

The following Sunday, I ran into "Norman Fein," a case officer assigned to Phnom Penh. Fein, an alumnus of the State University of New York at New Paltz, was a friend I had worked with during his previous tour in MR/4. Fein happened to mention that the word back in Phnom Penh was that Holt had a good asset. I told Fein that I had just tested an asset for Holt, and the results were inconclusive. No more was said.

Four days later, John Stockwell, the POIC in Tay Ninh and Holt's boss, contacted me and told me that Holt was waiting for me at the Duc bar. When I arrived at the bar, the first thing Holt said was, "I have a problem." He told me that, on the previous Monday (the day after my conversation with Norm Fein), he had gone to Phnom Penh and been severely chewed out by deputy COS "Oleg Toll." According to Holt, the reason for the chewing out was that the test I had run for him had been reported to Phnom Penh as favorable.

"How did that happen?" I asked.

Holt said that prior to my final call on the test, Bill Mangone, the C/OPS in Bien Hoa, had asked him how the test was going. Holt had told Mangone that the test was going "okay," and based on that, Mangone had cabled Phnom Penh that the test was favorable. Holt's story did not make sense, but I let it go.

"Did I say anything to you, during or after the test, that would lead you to believe that the test was favorable?" I asked.

Holt could not recall me doing so. He then suggested that he would have preferred that I not discuss the test with Fein. In some ways, I could see his point, but in my opinion, what took place between Fein and me had rectified an erroneous impression created by Holt. Fein had mentioned a test I had done, and Holt had misrepresented the results. I felt it incumbent on me to set the record straight.

About a month later, I went to Bien Hoa to conduct one of my seminars on how we might better use polygraph testing. Case officers from

Vung Tau, Tay Ninh, Hau Nghia, and Bien Hoa were there. Things were going well until midway through the session, when Stockwell stood up and strongly berated me for "discussing one of his cases." After listening to him for a few minutes, I reminded Stockwell that when a case officer misrepresents the results of a test, that case officer is not only failing to follow proper procedures but usually lying and trying to cover up something.

Stockwell and I had never been particularly close. I had worked with him before and perceived him to be an idealist with some admirable qualities. Frank Snepp's characterization of Stockwell in *Decent Interval* led me to conclude that Stockwell was somewhat of a Don Quixote, which, based on my contacts with him, was not far off the mark. After that day in Bien Hoa, our relationship deteriorated.

A month later, Rob Creed tested Holt's asset in Phnom Penh, and the man admitted that he had fabricated all the information provided to Holt. Rob worked for twenty-four hours straight on that second test.

Being perceived as an adversary goes with the territory, but the problem was exacerbated in Vietnam. The pressure to recruit was extraordinary, and the rewards for a successful recruitment equally so. FIREBALL's first case officer was promoted to GS-13 as soon as the operation was authenticated. Also, the lack of anything close to a good operation made coming up with one all the more imperative.

Case officers' job is to recruit agents who can provide significant information. Their performance is evaluated based on the number of agents they recruit, as well as the quality of the information the agents provide. Polygraph examiners, in contrast, are responsible for trying to authenticate or validate case officers' agents. Our performance is evaluated on the number of admissions we obtain and the amount of information developed from those we test.

Although it is a bit of an oversimplification, it can be said that our successes—getting agents to admit that they are not who they say they are—are case officers' failures. When an agent or asset fails a polygraph test, the case officer's roster of agents is diminished; he might have to retract previously reported information, and he might be criticized for poor agent handling. This is particularly difficult for a case officer to accept when the agent makes no admission. Polygraph is more art than science, and unless an admission is obtained, the final determination is frequently what we refer to as a scientific wild-ass guess (SWAG).

Case officers have berated me in front of their agents that I have just tested, bad-mouthed me behind my back, accused me of costing them promotions, withheld relevant information, and actually lied to me about their agents. When I arrived in Vietnam, the precedent for passing agents had been set, and my Saigon Station clientele was not receptive to change.

I do not recall many case officers thanking me when an agent failed a test, but that did not bother me. Occasionally, however, a case officer went over the line. During a trip in January 1973 to Pleiku, where I had gone to test some Montagnard reconnaissance teams, I had a real run-in with "Bob Armstrong," the POIC there. In his fifties, he was more than six feet tall and bald, with spindly legs and a huge potbelly; he reminded me of Babe Ruth. Armstrong had constructed the obstacle course at the Farm and was known for his weekend treks through the Great Dismal Swamp.

Armstrong's go-between with the Montagnard reconnaissance teams was a woman named Kdam, a Montagnard who had been raised by missionaries. She spoke excellent English and had a beautiful soprano voice that could have graced a concert stage. Armstrong and I had our first go-round when I told him that I could not use Kdam as my interpreter because operational interpreters must undergo polygraph testing before they can work for an examiner. Armstrong was angry, but when I would not back down, he grudgingly agreed that I could test Kdam. She did not pass the test, which clearly indicated that she was fabricating the reports from the team. When I told Armstrong how the test was going, he ordered me to stop the test and not to interrogate her. That evening, Armstrong told me that he had talked with Kdam, and she was ready to take another test.

When Kdam showed up the next morning, she seemed cheerful and in no way concerned about taking another polygraph test. Before beginning, I asked her, "What did Mr. Bob tell you about this test?"

"He told me that no matter how it comes out, he won't fire me, and I will have a job," she answered.

I told Kdam that there would be no test and went looking for Armstrong. This time, we argued heatedly nose to nose, and the situation became tense. "Bob, how the hell could you tell Kdam that it doesn't make any difference how the test comes out?" I asked. "You took away any leverage I might have had. I know she's lying, and the only way I can get her to admit it is with your support."

Armstrong made it clear that I did not have his support and asked me if I was ready to start testing the team members.

"Who will interpret for me?" I asked.

"Kdam," he said.

"Not for me, she won't! How can I trust her to translate correctly?"

Armstrong could not seem to grasp that idea and claimed that there was no one else who could interpret. I told him that my visit to Pleiku was over. Armstrong then remembered an interpreter who might be available—someone in Pleiku who had been sick.

Armstrong called in the interpreter, an articulate Montagnard, and I asked him if he had been polygraphed and if he was well enough to interpret for me. He gave me assurances on both counts. The first thing I had noticed about the interpreter were two distinctive scars over his right and left biceps and what appeared to be a scar that parted his hair in the middle of his skull. I asked him what had happened, and he said that during the invasion into Laos (Lam Son 719), he had been hit by three M-60 rounds—the first hit him in one arm, the second hit the other arm, and the third parted his hair.

I ran those tests on January 26, 1973, the day before the Paris Peace Accords were signed. That night, Pleiku was like the Fourth of July. The airfield was rocketed all night long. When I woke up the next day, rockets were still hitting the airfield. Armstrong did not speak to me at all and told the compound manager to take me out to the airfield. The manager thought it was too dangerous and suggested that we wait. Armstrong thought otherwise. "You'll be okay," he said. "Just get in and out of there as quick as you can."

By the time we arrived at the airfield, the rocketing had stopped, and I had no problem getting out. I flew from Pleiku to Nha Trang, where I did a test, and then flew on to Saigon the next day.

On returning to the office, I learned that Armstrong had sent a cable to the C/OPS in Saigon and to Barry in which he was very critical of my handling of Kdam's test. He also claimed that I had forced an interpreter out of a sickbed to assist me and that my slave-driver tactics had resulted in the interpreter's having a fatal heart attack.

Conn, the ROIC, had been very supportive of my handling of Kdam, as was the other case officer who had been in Pleiku at the time. Even so, Armstrong's cable was a downer.

Polygraph examinations sometimes uncover deceptions that have nothing to do with the question at hand. One time, I tested the wife of a VC who had been in custody for over a year. The Special Branch suspected that the woman was a communications link between other VC and her husband.

The wife was an attractive eighteen-year-old peasant girl, and her mother brought her to Bien Hoa for the test. Before I started the test, I asked her if she was feeling well, if she had taken any medication, and if she was pregnant. She answered no to the last question, but I noticed a change in her demeanor. Suspecting that she was lying, I decided to ask that question on the test. The charts were of rather poor quality, and I could not make a conclusive call. I stopped the test and asked the girl again if she was pregnant. She again told me no, but seemed very nervous. I told her that we would try again in a couple of days. Two days later, the girl's mother showed up alone. She said that the girl had gotten pregnant by another man and had run away. I never again used that question on a test.

Another test was more like a miscarriage or a stillbirth, and I have grieved over it for more than twenty-five years. Of the approximately 6,000 tests I have conducted, this is one that I cannot forget—nor do I want to. It serves as a constant reminder that what I do can have serious consequences.

The coordinator for MR/1 had requested that I make myself available for a test on Sunday afternoon. The MSS was bringing the wife of a fairly high-ranking VC into Saigon for questioning about her husband's whereabouts. Bruce Green would sit in, and Lynn Bell would interpret.

Lynn picked me up at the Duc at about 1 P.M., and we drove to the safe house. After introductions to the MSS detail, Lynn and I met the subject, a lovely peasant woman of about twenty-five. She had her four-year-old son with her, and seeing him sitting on her lap diminished my enthusiasm for the test. Lynn was wonderful with her and explained exactly what would happen. If she was apprehensive about taking the test, I could not detect it. Her little boy stayed in a bedroom during the test.

When we questioned her about her husband, she said that she had not seen him in a year and had no idea where he was. The test indicated that she was lying. Neither Lynn nor I raised our voices to her, and we tried every possible way to get her to tell the truth without leaning on her. After about an hour, she began to cry, and Lynn suggested that we break it off. I agreed, and we told the MSS that we would try again the next day.

Barry was waiting in the hall when I arrived at work the next morning. "That woman you tested yesterday—how was she when you left?" he asked in a somewhat excited voice.

I told him that she was fine. "She cried a little, but she was okay when we left," I said.

"She hanged herself in the shower last night," Barry said.

I was slow in reacting but remember thinking, "Oh God, no! No way!"

I told Barry that I found it hard to believe. She had been in good shape when we left. We had not pressured her in any way, and with her little boy there, I could not imagine her doing that. Barry then showed me pictures of her hanging from the shower nozzle. The first thing I noticed was the perfect hangman's noose around her neck and the way the rope was tied to the shower nozzle. She had not struck me as the sort of person who would know how to tie such a knot. Also, the nozzle would not have supported her weight if she had hanged herself. A hangman's noose, as I understand it, is supposed to break the person's neck, but the woman's feet were on the bottom of the tub, and there was not enough of a drop to have broken her neck. Also, from the photos, the woman's neck did not appear to be broken. Her face was relaxed, with no swelling, so it was unlikely that she had died by strangling herself with the rope. Barry said that she had left a suicide note asking that we take her son back to his grandmother in Da Nang.

As I walked back to my office, I ran into "Don Sales," a CIA liaison officer. He was struggling with a couple of cases of whiskey. I offered to help carry the booze to his car. "We are giving these to the police who investigated the suicide last night," he said.

When I talked to Bruce Green, he said that he thought the MSS people might have killed the woman because they were afraid she would identify VC penetrations of the MSS. In any event, I do not believe that she committed suicide.

Sleep was hard to come by for many nights. I could not escape the fact that had I not tested her, in all probability she would still be alive. Knowing that I had not mistreated this lovely woman did little to assuage my guilt. Visions of her sitting with her little boy on her lap continue to recur, and each time, I become depressed. If, in the course of my interview, she had provided us with the name of every VC mole from Quang Tri to Ca Mau, I still would not have felt any better. That incident was the nadir of my tour in Vietnam.

The aforementioned is what I did, and it defined, at least to those I worked with, who I was.

12

. . . .

AIR AMERICA

Author Christopher Robbins, in *Air America*, claims that Milton
Caniff's comic strip *Terry and the Pirates* and the airline depicted therein,
Air Expendable, was modeled on Air America.[1] From what I remember
of that comic strip and what I know about Air America, I do see some
similarities.

Most of what I have read about Air America since 1975 has been negative, particularly allegations pertaining to Air America's involvement in
drug trafficking. Robbins makes a convincing case that in Laos, in particular, Air America planes regularly carried opium to a processing plant
in Long Tieng, the headquarters of Vang Pao.[2] Whether any Air America
pilots profited is not clear, but there is no question that the CIA looked
the other way regarding Vang Pao's drug trafficking. William M. Leary

1. Christopher Robbins, *Air America: The Story of the CIA's Secret Airlines* (New York:
G. P. Putnam's Sons, 1979), p. 17.

2. Ibid., p. 233. However, Robbins retracted his statement about Air America carrying
opium to Long Tieng in a *New York Times* editorial, August 29, 1990.

calls allegations that Air America personnel were "involved" in drug trafficking a "bum rap."[3]

Air America came into being in August 1950 when the Directorate of Plans decided that it needed an airline to carry out some of its clandestine functions, particularly paramilitary operations. To carry out these functions, the CIA purchased Civil Air Transport (CAT), an airline started in China after World War II.[4] Air America was an offshoot of CAT. "At its zenith, Air America was, in terms of the number of planes it either owned or had at its disposal, *the largest airline in the world.*"[5]

My contacts with Air America personnel in Vietnam involved two groups: the men who flew and maintained the planes, and the CIA air ops people who scheduled flights. The air ops people were, for the most part, contract employees who were assigned to Air America and set up shop in CIA facilities. I had almost daily official and social contact with air ops personnel but only a passenger-pilot relationship with the pilots.

My first contact with Air America took place in May 1969, when I went to Laos to help Rob Creed. I arrived in Udorn, Thailand, on a Sunday afternoon, and Kay, Rob's wife, took me to the airstrip to board an Air America Pilatus Porter that would take me to Vientiane. Just before I boarded the plane, Kay said, "Gee, John, the last time I took someone here to pick up a Porter flight, the plane crashed and everyone was killed."

With that happy thought in mind, I took off for Vientiane. For the next five weeks, I flew almost every day in a Porter, usually from Long Tieng to Pha Khao or, occasionally, down to Vientiane or back to Udorn. Laos was not a pilot's dream, and flying in that mountainous terrain was a constant challenge. During my time in Laos, I developed a strong respect for the flying skills of Air America pilots.

My exposure to Air America in Vietnam was much more extensive and enhanced my appreciation of and respect for the Air America pilots. Air America was a very big operation in Vietnam, and at the height of the war, there were 240 Air America pilots in Saigon.[6]

3. William M. Leary, "CIA Air Operations in Laos, 1955–1974: Supporting the 'Secret War,' " http:/www.odci.gov/csi/studies/winter99-00/art7.html. In addition, the CIA inspector general investigated charges of drug trafficking in 1972 and concluded that they were unfounded. In 1976, the Church Committee came to the same conclusion.

4. Ibid.

5. Robbins, *Air America,* p. 16.

6. Ibid., pp. 149–50.

In the fall of 1971, I took a Porter flight into Rach Gia, where Charley Moses, the POIC, boarded the plane. Moses was about five feet, eight inches tall, weighed no more than 150 pounds, was in his mid- to late thirties, wore glasses, and was quite intense. We flew on to Ha Tien, a small fishing village near the Cambodian border, where I was to test one of his assets. We arrived at about 9:30 A.M. and landed on what appeared to be a marshy meadow a couple of miles outside of Ha Tien. Moses told the pilot to be back in four hours. Then we walked over to a one-lane road running past the meadow and hitched rides on the backs of mopeds into Ha Tien.

The interpreter met us in front of the hotel, an eight-room wooden structure with no running water or electricity, and told us that the asset was upstairs. The test did not go well. The man claimed to be a VC, and the test clearly indicated that he was not. After Moses and the interpreter conducted some business, we caught rides back to the meadow. Clouds had moved in, and it was starting to rain. We were about fifteen minutes early, but I was getting a little antsy.

Earlier that year, Mel Heath had been doing a test in the same Ha Tien hotel when a firefight broke out between some VC and the local police. There had not been a lot of VC activity in the area, but there was some. Here we were, two CIA employees, waiting in the middle of a meadow for a Porter. The rain was becoming a downpour, and the pickup time came and went. "What happens if the plane doesn't show?" I asked.

"I don't want any negative vibes," Moses said.

"Charley, do you have a radio with you?" was my next question.

"John, no negative vibes. He'll be here." Moses did not have a radio.

Twenty minutes later, I heard the familiar whine of the Porter's engine. The rain was coming down in windblown sheets, and Moses and I were drenched by the time we boarded the plane. I was a little irritated at Moses but more relieved to be in the Porter.

The clouds were very low as we took off. We could not have been 200 feet up when what seemed like a giant fist hit the plane and shook it. The motor sputtered and seemed to be stalling out. I looked at Moses, and he was chalk white. I assume that I was equally pale. The pilot radioed to Can Tho and said that we might be "going in." We were losing altitude when, miraculously, the motor stopped sputtering. The pilot somehow set things back on track, and we headed toward Rach Gia.

During the flight, I commented, "Charley, I would have been more than just a little pissed if we had had to spend the night in that meadow, and even more so had we been captured by the VC."

"No negative vibes," Moses said.

That was the first time I can recall thinking that I was going to die. We had probably run into wind shear, and when it hit the plane, I had thought, "This is it." I am glad that it was not my time and feel that I survived because of the skill of the Air America pilot. I do not recall his last name, but his first name was Bob. He was about twenty-eight years old, more than six feet tall, and an Air Force Academy dropout. I tried to send a letter of appreciation to him, but the front office killed it. The explanation Gordon gave me was that we (the CIA) did not want it known that we had been in Ha Tien.

On another occasion in Svay Rieng, Cambodia, I had just finished testing the POIC's paramour/ops assistant and told him that she was stealing money from him. He was not pleased. The next morning, he gave me a ride on the back of his motorcycle to the military airstrip where I was to be picked up. He just left me there and took off. A lot of Cambodian military personnel were at the airstrip, and several Cambodian planes were lining up to take off. I was the only American on the scene. As one of the Cambodian planes cleared the end of the runway, I heard gunfire—not rapid, like an AK-47, but the slow "thud, thud" of a heavier weapon. One of the Cambodian officers told me that a Khmer Rouge was hiding somewhere off the runway and firing at each plane as it took off.

China Airlines had a contract with the CIA to conduct flights between Vietnam and Cambodia, and one of its planes was supposed to pick me up. When the pilot was advised of the ground fire, he refused to land. I had no way of knowing what would pick me up or when or how, nor did I have any means of contacting anyone, so I just sat down to wait.

About half an hour later, a Porter landed. Although relieved, I was more than a little anxious as we took off. The pilot used the absolute minimum amount of runway to get off the ground, and the plane corkscrewed into the air. I do not know if we were shot at or not, but my sphincter had a good workout.

Most of the skies over Vietnam were pretty friendly, but on two occasions, I came under fire in an airplane.[7] The first occurred in November

7. The second, during a helicopter flight in MR/3, was described in chapter 8.

1971. The plane had just taken off from Moc Hoa, in MR/4, when I saw three green streaks go by the left wing. Lynn Bell, my interpreter, also saw them and yelled, "What was that?" Another passenger yelled out, "Were those tracers?"

I guess the pilot also saw them, because he immediately took evasive action. At the time, I did not think much of the incident, and we kidded about it on the flight back to Saigon. After we landed and I was walking to the Air America terminal at Tan Son Nhut, it suddenly hit me that those tracers could have knocked the Porter out of the sky, and me with it.

In early 1975, I was up-country in Cambodia when a Danish correspondent was severely wounded. An Air America pilot braved some serious ground fire to come in and evacuate him. In both Laos and Vietnam, I was on Air America planes that were evacuating the wounded.

Perhaps an analogy could be made between the Air America pilots and the stagecoach drivers and Pony Express riders of the nineteenth century. Most of them were hard living, adventurous, and independent. The hard-living part once gave me cause for concern. I was in Nha Trang and was scheduled to fly back to Saigon the next morning. That night, I was in the recreation room of the compound playing pool when I became involved in a conversation with a pilot who was blind drunk. At 7:00 the next morning, I was sitting in the C-46 when the same pilot boarded. I almost got off the plane.

Although I never really knew any of the pilots well, they often let me fly in the right-hand seat of the cockpit with them. That gave me a different perspective on both flying and the pilots. Sitting next to them and talking to them as they piloted the Porters allowed me to see how much they loved flying and how skilled they were. From the cockpit, I could see how poorly marked and in what bad condition some of the landing strips were—and what skill it took to land and take off.

On occasion, CIA case officers could be rather demanding. For the most part, the pilots put up with them, but I remember when one of our "cowboys" went too far. Paul Ingalls (introduced in chapter 2) was one of the "wild men" in the CIA. In his forties, he was a tall, bespectacled, balding redhead with a mustache. He went through seven packs of cigarettes a day. He saw himself as a real soldier-of-fortune type and could be a dangerous person to have around. One Saturday, as I was leaving the office to go back to the Duc, I ran into him. "John," he said, "I need you to go to Song Be right now. This is really critical."

I said that I had to go to MR/4 on Sunday and suggested that we talk to Keith Barry about this emergency. Ingalls told Barry that he had given a beacon (radio transmitter) to one of his agents to place in the vicinity of NVA troops. The beacon was a device for B-52s to home in on and find their targets. "I want to find out if my guy put it out there, and I think John can help," Ingalls said.

Barry knew that Ingalls was a nut, and he deferred to me. I told Ingalls that I would go to Song Be and delay my trip to MR/4 until Monday.

At that time, Ingalls was not popular with Air America pilots. The week before, he had carried an M-60 machine gun onto a Porter and told the pilot to fly at treetop level to see if he could "nail" any VC. The pilot refused, and an altercation ensued. The pilot coldcocked Ingalls. In *Air America*, Robbins makes it clear that Air America pilots did not think highly of CIA case officers and cites an example of an Air America pilot knocking out a CIA case officer's two front teeth.[8]

Song Be was not a good place to be. Close to the Cambodian border, the area was heavily traveled by the VC. The airstrip was not clearly marked, and on one trip, an Air America pilot put his plane down in Cambodia instead of Song Be.

After getting off the plane, I saw an armored personnel carrier that looked as if it had been sliced open by a giant can opener. The sight was gruesome, with blood, flesh, and bone splattered around. According to Ingalls, it had taken a direct hit with a recoilless rifle that the VC had captured from the ARVN.

The test on Ingalls's agent was inconclusive. My opinion was that he had given the beacon to someone else to place for him. After much ado about nothing, the pilot got us in and out of a nasty place and, once again, earned my respect.

Only once during my four years in Vietnam did an Air America pilot turn around before getting me to my destination. We were flying from Da Nang to Hue, and the fog was as thick as pea soup. There was no visibility at all once we descended for our landing. I was in the cockpit and could see nothing. All of a sudden, I heard the pilot mutter, "Fuck this! No way, Jose!" He took us up, up, and away, back to Da Nang.

8. Robbins, *Air America*, p. 216.

When we landed at Da Nang, the pilot said, "I'm sorry we had to turn back, but that was just too dangerous." I told him that I was more than pleased that he had not tried to make the landing.

Of all the air ops people I met, O. B. Harnage is probably the most memorable. One of the more famous pictures to come out of the war shows a man helping Vietnamese into a helicopter during the evacuation of Saigon. O. B. is the man in that picture. He was a contract employee assigned to the Air America office in the Norodom Complex, and he worked mainly out of Saigon. When one of the regional air ops officers went on leave, O. B. would fill in for him.

A "good old boy" from Georgia and a former U-2 pilot who had been a POW during the Korean War, O. B. was gregarious, macho, and a bull-shitter of the first order. He was a suds sipper of renown, and although I saw him drunk on more than a few occasions, he never got unruly or out of line.

On one of my trips from the airfield into Da Nang, O. B. gave me a ride. While going through downtown Da Nang, someone threw an empty beer can into the jeep. O. B. almost bailed out. It added a little spice to my day.

"Floyd Brower" was the regular air ops in Da Nang. He was just as unforgettable as O. B., but for different reasons. Brower was as dour as O. B. was ebullient, and he was usually confrontational. A lot of it was bluster, but on first meeting Brower, his behavior was disconcerting. He was very profane and not one of our more sensitive types. To Brower, I was an FNG and had to prove myself before he would cut me any slack.

He was also the most outspoken racist I met in Vietnam and made no secret of the fact that he hated African Americans. In the compound bar one night, Denise Bennett, a white secretary, became upset about the way Brower was disparaging African Americans. "Floyd, you can't say things like that," she said.

"You can disagree, but I hate blacks," Brower said. "They were the ones who beat me up every day and stole my lunch money on the way to school, and I do hate them."

One day at the terminal, some missionaries were looking for a ride on one of our planes. If there was room, our air ops would try to accommodate people who needed rides, but Brower called the missionaries a "bunch of goddamn freeloaders" to their faces.

In stark contrast to this belligerent image, Brower was an opera lover. He was at his most mellow when discussing opera and was almost fun to be around.

Brower was not particularly warm and fuzzy toward the Vietnamese, however. He kept a big German shepherd in a little enclosure at the terminal. Every day at around noon, a VNAF lieutenant passed the enclosure and dragged a stick along the fence to excite the dog. The dog went nuts and tried to get at his tormentor every time. Brower could have simply asked the lieutenant not to bother the dog, but he had something else in mind. One day, while I was waiting for a flight to Quang Ngai, Brower said, "John, watch this."

The lieutenant showed up and dragged the stick along the fence. The dog reacted as usual, but this time, the gate of the enclosure had been left open. After the dog had a brief snack, Brower called him off.

On several of my trips to Da Nang, I saw an American girl in our compound. I only met her once, but I believe her name was Michele. She lived in a Vietnamese orphanage and tried to arrange adoptions by Americans. Our people in Da Nang liked her and spoke highly of her. One of the adoptions she arranged was for the child of a prostitute and her Filipino boyfriend. Shortly after the adoption, Michele showed up at the compound, scared and crying. She told Brower that the Filipino was trying to extort money from her. Brower and "Roy Tyre," another CIA officer, had a talk with the Filipino, and he was never heard from again.

I "made my bones" (proved myself) with Brower by testing one of his people and finding out that he was dealing drugs. From that point on, Brower and I got along.

"Cam Payne," a retired air force major, was my favorite air ops officer. He worked out of Pochentong Airport, just outside of Phnom Penh. From late 1974 until April 1975, the Khmer Rouge was close enough to shell the airport and did so on an almost daily basis. This made Payne's working conditions less than ideal, but it never seemed to get to him. I think his sense of humor kept him sane. As things came to an end in Cambodia, Payne performed in exemplary fashion, making sure that our people in the provinces got evacuated and keeping a cool head when things started to fall apart.

I disliked one regional air ops, "Gus Dillon." He was not interested in social amenities, and I never had a one-on-one conversation with him. Physically intimidating, he weighed at least 200 pounds and, at about five feet ten inches tall, was built like a large fireplug. Dillon was also a mean drunk. Once, I saw him pick a fight with case officer Rob Young, who weighed no more than 130 pounds.

Some of my colleagues referred to Air America pilots as overpaid mercenaries and resented the fact that they were so well paid. But during the last panic-filled day in Saigon, Air America chopper pilots ferried more than 1,000 people from pickup points throughout the city to evacuation points. Air America pilots earned every penny they were paid.

Air America was my means of getting back to see Lee and, later, our son John. When I had finished my work in a province, the high-pitched whine of a Porter's motor was the greatest sound in the world. During my four years in Vietnam, Air America never let me down. For that, I will be forever grateful. In May 1988, I attended a ceremony at CIA Headquarters in which a plaque honoring Air America was installed in the main corridor. It was a ceremony long overdue.

13

. . . .

THE LIGHT AT THE END OF
THE TUNNEL

January 1973 began with thoughts of the Paris Peace Accords and
home leave. Part of our second tour was forty-five days of home leave,
and we were looking forward to it.

The accords were signed on January 27, 1973 (Saigon time), and although large confrontations between the ARVN and the NVA abated,
there were daily skirmishes, and the ARVN was taking substantial casualties. The bombing halt gave the NVA free rein to extend and improve
the Ho Chi Minh Trail and build a fuel pipeline from North Vietnam to
Loc Ninh, sixty-five miles north of Saigon. President Nixon characterized the signing as the first glimmer of light at the end of a long, dark
tunnel.

Less than a month after the Paris accords were signed, a cease-fire
ended the war in Laos. NVA road builders could now work unimpeded
and began to improve and extend the trail.

Most of us felt that with the signing of the accords, we were in less personal danger (if that was possible). We posed no threat. Congress and the American public wanted the war to end, and attacks on American civilians would be counterproductive. Although there was a diminished sense of personal danger, I and many of my colleagues felt that when the U.S troops left Vietnam, our safety net went with them.

Tet of 1973 was a nonevent. Our analysts were saying that the NVA had not recovered from the losses it had incurred during the Easter Offensive of 1972 and that it would be some time before the North Vietnamese could launch another major offensive.

The last American combat soldier left Vietnam on March 30, and the last POW left North Vietnam on April 1, leaving a little over 8,000 American government officials still in-country. The drawdown of U.S. forces had been going on for more than two years. As U.S. bases closed, thousands of Vietnamese lost their sources of income, the Vietnamese piastre (unit of currency) lost its value, and the economy went south. Drug dealers, prostitutes, shoeshine boys, maids, cooks, and construction workers had to find new sources of income. The Vietnamese economy had exploded as American involvement in the war expanded, and it imploded as the Americans left. One result was an increase in the influx of refugees into Saigon and other large cities. Inflation and unemployment, two horses of any economic apocalypse, were beginning to run as early as 1972, and the situation did not look good.

Sociologically, Vietnam had not been able to absorb the impact of more than 500,000 American GIs. Vietnamese shoeshine boys and their sisters who became prostitutes made more money than their parents did. Marriages between Americans and Vietnamese and the children sired by Americans and abandoned also did much to disrupt Vietnamese society.

With those thoughts in mind, Lee and I left for Laredo, Texas, and home leave. While in Laredo, we found out that Lee was pregnant, and there was much rejoicing. The doctor told us that we could expect the baby around Thanksgiving.

The aftermath of the Watergate break-in started to be felt while we were home. H. R. Haldeman and John Ehrlichman, Nixon's two top aides, resigned in April, and the possibility of Nixon being impeached became a reality. Just before leaving for Saigon, Congress voted to block all funding for military aid to Vietnam.

During our flight back, the elation over Lee being pregnant buoyed me, but I had a couple of not so happy thoughts. It occurred to me that the ARVN could not protect the remaining American civilians in Vietnam, and that Congress's blockage of funds for military assistance impaired the ARVN's motivation to do so.

En route to Saigon, we stopped over in Hong Kong for a couple of days. While standing in line for our flight to Saigon, we had an encounter that might be considered an omen. Immediately in front of me was a man hitting on a woman. Appearing to be in his mid to late forties, he had the flushed face and slurred speech of someone who was clearly drunk. When he realized that he was striking out, he turned to me and asked, "Are you going to Vietnam?"

"I sure hope so. This is Air Vietnam, and I don't think it goes anyplace else," I said.

"Do you know Bill Mangone?" he asked.

When I said that I did, he announced that he would be taking Mangone's place in Tay Ninh and introduced himself as Dave Carey. Carey then proceeded to question me about life in Vietnam in general and about MR/3 and Tay Ninh in particular.

Although we are not drinkers, Lee and I have alcohol in our home for guests, and I have no moral compunctions against drinking. I have been drunk four times in my life, the last time in August 1966 while I was in the army. I do have a disdain for "pain-in-the-ass" drinkers, however, and Carey was becoming a pain in the ass.

When he learned that I had worked with Mangone, he knew that I was CIA and felt that he had found a friend. After about twenty minutes, Carey seemed to sense through his alcohol fog that I was getting tired of him. He turned to pick up where he had left off with the woman in line, but offered this parting shot: "John, grab an M-16 and come on up to see me in Tay Ninh. We can kill a lot of communists!"

We had no further contact with Carey on the plane, and I went back to my musings on the future of Vietnam. As our plane touched down at Tan Son Nhut, I thought back on something one of our lecturers had said during the VNO course: "Vietnam is an accident of geography caught jaywalking across the twentieth century." My sense was that a lot of jaywalkers were about to be run over by an eighteen-wheeler.

We arrived in Saigon at about 8 P.M. As we cleared immigration, we ran into "Judy Kohl," one of our personnel officers, who was there to pick up Carey. "John, Lee, have you seen a guy named Dave Carey?" she asked. "I've been looking all over for him. I know he was on the plane."

We told her that he had been on the plane with us and should be in the reception area. Kohl was unable to find him and left without him. The next morning, "Eileen Fagan" from Personnel called Barry and told him that Carey was missing.

Barry sent Bill Evans and "Jeff Roman" to Tan Son Nhut to look for Carey. The Pan American Airways manager had Carey's bags, but there was no Carey. Roman went into the men's room and found a man passed out in the filthy urinal trough. He was a mess and had been urinated on. Roman had found Carey—reeking of alcohol and urine, filthy, and a little banged up.

Evans called Barry and told him to have a doctor waiting for them at the Duc. They half carried, half dragged the incoherent Carey outside the terminal and hosed him off. At the Duc, they gave him a shower and put him to bed. The next day, Carey was clearly suffering from delirium tremens. Dr. Shore was about to give him a glass of bourbon when Evans took the glass and emptied it in the sink. "The last thing this poor bastard needs is a glass of bourbon."

Shore told Evans that he had paid $5 for the bourbon and was going to tell Barry what Evans had done.

While this was happening, I was checking in from my trip and telling Keith Barry and Art O'Leary about my experience with Carey in the airport in Hong Kong. I pointed out that he was the last person in the world who should be sent to Tay Ninh. "Tay Ninh is right on the Cambodian border and not the place to be sending someone with a drinking problem. And this guy has a real drinking problem," I said.

Barry and O'Leary gave me an almost verbatim replication of what my old boss Jack Gordon had told me when I reported a similar situation on my first trip to MR/4: "John, you're not a drinker. You just don't understand."

While Barry and O'Leary were blowing me off, they knew that Carey was at the Duc being cleaned up by Evans and Roman. By Sunday, they knew that they had a nonfunctioning alcoholic on their hands, and they still sent him up-country. Sending Carey to Tay Ninh was bad enough, but as the POIC there, he would be handling FIREBALL, the station's premier agent. I found that mind-boggling.

My final word to Barry and O'Leary was that Carey would get into trouble in Tay Ninh. Thirty days after his arrival, he stuck the barrel of an M-1 carbine in his mouth and blew his brains out.

During his month in Vietnam, I had run into Carey a couple of times at the Duc, and he was drunk on both occasions. I had also seen him in Tay Ninh once, and he was sober as a judge.

Shortly after Carey's suicide, Lee and I had Jack Lehr and Art O'Leary over for dinner. Knowing that O'Leary was the deputy chief of security, Lehr got on him about Carey's even being in Vietnam. Lehr said that he had known Carey for almost twenty-five years, and for at least twenty of those years, Carey had been an alcoholic. He loudly wondered how the Office of Security could have signed off on Carey's assignment. O'Leary became a little flustered and said that maybe Carey had dried out. Lehr took exception to O'Leary's comment, and our dinner was a bit subdued.

First on our agenda after getting back to Saigon was letting our medics know that Lee was pregnant. Dr. Bush arranged for Lee to get her prenatal care at the Seventh Day Adventist Hospital, and her obstetrician predicted a late November birth.

Mark Verity, Amos Spitz, and I were pretty busy, and I was out of town about 50 percent of the time during Lee's pregnancy. In August, Amos left, and later that month, Rob Creed arrived to replace him. The working relationship that evolved among the three of us was the best I have ever had.

Saigon was beginning to look more run-down. There were more panhandlers, more prostitutes, and fewer bars on Tu Do. Gasoline prices had skyrocketed, and our maid told us that the price of rice had gone up so much that she could barely afford it.

An event that took place in Washington on November 7 had significant implications for the South Vietnamese. Congress overrode Nixon's veto and passed the War Powers Act, which, for all practical purposes, nullified the Paris Peace Accords. From that point on, the president could not send American troops overseas for more than thirty days without the prior approval of Congress.

Thanksgiving came and went, with no rush to the hospital. The doctor told us that if Lee did not give birth by December 1, he would have to induce labor. He also said that he might have to do a cesarean. One of my major concerns was that I would be out of town when Lee went into labor. But Stonewall Forrest was in Saigon on a TDY and assured me that he would get Lee to the hospital. Steve Bray, the mission warden, had a car standing by while I was out of town. On November 30, the doctor told us that he would do a cesarean on December 4.

On Monday night, I brought Lee to the hospital and checked her in. I was back before 8:00 the next morning. Lee went into the operating room at about 8:45, and it seemed as though only half an hour had passed when the doctor came out to the waiting room and told me that I had a healthy son. I was absolutely euphoric.

I went into the recovery room to see Lee, and my main recollection is of how cold it was. The air-conditioning was going full blast. Lee was naked with just a thin blanket over her. She was shivering, and her teeth were chattering. She later told me that two Vietnamese nurses had been arguing in the recovery room, and when they finished, one of them folded the blanket down below her breasts, making her even more uncomfortable. Lee was still in pain and unable to move.

As I left the hospital after visiting Lee and John, I could see huge billows of smoke off in the distance. The VC had launched a rocket attack against the logistics supply facility at Nha Be. When I returned to the embassy, I went up on the roof to get a better look. I could see explosion after explosion as pallets loaded with ammunition blew up. A huge detonation occurred when 35 million liters of gasoline went up in a tremendous sheet of flame. (I guess the VC were welcoming John.)

That night, when I went back to see Lee, she had been put in a room with a Vietnamese woman who was about to give birth. Lee seemed to be recovering well, and she had John with her. Her roommate had a female visitor. They both admired John in Vietnamese and then chattered on. When I went to see Lee the next morning, she told me that after I left, her roommate's visitor stayed beyond the curfew. She got into bed with the pregnant woman and spent the night.

On Lee's third day in the hospital, an American dietitian rushed into Lee's room and said, "I'm sorry. We didn't know you were American. What do you want to eat today? Do you want a steak dinner?" Too late. Lee was released that day.

Two of the other married CIA couples in Saigon had children—both girls—and almost everyone was predicting that we would have a girl too. There was some celebrity attached to having a boy, but in my euphoria, it went over my head. Around the Duc and the embassy, I passed out cigars and candy and basked in the glory of fatherhood.

Life after John's birth was better than I had ever known, but he certainly changed our routines. Lee was no longer working, and she was spending every minute with John. As much as she enjoyed being with him, the total lack of adult contact was stressful. As soon as John was big enough, we bought a back carrier and took him everywhere; he was like an appendage. The Vietnamese maids in the Duc became enthralled with him. When John was about ten months old, our maid began taking him to the roof to have lunch with the other maids. I guess that was the beginning of his taste for Asian food. We were pleasantly surprised when the waitresses from the Duc brought us a gift—a Chinese good-luck symbol. We still have it. On Tu Do, when I took John with me, bar girls came out on the street and swarmed around him.

"Sean Dolan," a case officer in Pleiku, and "Julie Ortega," a friend of Lee's from El Paso, Texas, were the godparents, and we had a great christening party. Donna Beard, one of my favorite secretaries at the CIA, served as proxy for Julie, who had left Saigon.

John made his first public appearance at the Duc Christmas party. As happy as that occasion was, there was a sobering note. While discussing the situation in Saigon with "Hazel Glass," a reports officer we had met at the VNO course, she said, "There may be peace on earth, but it sure isn't here. Do you know that the ARVN had almost 25,000 killed in action this year? It can't continue to take those kinds of casualties." This was not a good harbinger of things to come.

The year 1974 started as 1973 had ended—no outward sign of increased military activity, and a continuing downturn in the South Vietnamese economy. One situation I had not been aware of during the last months of 1973 was the rate at which desertions from the ARVN were growing. As I traveled throughout Vietnam in early 1974, POICs and case officers were telling me that many of the ARVN units were at half strength and that more soldiers were lost through desertion than through combat.

Watergate was the main topic of interest among most of the American civilians in Saigon, and most were betting that Nixon would not be impeached. When the impeachment hearings began in May, some began to see the implications for Vietnam if Nixon were to be convicted. My impression of the South Vietnamese reaction to Nixon's resignation was that they were amazed by the calmness of the transition from Nixon to Ford. Amazed though they were, they were also frightened. Would the promises Nixon made in the Paris Peace Accords be kept? Who was Gerald Ford? Virulent anticommunist that Nixon was, his resignation gave the North Vietnamese a boost and demoralized the South Vietnamese.

As if things were not bad enough, in October, a Catholic priest incited anticorruption protests in Saigon. These protests were supported by several newspapers in Saigon and became a thorn in Thieu's side. By the time American officials recognized the full impact of the corruption, it had become an inoperable, incurable cancer that was destroying Vietnam. The drawdown of American forces brought about an economic paralysis, and congressional cuts in aid sucked the will to live out of a country already at death's door.

President Ford was an unknown quantity to the North Vietnamese, and in December 1974, they decided to test him. In a clear violation of the accords, they attacked Phuoc Long province, sixty miles north of Saigon, and waited for an American reaction. There was none, and the descent down the slippery slope continued.

Phuoc Long province fell in early January 1975, and it appeared that the NVA might be preparing for large-scale military activity during Tet. Although Phuoc Long was not of particular strategic significance, the Americans' failure to respond to such an egregious violation of the Paris Peace Accords was a green light for the North Vietnamese to continue their offensive.

In mid-January, I was talking to a Vietnamese interpreter in Bien Hoa. "Mr. John," he said. "Mr. Polgar was just here. He tell us that the NVA aren't going to do anything this year. He also say things under control. I think he wrong."

On February 20, Polgar spoke at a meeting of the station wives regarding Tet of 1975 and what could be expected. Lee attended the meeting, which was held poolside at the embassy compound. According to Lee, Polgar assured the wives that things were going well and that there was no imminent danger. He actually went so far as to say, "I'll go out on a limb and say [South] Vietnam will still be here in the next [unintelligible] years." Lee was not sure if he said fifteen or fifty years.

Marta Fuentes, the wife of an operations officer and one of our neighbors in the Duc, was Basque. She spoke native French and communicated well with the maids. On the day of Polgar's briefing, Marta told Lee that her maid had said that the Americans had better get out of Vietnam, because she was seeing more VC in the marketplace every day. Marta was concerned about the baby and told Lee that she should consider getting out now instead of waiting until our tour was up.

At dinner that night, I spoke with the wife of a provincial case officer. She had attended the briefing and commented that Polgar's prognosis was much different from what her husband was telling her.

In late February, Frank Snepp, Polgar's anointed spokesman and one of his personal favorites, was at Can Tho to deliver Polgar's "all-is-well" message. I attended his briefing, as did almost every officer in MR/4. Snepp gave the appearance of being the epitome of the dashing CIA operative. He was young, handsome, and well spoken. To the uninformed, he gave the impression that he knew what he was talking about. Among the CIA employees in Vietnam, Snepp's main claim to fame was his dating Carla Christiansen, a lovely reports officer who worked in Saigon.

Snepp's Can Tho briefing was well presented and by the book. His maps and charts went along with what sounded like a canned speech about how well the war was going. He predicted that South Vietnam would hold free elections in October. Jeff Starrett, who had replaced Chris Hanlon as POIC in Chau Doc, called him on that. "Frank, if you attend elections in October, you're going to be the only American here, because we are on the way out."

Snepp described a military action that had taken place in the Delta the previous day as insignificant. On his way to Can Tho, Starrett had flown over the battle site and had seen the bodies. He invited Snepp to fly over the area with him, count the bodies, and see just how insignificant the action was.

Snepp was in the midst of his presentation when "Cesar Cervone," a case officer in Can Tho, interrupted him. "Frank, that may be what's going on in the rest of the country, but it sure as hell isn't what's going on down here. Since January, the ARVN has lost over 60 percent of the Delta."

Another POIC spoke up. "When Polgar, Nixon, and [Secretary of State Henry] Kissinger met at San Clemente, Polgar was given the word, *'Vietnamization is working,* and we don't want anything coming out of Saigon that says otherwise.'"

A number of other officers joined in. The crux of their comments was that they had been reporting NVA infiltration into the Delta and the concomitant deterioration of the ARVN for more than a year, and most of those reports were being rejected by Saigon. Snepp did not disagree but smiled, shrugged his shoulders, and said, "Guys, I'm just quoting the party line."

Snepp's view was certainly different from mine and, from what I was hearing, from that of the other people at the briefing. In fairness to Snepp, however, I have to acknowledge that he had access to a lot more intelligence than anyone at the briefing and may have known things that we did not. Fairness notwithstanding, after the briefing, it occurred to me that Snepp was preaching the message of a paternalistic management that did not trust labor with the truth about the gravity of the situation.

From what I had seen, each military region operated pretty independently, had its own agenda, and had a slightly parochial view of the situation in Vietnam. Snepp's presentation seemed to contradict the intelligence that MR/4 had been trying to disseminate, which could have negative implications for evacuation preparations. Snepp's "big picture" view was juxtaposed with MR/4's snapshot. Right or wrong, Snepp's presentation did not go over well.

Earlier that month, I had tested a source who identified an NVA unit that had just arrived in the Delta, and the test supported his claims. The source's case officer subsequently told me that Saigon had rejected the report with the statement, "We have no collateral information that the unit your agent claims to have seen exists. Without collateral information, we cannot disseminate your report."

In addition to reporting that NVA units were showing up in the Delta, many of the POICs reported that their local employees were telling them that they were seeing more and more "Northerners" in the Delta every day.

On February 24, 1975, a congressional delegation arrived in Saigon on a fact-finding mission. In his meetings with the delegation, Ambassador Graham Anderson Martin not only turned the congressmen off but also caused some of them to ask for his removal. CIA people were complaining that Martin was trying to dominate the meetings and was having a tough time with the delegation. Snepp claims that he himself saved Polgar's job by praising him to the delegation.[1]

Thieu's arrest of eighteen journalists earlier that month also came up. A few members of the delegation visited the journalists in prison, after

---

1. Frank Snepp, *Decent Interval, an Insider's Account of Saigon's Indecent End Told by the CIA's Chief Strategy Analyst in Vietnam* (New York: Random House, 1977), p. 166.

which Rep. Paul McCloskey and Sen. Dewey Bartlett both concluded that Thieu's repressive measures were contrary to everything America stood for and therefore should preclude Congress from appropriating more money.[2] On January 28, 1975, President Ford had asked Congress for an additional $722 million, and Congress turned him down.[3]

My best memory of the congressional visit is hearing that Rep. Millicent Fenwick had her wallet stolen while attending a meeting with members of the Vietcong's Provisional Revolutionary Government at Tan Son Nhut and that Rep. Bella Abzug was more absurd and rude than expected. Polgar claimed that her conduct, as well as that of Rep. Donald Fraser, was inexcusable. They failed to attend a dinner that Thieu had arranged for the delegation without letting anyone know that they would not be there.[4]

After capturing Phuoc Long, the NVA did not press forward with any large attacks and seemed to be lying low. By the second week of March, Tet was over, making it the second consecutive Tet without major military activity. Some CIA people, beginning to breathe sighs of relief, thought that perhaps the U.S. presence in Vietnam would continue for at least another year. Although the situation in South Vietnam was still bad, the North Vietnamese had given no indication of making an all-out push during 1975.

Early on the morning of March 10, an NVA attack began on Ban Me Thuot. Just as it had at Phuoc Long, the NVA used armor, artillery, and infantry in coordinated attacks. At about noon, I ran into O. B. Harnage. He said that one of the Air America pilots had radioed that something big was happening in MR/2. Later that day, a reports officer told me that the NVA appeared to be launching a major attack on Ban Me Thuot. "If the ARVN doesn't hold, things could get very bad," he added.

More so than during the twenty-four-day battle for Phuoc Long, we were aware of what was going on in Ban Me Thuot and the implications of losing the province. Phuoc Long was rather isolated, we had no people there, and it was not as strategically important as Ban Me Thuot.

2. Arnold R. Isaacs, *Without Honor: Defeat in Vietnam and Cambodia* (Baltimore: Johns Hopkins University Press, 1983), p. 337.

3. George Donelson Moss, *Vietnam, an American Ordeal* (Upper Saddle River, N.J.: Prentice-Hall, 1990), p. 468.

4. Larry Engelmann, *Tears Before the Rain: An Oral History of the Fall of South Vietnam* (New York: Oxford University Press, 1990), p. 61.

I thought it unusual that the attack came after Tet. When I mentioned my concern to Art O'Leary, he assured me that the attack was no more than saber rattling on the part of the NVA. "This too shall pass," was his assessment of the situation.

By the close of business that day, we heard that some ARVN units were fleeing the area around Ban Me Thuot, and the situation was not promising. Although some ARVN units fought well, Ban Me Thuot had been almost completely overrun by noon the next day, and the NVA was mopping up.

The battle for Ban Me Thuot ended on March 14, and immediately afterward, there was a lull in the fighting. None of the CIA people I spoke with seemed to know what was happening. I heard one person express the idea that the NVA was not going to do anything big until 1976 and probably would stop its offensive at Ban Me Thuot. A mood of waiting for the other shoe to drop prevailed among CIA people in Saigon. I did not learn the reason for the lull in the NVA push after Ban Me Thuot until years later: NVA officers thought they were being led into a trap. The attack on Ban Me Thuot had been too easy, and they could not believe that the ARVN had run as it had.

I also concluded that, until the fall of Ban Me Thuot, the NVA had had no intention of launching an all-out, balls-to-the-wall offensive like the Tet Offensive of 1968 and the 1972 Easter Offensive. But when the ARVN caved in as rapidly as it did, and then Thieu compounded the problem by ordering the abandonment of the highlands, the NVA was presented with an offer it could not turn down.

On the morning of March 15, there was no news of more military activity. Around 8:45, I was walking to the embassy when I ran into "Jeffery Innes," chief of reports for Saigon Station. Innes impressed me as having one of the better minds I had encountered in Vietnam. His wife and young son were with him in Saigon, and he gave every impression of having it all together. "It's all over. Things are back to normal. They took their shot and missed!" he said. Innes was upbeat and seemed sure of himself. Based on what I had seen since late 1974, however, I thought he was wrong, but I was unable to articulate my reservations. I told him I hoped he was right and continued on to the embassy.

About an hour and a half later, a collective "Oops!" seemed to echo in the compound. Rob Young reported from Pleiku to Nha Trang that one of his sources, an ARVN major code-named WHISPER, had just told him that Thieu was abandoning the highlands; if the Americans did not get out immediately, they would be trapped by the NVA. Claude Shin, the ROIC in MR/2, radioed Polgar with Young's report. Polgar ordered Shin to get our people out of Pleiku.

Scuttlebutt had it that Polgar then went to Chargé d'Affaires Wolf Lehmann to inform him of the situation and to tell Lehmann what he had done. Supposedly, Lehmann chastised Polgar and said that he had just spoken to Thieu, who had said nothing about pulling out of the highlands.[5] Polgar allegedly said, "That's what happens when you go in the back door to get information."

Regardless, Lehmann did not countermand Polgar's orders. In the highlands, the ARVN was in full flight by 2 P.M., and the rout was on. Later that afternoon, we heard that Thieu had made the decision to abandon the highlands on March 14, at a meeting in Cam Ranh Bay. Snepp mentions that General Phu, the MR/2 commander, specifically ordered Gen. Pham Van Dat not to inform the Americans about the withdrawal.[6]

At the Duc that afternoon and evening, the main topic of conversation was Thieu's order to pull out of Pleiku without letting the Americans know. I saw no one panicking, but it was mentioned that the only thing between us and the NVA was the ARVN rabble. A commo tech voiced a concern that many of us felt but were reluctant to bring up. "Do you think the South Vietnamese are going to let us just walk away? If they ever get the idea that we are ditching them, I don't want to be around. Who is going to save us?"

Polgar had assured us that there would be no major offensive in 1975. His position was that a negotiated settlement would take place. What had already happened at Ban Me Thuot and what was happening in Pleiku did not seem to change his position.

The green light given the NVA by the American nonreaction to the attack on Phuoc Long was still on, and the offensive started to gather momentum. The North Vietnamese knew that American B-52s and troops would not be coming to bail out the ARVN, and they felt safe in attacking Ban Me Thuot. They also thought that the South Vietnamese would put up some semblance of a fight and, when they did not, felt that they were being led into a trap.[7]

5. Oliver Todd, *Cruel April: The Fall of Saigon* (New York: W. W. Norton, 1990), p. 144.

6. Snepp, *Decent Interval*, p. 195.

7. Engelmann, *Tears Before the Rain*, p. 302.

Along with many other CIA people, I had been shouting for years that Vietnamization was not working, and the South Vietnamese military seemed to be doing its best to prove our point. By the time I went to bed that night, I did not feel that my family and I were in imminent danger, but I felt uneasy about the current offensive. Most of all, I had diminished confidence in my leaders because I thought that they were taking the current situation too lightly.

Among my recollections of those first days of the final offensive, my sharpest memories are of the refugees. All roads out of the highlands to points south were jammed with fleeing civilians and military rabble that had once been troops. A Defense Attaché Office analyst, who had been flying over the roads, described a horror show: "There were dead people all over the roads, and stalled cars, trucks, mopeds, tanks, carts, and anything a human can travel on, everywhere. On our last flyover, NVA artillery shelled the road, and there wasn't any place for those people to hide. God, it was awful."

In Saigon, we heard such stories from many sources, but no one seemed to realize the severity of the situation. None of our people in Pleiku had arrived in Saigon, and Nha Trang had not been evacuated or, at that point, even threatened.

The abandonment of An Loc, however, did get our attention. The fight for An Loc had been the preeminent battle of the 1972 Easter Offensive and a tremendous symbolic victory for the ARVN. On March 18, 1975, the ARVN withdrew from An Loc without being attacked by the NVA, and the thought took root that the withdrawal could be the start of something big. Before the end of the week, we believed that if the ARVN did not make a stand soon, all of us would be in danger. If Polgar felt that the situation was deteriorating, he did not share his thoughts with anyone at my level.

Just as it had done after Phuoc Long in January, the NVA seemed to pause as the ARVN pulled out of Ban Me Thuot. It turned out that the North Vietnamese were only regrouping and trying to figure out where to go next. By the end of the week, it was clear that, sometime between March 15 and 20, Hanoi had made the decision to go as far as the NVA's current momentum would take it.

A reports officer told me that a tremendous amount of traffic was coming down the Ho Chi Minh Trail and that the ARVN did not seem to be putting up much of a fight. "Jesus, John, if I were them [the NVA], I wouldn't stop. By the time Thieu gets the message that we [the United States] are not going to bail him out, it's going to be too late," he said.

I still thought, however, that if the situation became serious, the U.S. military would get the Americans out of South Vietnam. At the Duc, the main topic of conversation was not the collapse of the ARVN but the seeming lack of any sense of urgency on the part of Martin and Polgar. Also, Thieu's leaving our people hanging in Pleiku evoked real anger. I heard several people make negative comments about the Vietnamese: "We're here trying to help them, and they stab us in the back like that." "How the hell can they do that?" "Our people got out of there by the skin of their teeth." "Maybe they [Thieu and the South Vietnamese] thought that if some of us got killed or captured, it would get them some aid."

Shortly after the fall of Ban Me Thuot, I got a letter from "Al Tremaine" and his wife. Al had been named to replace me, and in his letter, he expressed some concern about the current situation and asked me if they should continue processing. I went to Art O'Leary and told him that we should tell the Tremaines to hold off.

"The pipeline is still open," said O'Leary. "Tell them to keep processing."

At that point, I did not know how far the NVA would be going, but I suggested to O'Leary that it would do no harm to have the Tremaines delay their processing, at least until we had a clearer picture of what was going to happen. O'Leary thought that I was being "alarmist" and rejected my suggestion. The Tremaines moved out of their home and sold their cars, and Mrs. Tremaine quit her job. They were in Hawaii when they were notified that their tour had been canceled. Their household effects were lost when the Khmer Rouge seized the *Mayaguez* (a commercial freighter) off the coast of Cambodia.

On March 24, six days after An Loc was abandoned, NVA activity in MR/1 took a dramatic upturn. Between March 24 and 29, Hue, Tam Ky, Quang Ngai, and Da Nang fell to the North Vietnamese.

Gen. Ngo Quang Truong, the ARVN commander in MR/1, had an outstanding reputation. One author described him as "probably the finest general in the RVN armed forces."[8] Thieu, after the meeting in Cam Ranh on March 14–15, ordered Truong to abandon the northern prov-

---

8. Moss, *Vietnam, an American Ordeal*, p. 378.

inces, but on March 20, he reversed himself and ordered that Hue be held at all costs. By then, it was too late.[9]

On the evening of March 25, I was having dinner in the Duc dining room when Monica Beal, wife of the ROIC in MR/1, came in. She looked emotionally and physically drained. I had seen her only twice before and had gathered that she was a bit aloof. That night in the dining room, her emotional greeting of another CIA wife seemed a bit melodramatic to me. When I subsequently learned what Monica and many other people had faced in Da Nang, I was ashamed of myself. She conducted herself with dignity and grace, and her husband had performed heroically. At great personal risk, Bob Beal repeatedly went back into Da Nang to try to find local employees and take them to an evacuation ship.

During those five days in March while MR/1 was going down the tubes, it was disquieting to see how easy it was for the NVA to roll over the best the ARVN had to offer. Only years later did I learn how Thieu's conflicting and insane orders to Truong had castrated the general and his troops.

There is no greater testament to the failure of Vietnamization than the poor performance of the South Vietnamese military during the last three weeks of March 1975. As negative as I had been about Vietnamization, I had always thought that the ARVN would offer *some* resistance. The fact that it did not was scary. As the South Vietnamese military disintegrated, so did whatever protection it offered.

If there had been any doubts about the intentions of the NVA, they were dispelled with the fall of Da Nang. The North Vietnamese offensive was a juggernaut reminiscent of the German blitzkrieg of World War II. The loss of Hue, the old imperial capital and the cultural heart and soul of Vietnam, was both symbolically and militarily significant. It had been occupied during Tet of 1968 and again in 1972. This time, however, no Americans were available to help get it back, and there were no South Vietnamese troops with the ability or wherewithal to do so.

On March 28, Gen. Frederick C. Weyand and his delegation arrived in Saigon for consultations with Thieu. Ted Shackley and George Carver, former special assistant for Vietnam affairs and senior Directorate of Intelligence officer, represented the CIA. Ambassador Martin was also on the plane.

---

9. Stanley Karnow, *Vietnam, a History* (New York: Penguin Books, 1991), p. 700.

Polgar had a reception for Shackley at the Duc, and I managed to catch sight of Carver sitting by himself at the Duc pool. The only information I had about the delegation's discussions was that Shackley had recommended sealing off Saigon from refugees.

I also heard one of the CIA logistics men complaining about an ARVN colonel. "We're working all day and night to rearm the troops that made it back here," he said, "and this asshole leaves at 4 P.M. It's as if he doesn't give a shit."

For four days prior to the fall of Da Nang (March 29), we had been receiving radio messages telling us how desperate things were there. We saw pictures of ARVN soldiers hanging onto helicopter skids in their chaotic flight, and we received a lot of secondhand information about the hell that Da Nang was becoming. As our people from Da Nang straggled in, a horrific picture emerged. For me, the worst part was what I heard about the South Vietnamese military. The ARVN troops and other South Vietnamese military units in MR/1 had become murderers, rapists, and looters. Because we might have to depend on the ARVN for protection, I realized that it was now time to get Lee and John out of Vietnam.

14

FAREWELL

The fall of Da Nang on March 29, 1975, dispelled any remaining doubt I had about the outcome of the war. I knew that what had happened in Da Nang could happen in Saigon. I did not want to be in Saigon when that day came, but it was my job to stay. Lee and John did not have to stay, so that afternoon, I told Art O'Leary that I wanted my wife and son out of there.

If we did not have John, I am sure that Lee would have stayed, but we both agreed that under no circumstances was John to be put in harm's way. Another couple, "Bill" and "Mary Elder," had a son, Tony, a few months younger than John and an infant son, Nicholas. Mary and the boys would also be leaving.

During the next few days, the situation became worse. With the fall of Da Nang, the NVA refocused on MR/2. On April 1, Qui Nhon fell. Two days later, the NVA captured Nha Trang. On the morning of April 3, I took Lee and John to Tan Son Nhut, and we connected with the Elders. At 10:00, we said a difficult good-bye.

My trip back down Cong Ly was a bit different from my first trip on

April 10, 1971. This time, there was no Bo Mooney telling me how well the war was going. The din from the streets was muted; it was not a joyful noise. As the car wended its way, I thought of Lee and John and of how much I would miss them, but I also thought, "This could get exciting, and I want to be a part of it." I had no skill that would be useful in a Saigon going down the drain, but I wanted to be there. This was "my war," and I wanted to see it through. I had never seen myself as a heroic figure, but this might be my one and only chance. Had James Thurber been looking for a model for his Walter Mitty in April 1975, he could have done a lot worse than I.

When Lee and John left on April 3, I had no idea that I would be leaving exactly one week later. As soon as I got back from Tan Son Nhut, I went to the office. The lines of people waiting for passports were stretching down Thong Nhut. There was a sense of urgency but no panic.

On March 29, when I had told O'Leary that I wanted Lee and John out, I had also suggested that we start getting rid of our classified material. In Da Nang and Pleiku, there had not been enough time to dispose of classified documents. O'Leary said that I was being a bit premature. "We can't let the Vietnamese think that we are getting ready to leave." Now, destroying classified documents became a round-the-clock exercise. We had one large paper shredder in Norodom. During the next few days, it became one of the most sought-after pieces of equipment in Saigon.

The Duc was beginning to fill up with CIA people coming in from MR/1 and MR/2. That night (April 3) after the movie, I went to the Duc bar. It was more crowded than usual, and those who had escaped from MR/1 and MR/2 were receiving a lot of attention.

Several of those from MR/1 spent their first few days in Saigon writing up recommendations for commendations for one another. More power to them—they were entitled. Hearing their stories convinced me that I had made the right decision in getting Lee and John out of Vietnam. I heard no one bragging about their exploits, but their sense of desperation during those horrible days in Da Nang came through very clearly.

I saw no "siege mentality" among the people in the bar that night, but rather what I would call a "ship of fools" mind-set—people sitting in a bar, a bit frenetic, talking too loudly, drinking too much, and afraid to bring up what might happen. Many people there were feeling guilty about leaving behind their Vietnamese friends, colleagues, and lovers.

Others were bemoaning the loss of personal possessions. The people on contract knew that they would have to find other jobs when they returned to the States. "John, the ride on this gravy train is over," one contract employee said.

No one expressed any sense of personal danger. Because of the possibility of dangerous elements among the refugees, Saigon had been more or less cordoned off that afternoon to prevent more of them from coming into the city.

Because Creed, Verity, and I were not conducting tests outside of Saigon during those last days, we had a chance to sit back and observe. When we heard that Polgar was encouraging nonessential people to leave, our concern factor went up a notch. Supposedly, Polgar said, "You can go if you want to, but I don't guarantee it won't hurt your career."

At the same time, "Bill Carson," Saigon Station's chief of support, told the station branch chiefs, "Things are going to get real tough around here, and if any of you thinks he can't take it, stand up and say so now, and you can leave."

One branch chief who had been at that meeting told me about it and referred to Carson's words as "macho bullshit." "Yeah," he said, "I can see someone standing up and saying, 'I can't take it. Let me go home.' " There had been no takers.

Nha Trang fell that day, and the juggernaut continued to roll. Our people in Nha Trang had started getting out two days before, and they all made it, albeit less dramatically than those in MR/1.

"Jim Avery," one of our better interpreters, had been stationed in Nha Trang. The day after he arrived in Saigon, I saw him in the Duc dining room. We had lunch, and during the course of our conversation, his emotional distress was apparent. The main reason for his distress, he explained to me, was that during the previous two months, he had been debriefing a fairly high-level North Vietnamese defector and had developed a personal relationship with him. When the CIA pulled out of Nha Trang, the defector had been abandoned, which, according to Avery, was the result of incompetence and indifference. Avery told me that Shin had made a solemn promise to get the defector out, and he was almost in tears as he speculated on what the NVA would do to the defector when he was captured. I heard later that Avery resigned over this incident. I admire him for having the courage of his convictions.

With the fall of Nha Trang, the level of tension significantly increased.

People who had been talking in terms of *weeks* before the collapse now spoke of *days*. Neither Ambassador Martin nor Polgar was sounding any alarms, but those of us who were less informed did not believe that the NVA was going to stop in Nha Trang.

The next night, April 4, the Duc bar was crowded, but no one seemed to be in a panic. I was sitting with a Da Nang refugee when I heard a man at the bar say, "Do you know what that fucking Loan said? He said, 'If the Americans try to abandon us, our army will not let them go.' "[1]

On hearing this, I remembered what someone had said after the fall of Ban Me Thuot: "They aren't going to let us get out of here." It gave new life to a fear that had been at the back of my mind. Knowing how the ARVN had behaved in Da Nang and realizing that the fall of Saigon could be even worse caused me to question my desire to stay until the end.

Da Lat fell on April 4. Polgar had reorganized the Saigon staff and had put Bob Beal in charge of planning the evacuation. Despite Beal's heroic performance in Da Nang, many CIA people in Saigon thought that he was the wrong man for the job. He had not been assigned to Saigon and did not know any of the Vietnamese officials or, for that matter, many of the Americans there. One of Beal's first moves was to appoint "Frank Kohl," previously his C/OPS in MR/1, his deputy. He then told John ("Black Jack") Hallett that he would be working for Kohl. "Not only will I not be working for him, I wouldn't have him work for me," was what Hallett reportedly told Beal.

Of the events that occurred during my last days in Saigon, none had the impact of the crash of the "baby-lift" flight. On the afternoon of April 4, an air force C-5A carrying 243 Vietnamese children and 44 female escorts crashed, and almost 250 of the passengers died. The flight was intended to carry Vietnamese orphans to the United States, where adoptions were being arranged. Although most of the children were orphans, some were children whose parents had arranged for them to be taken out of Saigon.

On the day of the flight, our secretaries had been discussing how some American women in Saigon had overcome Martin's obstruction of their

---

1. He was referring to Gen. Nguyen Ngoc Loan, chief of the South Vietnamese National Police. One famous photograph from the Vietnam War is of General Loan executing a VC in the streets of Saigon during Tet of 1968.

evacuation plans by volunteering as escorts for the infants. Some of the women were secretaries at the Defense Attaché Office.

I was in the dining room at the Duc when I heard about the crash. It was difficult to comprehend. I had not known any of the escorts, but hearing that more than 200 children, many of them orphans, had been killed sucked the wind right out of me. As a father who was missing his own son terribly, perhaps the crash affected me more than most. Twenty-five years later, I can still recall my sense of sadness when I heard the news.

One of the reasons for the baby lift, as cynical as it might sound, was to generate sympathy for the plight of Vietnam. It was thought that television coverage of the children's arrival in the United States might accomplish that goal.[2]

The night of the plane crash was the first time I heard the tamarind tree mentioned. Near the rear entrance to the American embassy stood a huge tamarind tree. The embassy parking lot was planned as a staging area for an evacuation, if necessary, and the tree would be in the glide path of helicopters coming in for a landing. Some saw that tree as a symbol of Martin's intransigence regarding evacuation plans, but Lehmann and Polgar take strong exception to that idea.[3]

On the morning of April 5, a pall settled over the embassy compound. "Karen Hary," one of our secretaries, was openly crying, and I saw many other women walking around teary eyed and dazed. People were coming in from Cambodia to transit back home, and station people whose tours were up were leaving. No new people were arriving, and Saigon Station was in a state of increasing anxiety.

Later, I was having lunch at the Duc with a TDYer from the Office of Logistics. "John," he said, "you did the right thing in getting your family out. This place is a sinking ship, and I don't think we have enough life rafts."

That afternoon, O'Leary called me into his office. "How would you like to take the station files out?" he asked. "We have five tons of files to take back to the States and need someone to escort them. Do you want to do it?"

---

2. Arnold R. Isaacs, *Without Honor: Defeat in Vietnam and Cambodia* (Baltimore: Johns Hopkins University Press, 1983), pp. 396–97.

3. Larry Engelmann, *Tears Before the Rain: An Oral History of the Fall of South Vietnam* (New York: Oxford University Press, 1990), pp. 42, 57, 72–73.

"If you tell me to do it, I will, but there's no way I will ask. I'm not going to be known as the security officer who asked to leave Vietnam," I said.

O'Leary then asked me to do it, and I said that I would. He did not know when I would leave but thought it would be on the tenth or eleventh.

Going home was an attractive proposition, but I had mixed feelings—seeing Lee and John was utmost in my mind, but I wanted to see the crisis through, if only to say that I had. I had no doubt that Saigon would fall and that there was nothing I could do to change that fact. That my tour was just about up might have influenced O'Leary's decision to ask me to accompany the files, but I think he also saw me as excess baggage, and in truth, I was. My departure meant one less person to worry about, and taking the files out would give me an excuse to leave.

My last weekend in Saigon turned out to be rather mundane, but one incident on my last Sunday morning there provided another illustration of how unprepared the South Vietnamese military was. Because the VNAF did not have enough trained mechanics to service its aircraft, it had contracted with an American company, Lear/Siegler, to do the maintenance. The Lear/Siegler mechanics were taken to Bien Hoa every day by bus. That Sunday, someone rolled a grenade under the bus. No one was hurt, but all the Lear/Siegler mechanics left Vietnam on Monday.

In *Decent Interval*, Snepp mentions two of his colleagues, "Pat" and "Bill Jensen," who had made what amounted to a mutual suicide pact. Pat was a senior analyst, and Bill was the CIA chief of Saigon Base. If capture were imminent, Bill was to kill Pat and then himself. That night, April 6, "Chris Howard," one of Jensen's subordinates, and I were having a hamburger in the Duc bar. Chris and his wife, "Debbie," were two of my favorite people in Vietnam. A graduate of Williams College, Chris had survived two tours as an infantry captain in Vietnam.

"John, do you know what I heard that idiot [referring to Jensen] say?" Chris asked. "He said he can see him and his boys backing up to a C-130 with machine guns blazing. I hope to hell he does not see me as one of his boys. He's nuts! If it ever gets to that point, we're not getting out of here."

When I went into the office on Monday, O'Leary said that I would be taking the files out on Thursday, April 10. O'Leary also told me that Martin did not know that we were removing the files. I checked with "Ted Dull" at Air America, and he said that a C-130 would come in

Wednesday afternoon, and the files would be loaded. On Thursday morning at 10:00, we would take off for Clark Field in the Philippines, overnight there, and fly the next day to Travis Air Force Base, California, with a refueling stop at Hickham Air Force Base, Hawaii.

That afternoon, I took our maid to the market, bought her a 100-pound sack of rice, and took it to her home. Before Lee left, she had given the maid our sewing machine. I gave the food and liquor that was left to our military detailees and the maid. By the end of the day, everything I had left could be packed in one suitcase.

On Tuesday morning, April 8, at about 10:00, I was walking down the stairs at the Duc when I heard a tremendous explosion, followed by the whoosh of a jet and machine gun fire. The maids and waitresses in the Duc started screaming. When I reached the lobby, a desk clerk told me that a plane had just dropped a bomb on the presidential palace.

On Tran Quy Cap, traffic had stopped, but I heard no sirens, and there was no more machine gun fire. Walking toward the embassy, I saw wisps of smoke coming from the palace grounds. At the embassy, I learned that a VNAF A-37 had dropped a 500-pound bomb on the palace grounds, but there were apparently no casualties.

Just before noon, four or five of us were outside next to the shredding room when another jet flew over. Someone yelled, "It's a MiG!"

When I went inside, I saw Jeff Innes and said, "Someone said that was a MiG."

Innes became angry and said, "Don't go spreading rumors like that! You're going to panic people."

I did not remind him of our conversation on March 15, when he had said, "Things are back to normal." Obviously, things were becoming even more tense. That afternoon, I went to the Cat Tinh tailor on Tu Do and picked up a coat I had ordered, and I had my last two jelly doughnuts at the Givral Café.

At the Duc bar that night, people were exchanging boozy farewells. One of the main topics of conversation concerned Polgar having his household and personal effects shipped out. "He's telling us there's going to be a negotiated settlement, but I guess he isn't taking any chances," someone said.

My impression was that everyone there realized that the situation was serious. By then, despite Polgar's assurances, no one believed that a negotiated settlement was going to happen.

On Wednesday, my last day in Saigon, I attended a briefing in Carson's office for final details on getting the files out. O'Leary said that I had to pick up a personal letter from Polgar to Shackley and hand-carry it to headquarters. I obtained my courier orders, a gun, and a $500 cash advance. For the rest of the day, I helped burn classified material.

Three years and 364 days after my arrival in Vietnam, I was ready to leave. Saying good-bye has never been easy for me, and I usually avoid doing so. This time, because the good-bye might be final, I took the time to make my farewells. I said good-bye to Fernandez, the Duc engineer. He had been very kind to Lee and me, and I would always remember him. Lee and I had also grown attached to the Duc waitresses, after seeing them two to three times a day for four years, and I was concerned about what would happen to them after Saigon fell. Would the North Vietnamese consider them tainted by the Americans and persecute them for having worked for us? I hoped not, but I was not optimistic. Would the Americans evacuate them? Because they were not key indigenous personnel, I doubted it. Snepp, in *Decent Interval,* claimed that some CIA men obtained sexual favors from the waitresses by promising to get them out. Although this is probably true, I expect that most of the promises were made with the intention of fulfilling them. To me, the waitresses were a group of lovely young women who made our lives at the Duc more pleasant.

Partying at the Duc that night seemed a little heartier than usual, but I could not get into it. After nearly four years, a long journey was coming to an end. Knowing that I would soon see Lee and John took the sting out of leaving, but not the shame.

When I woke up on Thursday morning, I was eager to move. I did not want to think about what would happen to the South Vietnamese, and I was not looking forward to my last breakfast in the Duc. It went better than I had expected. I gave each of the waitresses on duty $20, wished them well, and said good-bye.

At 8 A.M., I went to Polgar's office, picked up his letter to Shackley, and said good-bye to the secretaries. Polgar was on the phone as I went out the door, and the last words I heard him say were, "But they are putting up a fight?" There was a sound of exasperation in his voice, and I am sure that he was checking on the ARVN.

From the embassy, I returned to the Duc to pick up my suitcase. As I got into the Duc car, I saw Jim Lewis. I had polygraphed him when he entered on duty. He said that he was on his way to MR/2 to check on the advance of the NVA. The last thing I said to him was, "Keep your head down, Jim." Lewis was captured and taken to Hanoi. He was released in November 1975, but on September 20, 1984, he and his wife were killed in the bombing of our embassy in Beirut. Paul Daly, the first person I had met in Vietnam and someone else I had tested, had also been killed. Daly was the only one of my colleagues killed in Vietnam as a result of hostile action; two, "Dave Kemp" and "Bob Warner," died as a result of misadventure.

The ride out to Tan Son Nhut did not seem much different from the hundreds of others I had taken, with one exception. Cong Ly was no longer as bustling and vibrant as it had seemed to me on my first day in Vietnam. I heard no joyful noise but more of a muted accompaniment to a swan song.

I knew that my flight to Clark would not be pleasant. C-130s are not built for comfort, and the overpowering smell of oil almost made me nauseous. With a sense of melancholy, as well as one of relief, I buckled up for the journey home. As the plane nosed up from Tan Son Nhut, I got one last look at Vietnam.

15

· · · · · · · · · · · · · · · ·

HOMECOMING

"Lee and John, here I come!"

About halfway across the Pacific, any regrets about leaving Vietnam were gone. I could think only of seeing Lee and John. As soon I arrived at Travis Air Force Base, I planned to turn over the files to anyone who met me and be on my way.

The plane landed at 11 P.M., and "Larry Wane" and "Frank Goren" from the San Francisco field office were waiting for me. Goren said that the three of us had to unload the files and move them to the CIA storage facility in Sunnyvale. When I mentioned that we had five tons of files to unload, they both turned a little pale. Goren went over to the Travis transit lounge and somehow convinced an air force noncommissioned officer to find us some airmen to help with the unloading. Those young men were a godsend.

Help was waiting for us in Sunnyvale. By 6:30 A.M., the truck was unloaded, and "Dick Latta," the chief there, took me to his house so that I could take a shower. We drove to the San Francisco airport, where I caught a United Air Lines flight to Dulles International Airport in Virginia. When the plane landed at 1 P.M., I felt like a zombie. As excited as I was to be back in the States, I could hardly keep my eyes open.

One of Shackley's gofers was waiting for me when I arrived. I gave him Polgar's letter, and he drove me to headquarters. "Brad Adams," the chief of support for the Directorate of Operations,[1] was waiting for me when I checked in. He asked me to meet with "Ed Minor," the chief of support for EA Division. Minor and William R. Katopish, one of my OS bosses, were waiting for me in a conference room. "What in hell is going on out there?" Minor immediately asked me. "We charter planes to get people out, and no one wants to take the flights. Why aren't people leaving?"

My answer would come back to haunt me. "They are rearranging the deck chairs on the *Titanic*," I said. I then repeated what Polgar and Carson had supposedly said about leaving, that is, "You can go, but it might hurt your career," and "If you can't take it, say so and you can go." Under those circumstances, I told them, no one was going to leave unless ordered to go.

Minor seemed genuine when he thanked me for the information. He arranged for orders so that I could pick up Lee and John in Laredo. On the way out, I stopped in to see the people in Polygraph. In 1974, the OS had been reorganized, and IRD became the Interrogation Branch (IB). They welcomed me, but it was after 4 P.M. on a Friday, and they were eager to get out of there.

Al Tremaine, who had been scheduled to replace me in Saigon, gave me a ride to the Tyson's Holiday Inn in Tyson's Corner, Virginia, where I was booked for the night. On the way to the hotel, he told me, "John, I really wanted to go out there, but I wish they had told me to stop processing. We lost about $2,000. [Colin] King [OS deputy director] said, 'What's he bitching about? He got a free trip to Hawaii.' " I told Al that Lee and I had really wanted to tell them to delay their processing, but we had been countermanded.

All I wanted was to call Lee and get some sleep. On the way to my room, I passed the bar, where Friday afternoon happy hour was just beginning. Many CIA people, including a few I had served with in Vietnam, were in the bar. Terry Reese, who had been in our office in Saigon, saw me and called me over. For the next hour, I enjoyed the celebrity

1. The Directorate of Plans became the Directorate of Operations in January 1973.

accorded a recent returnee from Vietnam and brought my colleagues up to date on what was happening in Saigon. I enjoyed the attention, but I was dead tired and finally begged off to go to my room. I called Lee and told her that I would be arriving in Laredo the next day. I also called my brother Bill in Albany, New York. I had not spoken with him in more than two years, and it was good to hear his voice.

Ten minutes later, I was sound asleep, but at 2 A.M., I was wide awake. The excitement of the last days in Vietnam, the flight, the anticipation of seeing Lee and John, the guilt of leaving before the war was truly over, the gratitude for being the survivor of a sinking ship, and jet lag—all these combined to interrupt my sleep.

Early Saturday morning, I took a cab to Dulles and caught a flight to Laredo. With a stopover in Dallas, I arrived in Laredo at about noon and took a cab to a corner on Matamoros Street near my mother-in-law's house. I wanted to surprise Lee and John, so I walked the last fifty yards or so to the back door of the house.

The door was open. John was standing at the sink drinking a glass of water. I had not seen him in more than a week, and my emotion was indescribable. For several minutes, I stood at the door and watched him. For some reason, I just wanted to wait until he noticed me. Suddenly, he turned to his left to put the glass on the table and saw me. "Daddy!" he screamed and came running to me. The look on his face and obvious joy at seeing me evoked a feeling that everyone should experience at least once in a lifetime. Lee and her mother heard him and came running. Lee looked wonderful, and at that moment, I was as happy as I had ever been in my life.

Socorro, my mother-in-law, is a most gracious and lovely lady, and I dearly love her. She and the rest of Lee's family have always been wonderful to me and treated me as someone special. After five days of Laredo's heat, however, I decided that it was time to return to Washington.

Lee and I had talked about where we would live but had made no decision. Eileen Fagan, a good friend from Vietnam, had invited us to stay with her for a few days, and we did. I contacted a former colleague who was a real estate agent, and within three days, we had a house.

In mid-May, I checked back into IB. First on my list of things to do was to call Art O'Leary. Thinking that he had been in Saigon until the end, I wanted to know how it had gone and where the other OS people were. Kate, his wife, answered the phone, and after exchanging pleasantries, she put Art on. He told me that he had had to leave early to take Kate to Sloan-Kettering in New York for cancer treatment and that "Jack Hanes" had replaced him. When I told him about my conversation with Katopish and Minor, O'Leary said, "Yes, I heard, and unfortunately, your comments got back to Saigon."

"What do you mean, unfortunately?" I said in an angry voice. "I told it exactly the way it was."

"Oh, don't worry about it, John. It's no big deal."

"No big deal! You're saying that telling Katopish and Minor the truth was unfortunate!"

On that note, we bid each other good-bye. That was to be my last contact with O'Leary until 1984.

On my second day back in the office, Director of Security Robert W. Gambino interviewed me. Over the years, I had four more direct, one-on-one meetings with Gambino, and I always came away impressed with him. On three occasions, I had to brief him on cases I had done, and he was always very supportive. I thought that our first meeting went well. He immediately put me at ease and asked about my Vietnam experience and what I wanted to do careerwise. When I said that I wanted to stay in polygraph, he said that he saw nothing wrong with my decision, as I obviously liked what I was doing and seemed to be good at it. Just before leaving, I brought up my conversation with O'Leary and said that what I had told Minor and Katopish was the truth, and I resented being criticized for it. Gambino assured me that I had done the right thing. Although he might have meant what he said, my experiences over the course of my career led me to conclude that "telling it like it is" is not career enhancing.

Gambino's comments placated me a little, but the next day I got some news that put a real damper on being back in the office. "Don Cody," an examiner who had come into IB while I was in Vietnam, called me into his office. He said that because I had blown the whistle on Bo Mooney, I was at the top of the IB's shit list. He told me that IB management felt that I should have kept Bo's problems in-house and not brought them up with Ray Lenihan, the regional security officer. As a result, the knives were out for me.

I do not take negative comments well, especially when they are unjust. Cody's revelations were career threatening, and my reaction was to go directly to "Les Farrell," the new chief of IB. Farrell had given me my first briefing after I entered on duty in 1968, and I liked him. He was a former polygraph examiner who had been "wrapped up" (CIA for arrested) overseas while doing a test and spent thirty days in jail. The CIA paid $1 million to get him out but never recovered his polygraph instrument. Farrell had been a GS-14 and on his way up when I first met him. But while I was in Vietnam, Farrell had apparently rubbed someone the wrong way and been exiled to IB. For all practical purposes, his career had reached its zenith. When I broached the Bo Mooney story and told Farrell that I had made that situation known to the former chief, Bill Osborne, two years before saying anything to Lenihan, he said, "I'm glad you told me, John. Don't worry about it."

Later that day, one of the IB supervisors told me that shortly after I had preached the gospel of Bo to Lenihan in Saigon, Bo had run into "Joe Murray" in Hong Kong and pleaded his case. Murray was the godfather of the OS's "Irish Mafia"(a clique of Irish Catholics) and second only to the director of security in his power to make or break the careers of security officers. My take on the conversation with the supervisor was that if I ever needed support, I would be well advised not to seek it from Murray.

I had never met Murray, but I knew him by sight. Shortly after my return from Vietnam, I was walking by his office on the fourth floor and saw him sitting at his desk. I knocked on the door and introduced myself. His reaction was less than warm. Although I knew that he had heard only Bo's version of what had happened, I hoped that he might be fair-minded and ask for my side of the story. It did not happen.

As far as I know, Murray never did anything overt to hurt my career, but I also know that he never did anything to help me. Just before Murray retired, "Greg Milenski," my boss at the time, said to me, "Joe never wanted to do anything for you, and I could never get his support to promote you."

The aftereffects of Bo were not the only glitch in my homecoming. Another occurred when I tried to resolve an issue regarding Lee's contract with the CIA. Although her staff status had been restored, Lee had missed out on an automatic promotion and lost a fair amount of money during the time she was on contract status. Lee felt that she had been treated unfairly and, while in Vietnam, had written two memoranda to the inspector general. Neither one had been answered. On my second day back in the office, I went to the inspector general to see what had happened to them. A secretary said that she would check, and that afternoon, she called to say that neither memorandum had left Saigon but had been sent back to Lee by the personnel officer. But Lee had never received them. As we were discussing the situation that evening, Eileen Fagan called and asked Lee not to do anything rash. Personnel was working to resolve the problem, and ultimately, Lee received the money.

An OS personnel officer, when he first met me about a month later, kiddingly said, "You're the guy whose wife stuck it to EA!" If getting what she was entitled to was "sticking it to them," I guess she did, but I did not see it that way. That an OS finance officer even brought this up was disquieting.

Within two weeks, I was back on-line (conducting applicant tests) and doing two cases a day. I was one of the most (if not the most) experienced examiners in the branch, and I was adapting well to my new work environment. I saw a lot of new faces in the workplace. We had a new chief and four new examiners. I found myself in the position of being one of the most senior examiners in the division and, at the same time, being the new kid on the block.

The biggest shock for me and for any examiner returning to the division after an overseas tour is going back on-line. I had more or less made my own schedule in Vietnam, and after four years of doing it my own way, suddenly shifting gears and moving into a regimented system of doing two tests each day was a difficult adjustment. An even more difficult adjustment was going from a two-hour lunch break to a half-hour lunch break.

I also had to adjust to the types of CIA applicants being tested. Before my Vietnam tour, one in five applicants admitted to drug use. During my first month of testing after my return, just under four of five applicants admitted drug use. Prior to Vietnam, I never assumed that my younger subjects had used drugs. With the admissions I was now getting, my attitude began to change, and I found myself less inclined to accept denials of drug use. From what I could observe, my colleagues and I were not conducting the tests any differently. Were we getting better at our jobs, or had drug use become as pervasive as the test results indicated?

In Vietnam, I had had a modicum of status. I had been well known by those I worked with and even respected by some. Back in headquarters, I felt like I was starting all over again, and I was suffering from a case of bruised ego. Also humbling was the quality of some of the new examiners. One of the best was "Bill Bontiempo," a former police officer and former bodyguard for Secretary of State Henry Kissinger. I took an instant liking to Bontiempo. One of the reasons for becoming a polygraph examiner is to catch spies. I was listening to Bontiempo one day when his subject, a CIA employee, confessed to having been recruited by a foreign intelligence service and directed to apply for a position with the CIA. It was a masterful job. As happy as I was for him, however, I confess that I was a little jealous.

Two months after returning from Vietnam, I was back on the road doing operations work and dealing with case officers. Also, I was being asked to give briefings to case officers at the Farm and participated in a seminar dealing with the fabrication of operations reports.

Many case officers I had worked with in Vietnam were requesting me to do cases for them, and I was flattered, but there was another side to that coin. Some of those same friends would call me to complain about the treatment of their spouses or dependents during their polygraph tests. I had two callers ask me to tell them whether their dependents had admitted to drug use. Often, I received calls asking if I could get someone scheduled for a test. It was a way to keep in touch.

For many case officers returning from Vietnam, it was more difficult. They had been away from their home divisions for almost two years and were out of the loop. Because positions had to be found for them, friction sometimes resulted. When Shackley took over the Latin America Division, for example, upper-management positions had to be found for the people who came with him. A personnel officer from the Latin America Division told me that this was a real problem because he had to find jobs not only for Shackley's people but also for those whose jobs were being usurped.

During those first months back in headquarters after the fall of Saigon, a lot of questions were being asked. Friends in EA Division told me that Snepp was pushing for the inspector general to investigate what had happened during the evacuation. Snepp claimed that negligence on the part of Polgar and his cohorts had resulted in the abandonment of many of our assets. He definitely seemed to be a voice crying in the wilderness, and I found his position inconsistent with the content of his briefing I had attended in Can Tho in late February.

Historically, CIA people have been held accountable for their mistakes or errors in judgment. After the disastrous Bay of Pigs invasion,

DCI Allen Welsh Dulles was fired. In August 1970, the chief of station in Santiago, Chile, predicted that Salvador Allende Gossens, the Marxist coalition candidate, would lose the presidential election. Allende won, and the chief of station was replaced. Regardless of whose fault it was, Vietnam was a failure. And after a failure of that magnitude, heads usually rolled, but no heads were rolling in Langley. My initial thought was that no heads were rolling at the CIA because it would not end there. There was enough blame to go around, and from the White House to the halls of Congress to the State Department in Foggy Bottom to the Pentagon and beyond, no one wanted to open that Pandora's box.

Farewell luncheons and parties were a weekly occurrence during my first few months back in headquarters, and it was hard to keep up with them. People were retiring, or they were leaving because their contracts had not been renewed. I had only one problem with the luncheons. They were invariably in Chinese restaurants, and I do not like Chinese food. At Black Jack Hallett's farewell, he said, "Goddamn it, John. Just once I would like to go to one of these things at someplace besides a Chinese restaurant."

Whenever Vietnam was discussed in the corridors and cafeterias, the main topic was the evacuation. Having missed out on it, I had little to contribute, but I did hear a lot about what had happened during those final days. I heard that Mike Hearn and Ted Dull had "bugged out" (left without giving notice or being ordered to do so) and that it was only by pure luck and the grace of God that none of our people was killed.

As an entity, the CIA's way of adjusting after Vietnam was to downplay what had happened. In an attempt to make its actions in Vietnam more palatable to those who might be critical, it held an awards ceremony for Vietnam veterans in the "Bubble" (main auditorium) in December 1975. I was unable to attend, and my Vietnam Service Medal was sent to me through the internal mail, which I thought was a fitting symbol of the CIA's attitude regarding my service in Vietnam.

When one of the attendees told me that he had been given a medal for assisting the victims of the baby-lift crash, he added, "John, I tried to get out to the airport but got stuck on Cong Ly and never made it."

Jim Warren, the ROIC in MR/4 who had performed so well, was totally ignored because he had disregarded Polgar's orders. Frank Snepp and John Stockwell, two of the more outspoken critics of CIA performance in Vietnam, were both commended. Many of our people performed heroic deeds in Vietnam, and they should have been honored. The way the awards ceremony was conducted, however, detracted from, rather than enhanced, the image of the CIA's performance in Vietnam.

An old ballplayer once said, "The older we get, the better we were." For me and for many of my Vietnam colleagues, those words reflect how, over the years, we have characterized our Vietnam experiences.

After 1975, the CIA's global focus changed. The oil embargo and the Iran hostage crisis presaged an emphasis on the Near and Middle East. Iran-Contra shifted the CIA's focus to Central America. Contract employees and case officers whose only operational experience had been in Vietnam were particularly hard-pressed to find jobs.

In the short term, those who served in Vietnam did not suffer any career damage, but as the years passed, it seemed to me that we were not getting our fair share of the top-level jobs. When annual promotions to the Senior Intelligence Service were announced, the absence of the names of Vietnam colleagues was noticeable. President John F. Kennedy once said, "Success has many fathers; failure is an orphan." Many of those who served in Vietnam were tainted by the experience, exiled to dead-end jobs, and orphaned.

As good as life in Vietnam had been, it was never home. My assignment in Vietnam gave me an appreciation of how great America is, and nothing has happened during the past twenty-five years to cause me to change my opinion. By December 1975, I had found a niche in Polygraph that would serve as my workplace home for the next twenty-four years, but I never attained the status or job satisfaction I had had in Vietnam.

EPILOGUE

We may not have gone to Vietnam for the right reasons, and we may not have stayed for the right reasons, but we left for the right reason—the American people wanted us out of there. As badly as we failed to convince the South Vietnamese that it was their war, we had less success in sustaining the American people's support for the war.

America became war weary, disillusioned, and angry about our involvement in Vietnam. As the number of crosses at Arlington increased exponentially and our Veterans Administration hospitals filled with wounded and drug-addicted Vietnam veterans, the proposition that we were winning the war was repudiated. By 1968, the American people were already war weary, but with the realization that they had been deceived came disillusionment and anger. That anger translated into a plank in Richard Nixon's 1968 presidential platform—"peace with honor," and getting out of Vietnam.

Congress also read the American mood, and as disillusionment and anger increased, its willingness to appropriate funds for Vietnam decreased. Diminishing public support and growth of the antiwar movement were primary in convincing the North Vietnamese that if they held on long enough, they would win.

The Vietnam War was the first war in our history in which there were so many American civilians not only on the scene but also actively participating in the war. The State Department and the CIA had large contingents in Vietnam, and each had its own agenda. In addition to U.S. government civilians in Vietnam, there were hundreds of media people, oil speculators, timber buyers, missionaries, moviemakers, construction workers, private contractors, ex-GIs, and adventuresome tourists throughout the country. Their presence created an atmosphere that made it easier to forget that there was a war going on.

American troop withdrawals began in 1969, and the last American combat troop left Vietnam on March 30, 1973. For the last two years of the war, America's role was directed by civilians, who, for the most part, were not up to the task.

Not having witnessed or participated in any combat in Vietnam, I am uncomfortable saying that our strategy and tactics were factors in our losing the war, but I believe it to be the case. The model that American advisers used to train the South Vietnamese was the Korean War, an inappropriate model for fighting a guerrilla war. The American generals who directed that training had attained their ranks fighting conventional wars, and in Vietnam, they were faced with an enemy, terrain, and tactics that were different from anything they had previously encountered.

General Westmoreland promoted search-and-destroy operations as a major tactic against the communists. Sending large-scale units into the countryside to look for the enemy allowed the NVA and the VC to pick and choose when and where to engage the Americans. By so doing, they limited their casualties and wore out the Americans. The most ironic factor regarding our military's performance in Vietnam is that we lost a war in which we never lost a battle, at least by our definition of winning.

Conflicts among the State Department, the CIA, and the U.S. military were also a factor in why we lost the war. In 1995, NVA Col. Bui Tin claimed that if President Johnson had allowed General Westmoreland to enter Laos and block the Ho Chi Minh Trail, "Hanoi could not have won the war."[1] The U.S. ambassador to Laos, William Sullivan, severely limited U.S. military operations against the Ho Chi Minh Trail, and the CIA resisted the U.S. military's wish to expand its operations in Laos because Laos was the CIA's bailiwick.

---

1. Richard H. Shultz, Jr., *Secret War Against Hanoi* (New York: HarperCollins, 1999), p. 205.

The "big lie," in conjunction with the failure of Vietnamization, outdated strategy and tactics, and interagency turf wars, blunted the efforts of the most technologically superior, best equipped, and most well supported military force in history.

An understanding of how and why we lost the war can help put the war behind us and keep us from repeating the mistakes we made, but the postwar effects make real closure very difficult. There are more "leftovers" from the Vietnam War than from any of our previous wars. Post-traumatic stress syndrome, drug problems, Amerasian children, victims of Agent Orange, and the POW/MIA (missing in action) issue are constant reminders of that epoch. The POW/MIA issue has done the most to keep memories of the war alive. When I left Vietnam, I was 70 percent sure that there were no living POWs in Southeast Asia. Now I am 99 percent sure. The main reason for my certainty is that the North Vietnamese could not afford to keep any POWs alive after promising that there were none. The political cost would be too great if more POWs were ever found in Vietnam. The fact that no *credible* evidence has been found to support any claims of POWs still living in Vietnam also sways me.

Americans' lack of trust in the military carried over to the postwar era, and families of POWs and MIAs were convinced that they were being lied to. Some politicians have used the POW/MIA issue to achieve their own political ends, and others have been afraid to challenge claims that we left POWs behind—even though they knew better—out of fear of the political consequences. Movies were made, books were written, frauds were perpetrated, the agony of the families involved was prolonged, and our foreign policy toward Vietnam was negatively affected without any solid evidence of living POWs in Southeast Asia.

As many negatives as there are associated with Vietnam, I have found a couple of grains of hope. We will probably never fight another war like the one we fought in Vietnam. Mass commitments of ground troops may be a thing of the past. I know of two situations—in the Congo and in Afghanistan—in which certain CIA people pushed very hard to go into those areas as we did in Laos and Vietnam. The rationale for not doing so was, "Didn't we learn anything in Vietnam?" I suggest that we did.

On a more personal note, I believe that the Vietnam War was the worst thing that has happened to the United States in my lifetime. Being even a bit player in that sad chapter of our history has left me with a sense of ambivalence. On the one hand, I am ashamed of the way we let down our GIs and failed to live up to our commitment to our South Vietnamese, Cambodian, and Laotian allies. On the other hand, I take pride in the fact that I gave it my best shot. That we lost the war diminishes, but does not vitiate, my effort. Like the GIs who went to Vietnam before me, I was young, pure of heart, and in search of a Holy Grail. And like many of those GIs who were fortunate enough to survive, I came home older, a bit cynical, and unfulfilled in my quest.

I hated the war for what it did to my country and loved it for giving me an appreciation of how lucky I have been. There were some adrenaline rushes that I would never want to repeat, but on reflection, the events that caused those rushes allow me to think less badly of myself. I did not shirk my duty; I did my stint and paid my dues.

During the twenty-five years since my return from Vietnam, few days have gone by without something reminding me of that time—testing someone who was there, working with a colleague who was there, testing or interviewing the child of a Vietnam colleague, seeing a TV story, or reading a newspaper article about Vietnam or having a conversation with a colleague who was there with me.

Frank Snepp's *Decent Interval* did a great deal to keep the memory of Vietnam alive. In those first few months after Vietnam, back in headquarters, it was no secret that Snepp was writing a book and that he was pushing for an investigation of the CIA's performance during the evacuation. Polgar had offered him a position overseas, but Snepp resigned— partially in protest, but also to write his book. He and his book were the talk of the CIA, especially among the employees who had been in Vietnam.

On the day that *Decent Interval* appeared in the bookstores, I went out and bought a copy. The first thing I did was look for my name in the index. When I did not find it, I looked for any mention of polygraph. Finding none, I perused the index to see what other names I recognized. As I sat on a bench waiting for the shuttle bus back to headquarters, thumbing through the book, a shadow appeared on the pages. I looked up to see Tom Polgar standing in front of me. He reached down, opened the book to page eighty-five, and pointed to Snepp's characterization of him: "Short and squat, with a butcher's build and a sagging barrel chest, he looks more like an overgrown gnome than 'Special Assistant to the

Ambassador' [Polgar's official title]."[2] From what I remember of the Polgar-Snepp relationship in Vietnam, Polgar had treated Snepp like a son. My impression was that Polgar felt more betrayed than insulted by Snepp's comments. He said that his attorney had agreed to take his case pro bono if he sued Snepp (which he did not).

Although I felt that Snepp took a lot of literary license in describing his own role in Vietnam, there is a lot of good material in the book. Among the CIA Vietnam veterans I discussed it with at the time, I heard few ringing endorsements. Many of them felt that the book was too self-serving and that overstating his role weakened Snepp's credibility. Neverthless, *Decent Interval* is the definitive book about Vietnam written by a CIA employee. Although some of the criticism he levels at the CIA people who were there is justified, to my knowledge, he was never that critical while in Vietnam.

Because Snepp failed to get the CIA's prior approval for the book's publication, as required, it took him to court. The CIA won the case, and Snepp had to relinquish his royalties. As I understood the ruling, Snepp lost his suit because he had violated a contract by not getting prior approval. I had no problem with the verdict, but I think the CIA may have been overly harsh in the way it went after him. Had he presented the book for review, it probably would have been approved without being gutted. I saw little in it that was classified information. Snepp subsequently wrote *Irreparable Harm,* in which he made the case that the CIA violated his First Amendment rights in seizing his royalties. I believe that when Snepp wrote *Decent Interval,* he anticipated that the CIA would take him to court but was sure that he would win. Perhaps he also thought that the publicity of such a trial would help the sale of his book.

Not long after *Decent Interval* came out, Sean Dolan was visiting us and mentioned a contact he had had with Snepp. Sean had left the CIA with the intention of becoming a priest and was in a Catholic seminary in Maryland. On a weekend visit to Washington, he ran into Snepp, and Snepp asked Sean if he would appear on a television show in his clerical garb. Sean declined.

In a *Newsweek* article commemorating the twenty-fifth anniversary of the fall of Saigon, Evan Thomas mentions that Snepp was "declared a

2. Frank Snepp, *Decent Interval, an Insider's Account of Saigon's Indecent End Told by the CIA's Chief Strategy Analyst in Vietnam* (New York: Random House, 1977), p. 85.

pariah."[3] I had no sense of that among most of the CIA people I dealt with. Senior management felt that it had to make an example of him and, in my opinion, overdid it, but I know of no one in the Agency who thought that Snepp was being malicious in *Decent Interval*. Rather than a pariah, I thought the Agency's public view of Snepp was like that of a parent toward a wayward child who needed to be punished and serve as an example to others.

In contrast, John Stockwell did become a pariah. Stockwell also helped keep the memory of Vietnam alive, but he made his entry into the world of CIA authors a bit more dramatically. He had been raging about how poorly the CIA had performed during the evacuation, and there was concern about where his discontent might lead.

In the fall of 1975, I had lunch with "Ray Mallett," the former POIC in Pleiku. He mentioned that Stockwell's last boss in Vietnam, Gil Mayer, the last ROIC in MR/3, had called him for advice. According to Mallett, Mayer said, "Ray, I have a problem. They are really pushing me to write a great performance appraisal review for Stockwell, and I am having a real problem doing that." Mallett told Mayer to let his conscience be his guide. Subsequently, Stockwell was named chief of the Angolan Task Force, a prestigious position for a fairly junior officer, leading me to assume that Mayer had given him a good review. For the next year and a half, Stockwell was a high-profile and hard-charging officer, seemingly on the way up.

On the morning of April 10, 1977, I was in my office when an examiner came in and asked me if I knew a guy named Stockwell. I told him that I did, and he showed me an open and very critical letter of resignation published by the *Washington Post* that Stockwell had written to Adm. Stansfield Turner, the DCI. Stockwell's letter caused a lot of excitement, especially among the people in the Directorate of Operations. Stockwell followed up his letter of resignation with his book *In Search of Enemies*. For the next couple of years, he enjoyed some notoriety as a CIA renegade supposedly searching for truth.

Reminders of Stockwell also bring FIREBALL to mind. I left Vietnam with many questions about him and, until recently, was half convinced that he had been run by the VC. I thought that they might have used him not to pass us disinformation but as a conduit for information

3. Evan Thomas, "The Last Days of Saigon," *Newsweek*, May 1, 2000, pp. 34–42.

they wanted us to have. During the past few years, facts have come to light that answer some of my questions.

David Corn, in his book *Blond Ghost*, claims that "CIA people later heard that FIREBALL was killed after a South Vietnamese security officer betrayed him."[4] Another source, a former translator in Vietnam, wrote to me that he had heard that a principal agent in Tay Ninh had fingered FIREBALL. At the time, I thought that the agent could have been Albert, Stockwell's interpreter, or possibly Nguyen Van Phong, FIREBALL's Vietnamese case officer.

"The Fate of a Mole," an article published in the *People's Army Newspaper* (a North Vietnamese military newspaper) on July 22, 1995, describes in detail how FIREBALL was identified and subsequently died. According to the article, FIREBALL was given up by Nguyen Van Phong after Phong's arrest on April 30, 1975. The article identified FIREBALL as a district cadre for the Cao Dai Holy See region in Tay Ninh and went into great detail as to how the FIREBALL operation had been run. FIREBALL, according to the article, committed suicide before the North Vietnamese counterintelligence service could arrest him.

Based on what I knew of FIREBALL in Vietnam and what I have learned since, my take on him is that he was a VC whose uncle peddled him and his information to anyone who would buy it. At this point, I know that he worked for the U.S. Army, the National Police's Special Branch, and the South Vietnamese Military Security Service, and I surmise that he might have worked for other services as well. I do feel some sense of closure regarding FIREBALL, but some questions will never be answered.

In late June 1975, as I was going into the headquarters building in Langley, I heard General Timmes call to me. "John, how are you? Do you have a job?" he asked.

We shook hands, asked about each other's families, and commiserated for a few minutes. I told him that I was back on-line doing polygraph tests.

"You have a job. I wish I did," he said.

General Timmes died on October 20, 1990, at the age of eighty-three and was buried in an impressive ceremony at Arlington National Cemetery. He was a gentleman, and, personally, I liked him. In my opinion,

---

4. David Corn, *Blond Ghost* (New York: Simon and Schuster, 1994), p. 291.

however, he was part of the problem in Vietnam, and I wonder if he would have been part of any satisfactory solution had the tide gone the other way.

Once the furor over Snepp and Stockwell died down, it was business as usual, and I settled into my niche in IB (which became Polygraph Division in 1980). During the next twenty-plus years, I conducted more polygraph examinations than any examiner in the history of the CIA, and I take great pride in the fact that I never had a test subject make a complaint about me. After returning from Vietnam, I went on more than seventy TDYs and never lost my enthusiasm for doing operational tests. There came a time, however, when I felt that I was being overexposed. I suggested to my chief that I would not want to have to write a damage assessment if I were ever wrapped up.[5] Thereafter, my foreign travel decreased.

On one of those TDYs, I was transiting London and ran into Tom Clines. Clines had worked for Shackley in Miami; had been Shackley's base chief in Long Tieng, where I met him; and had been a business associate of Shackley's after Shackley retired in September 1979. "John," he said, "Ted and I went to brief Admiral Turner a couple of times. One time, Ted said, 'We don't do things that way around here.' When Turner said, 'What do you mean *we*,' I knew we were in trouble. The other time, Turner said to Ted, 'Don't talk to me like a plebe!' I knew, right then and there, it was time to go."

After retiring, Shackley wrote *The Third Option*, in which he made the case that when diplomacy failed, covert action was a logical and viable alternative to war. His point is valid, but his suggestions on how to implement covert action seemed simplistic.

The Shackleys were at the Lao reunion I attended in August 2000. Both he and Mrs. Shackley looked well, and he is still working on his memoirs.

Tom Clines was also at the reunion. In addition to running into him in London, I have seen him on two other occasions since he retired—once at JFK Airport in New York, and once in a restaurant in northern Virginia. Both times, he was very affable, and we had a nice conversation.

---

5. Whenever a CIA person is compromised, is arrested, or defects, a damage assessment has to be done. The purpose is to try to identify what CIA people, agents, or operations could be compromised.

Felix Rodriguez and I have stayed in touch. On Veterans Day (November 11) 1998, I attended the Heroes and Heritage Awards dinner at the Organization of American States as Felix's guest. The dinner was to honor Latin Americans who have distinguished themselves in service to the United States. Felix was honored with the Hero Award. Two of the other honorees were Alfred Rascon (Heritage Award), a Medal of Honor winner, and Lt. Comdr. Everett Alvarez, Jr. (Chairman's Award), the longest confirmed POW in the nation's history.

Don Gregg lived up to my expectations. When George Bush became DCI, he named Gregg to be his adviser on East Asia. After leaving the Agency, Gregg became U.S. ambassador to South Korea.

Bo Mooney, after being told that he would never be promoted or allowed to travel overseas, left polygraph. On the many occasions I saw him, he was always friendly. In 1989, he died of cancer.

On occasion, I run into Amos Spitz. He is neither friendly nor unfriendly, but he is still phlegmatic, taciturn, and stolid, just as I remember him. Amos never recognized that most people have a negative reaction to him. When a reduction in force occurred, he had no friends in OS to plead his case, and he was let go. Regardless of my personal feelings about Amos, he had gone to Vietnam when no one else would and had paid his dues. Something could have (and should have) been found for him so that he could receive his full retirement benefits.

Of the Office of Security colleagues I served with in Vietnam, Bill Evans is the one I have stayed in touch with. After Vietnam, Evans and Karen Hary married. Bill subsequently took a rotational assignment with the Directorate of Operations, where he made such a good impression that he was asked to stay—OS's loss. When he retired, he had attained a rank equivalent to that of a two-star general. He was one of my "lifeliners" and remains a friend.

After Vietnam, Keith Barry became very involved in the CIA's emerging counterterrorism program. He parlayed that experience into a position as chief of security in Paris and London for a major airline. He married a Vietnamese woman who worked in the Norodom Complex travel office in the Saigon embassy. Currently, he is a consultant in the security arena.

Things did not go well for Art O'Leary after he left Vietnam. Shortly before the fall of Saigon, he returned to the States to take his wife, Kate, to the Sloan-Kettering Cancer Institute in New York. Kate survived that bout with cancer but ultimately succumbed in 1990. In the late 1970s, Art suffered a stroke that left him partially paralyzed and impaired his speech. I last saw him in 1985, and he passed on in October 2001. My failure to develop a warmer relationship with him is an ongoing regret.

By the time Mark Verity returned from Vietnam, he was considered one of the CIA's best examiners. As a result, he was called on to do some of the highest profile cases. He received a $10,000 bonus for catching a double agent. Also, he took on the Defense Intelligence Agency when he accused a North Vietnamese refugee who claimed to have been an undertaker for American POWs of being a fabricator. Robert Russell Garwood, a U.S. marine who remained in Vietnam for fourteen years after the war, subsequently identified the refugee as a North Vietnamese interrogator.

Today, Mark, who never married, is happily retired to his beloved Rockies. He drinks only premium beer and hosts an annual trek in the mountains for Agency colleagues. His professionalism and ethical conduct set high standards that made the CIA's polygraph program the best in government.

Rob Creed became one of my supervisors in Polygraph Division (PD). He was as good a supervisor as he was an examiner. I learned a lot from him and came to respect him a great deal. It had been my hope that Rob would become chief of PD, and I do not understand why that never happened. He is a prime example of an officer whose career was impeded by his service in Indochina. I recently saw him and Kay at the Lao reunion. They looked great and are doing well.

Historians have treated Ambassador Martin very harshly. No one, it seems, has a good word to say about him. Neither Nixon nor Kissinger paid tribute to or even mentioned Martin in their memoirs. He was "their man" in Saigon, promoted their policies, and became their fall guy. As much as I agree with many of the criticisms leveled against Martin, Nixon and Kissinger should have acknowledged his efforts on their behalf. Martin died in 1990 of cancer, discredited, forgotten, and, I would assume, bitter.

After Vietnam, Greg Collins (the salt of the salt-and-pepper duo) became a case officer, and Catherine worked with the CIA as an interpreter/translator. I have kept in touch with them, and Greg was helpful with this book. One of their sons graduated from the University of Virginia, another from the U.S. Air Force Academy, and the third from the University of North Carolina. Greg and Catherine have four grandchildren and are enjoying retirement.

Lynn Bell, the pepper of the duo, sent Lee and me a Christmas card in 1976. We responded but have not heard from him since. Based on information I acquired since 1975, Lynn's positions on the war (as noted in chapter 8) seem to have been borne out—in particular, his position that the VC and NVA did not target women against Americans. In Larry Engelmann's *Tears Before the Rain,* Gen. Tran Bach Dang put it this way: "We [the NVA] did not use women who were sleeping with American officials or intelligence officers. We did find that our infiltrations of the American Embassy and the Central Intelligence Agency were not that important, because they really didn't know much about what was going on."[6] It may not be very flattering, but based on my experience, there is more than a grain of truth in what he said.

Tito Cortez became a deputy sheriff in Arizona after retirement, and I spoke with him at his retirement ceremony. He looked great and seemed to be enjoying life. Two years later, he died of a heart attack.

After retiring, Pedro Torres took a position as chief of security for a large corporation in South America. Torres became very involved in industrial security issues and did well as a consultant. He died in 1999.

Bruce Green became a very successful lawyer and state legislator. He currently works for the Department of Defense in a senior position.

Chris Hanlon was most helpful with this book, and I keep in regular touch with him. Chris told me that he had run into Paul Mathis (VIOLET's case officer) in an airport, and in a discussion of the VIOLET case, Mathis said, "I guess they just couldn't keep that operation together after I left."

It seems as though I am always running into people who remember me from Vietnam, or whose faces I recognize from Vietnam but cannot put a name to. One of them was our son John's Little League baseball coach. Such contacts, in conjunction with the more regular contacts, keep Vietnam constantly in my mind.

Since returning from Vietnam, I have attended the funerals of nine former Vietnam colleagues. I served in Vietnam with three of those killed in the embassy bombing in Beirut. It is unfortunate that so many

6. Larry Engelmann, *Tears Before the Rain: An Oral History of the Fall of South Vietnam* (New York: Oxford University Press, 1990), p. 307.

of my contacts with Vietnam colleagues take place at funerals and memorial services, but that is one of the prices of getting older.

As a senior examiner, I was given the opportunity to do some very good tests. In 1979, I did what I think was my best test. I caught an Eastern European double agent who had been working for the Federal Bureau of Investigation for five years. The agent was due to return to Czechoslovakia, and the FBI asked us if we wanted to take him over. The Agency was willing to take him, but he had to be polygraphed first.

During my tour with the 513th Military Intelligence Group in Germany from January 1965 until July 1967, one of our polygraph examiners, S. Sgt. Glen Rohrer, defected to Czechoslovakia. While investigating his defection, we learned that the Czechs ran a polygraph countermeasures program and that the head of the program was a Dr. Miroslav Dufek. Going on the assumption that if an agent were a Czech intelligence officer he would probably know or at least recognize Dufek's name, I constructed a test in which I asked the agent if he knew or had any knowledge of a Dr. Miroslav Dufek or six other doctors whose names I had taken from a Prague telephone book. When I pretested the questions with the agent, he denied recognizing or having any knowledge of the men whose names I used on the test. He also denied any contact with Czech intelligence before or since coming to the United States. The only name to which he reacted on the test was Dufek's. I confronted him, and after about an hour, he said, "I think Dufek debriefs diplomats when they return from overseas."

Based on his pretest denial of any contact whatsoever with Czech intelligence, this was information he should not have known. At that point, I brought the FBI agent and our case officer, Aldrich Ames, to the room where I was conducting the test and, without any hesitation, said, "This guy is a Czech Intel officer and has reported to them on his contacts with the Bureau."

The agent shrugged his shoulders and said, "Not me." I could not get him to confess, and the session was terminated.

When I got back to headquarters, I took some heat from the desk officer who managed the case, and two days later, the chief of the Soviet Europe Division, "Hank Geary," asked me to make a presentation at a meeting of all the division officers who had been involved in the case. The desk officer began the meeting by telling me that since the agent had made no admissions, I was premature in calling him a Czech intelligence officer. Geary then asked me to make my case. I explained the basis for my call and summed up my comments with, "There is not a doubt in my mind that the man I tested is a Czech double agent."

"That's good enough for me. We don't take him. Meeting's over," Geary said.

One week later, the FBI called to let me know that it had determined that the agent I had tested was a Czech intelligence officer.

At about the same time, one of the supervisors approached me and asked me to test the son of a manager in the Office of Security. He added a kicker. "John, he was tested by one of the other examiners, and we want you to do it over. We will send the other examiner out of the office, and we don't want him to know that the kid is being retested."

The first examiner had called the young man "favorable with no derogatory information developed." During the test, I developed disqualifying information about the young man, as well as information that contradicted the first examiner's report. I handed the original report to the supervisor who had assigned me the case and said, "This is a fabricated report."

He had been monitoring the case and said, "You're right." It came as quite a surprise when the original examiner subsequently became my boss.

In 1977, our second son, Jimmy, was born. He is a professional musician and a constant song in my heart. He and John are as different as day and night, but both have more than met every expectation we had for them.

I loved my job and many of the people I worked with. Deciding to stay in Polygraph Division may not have been the best decision in terms of career advancement, but in every other way, it was. I met Lee, traveled to more than forty countries, and managed to provide well for my family. If I ever told my mother how much money I was making without having to work outside or lift anything heavy, she would have thought I was robbing banks. When I retired, I left with the feeling that I had done a difficult job not only well but also the way it should be done. I look back with few regrets and look forward to an enjoyable retirement.

BIBLIOGRAPHY

. . . .

Cassidy, John. *A Station in the Delta*. New York: Scribner, 1979.

Corn, David. *Blond Ghost*. New York: Simon and Schuster, 1994.

DeForest, Orrin. *Slow Burn*. New York: Simon and Schuster, 1990.

The Demanding Years. Hanoi: Public Security Publishing House, 1988.

Engelmann, Larry. *Tears Before the Rain: An Oral History of the Fall of South Vietnam*. New York: Oxford University Press, 1990.

Grant, Zalin. *Facing the Phoenix: The CIA and the Political Defeat of the United States in Vietnam*. New York: W. W. Norton, 1991.

———. *Over the Beach: Air War in Vietnam*. New York: W. W. Norton, 1986.

Isaacs, Arnold R. *Without Honor: Defeat in Vietnam and Cambodia*. Baltimore: Johns Hopkins University Press, 1983.

Karnow, Stanley. *Vietnam, a History*. New York: Penguin Books, 1991.

Moss, George Donelson. *Vietnam, an American Ordeal*. Upper Saddle River, N.J.: Prentice-Hall, 1990.

Pimlott, John. *Vietnam, the Decisive Battles*. New York: Macmillan, 1990.

Robbins, Christopher. *Air America: The Story of the CIA's Secret Airlines*. New York: G. P. Putnam's Sons, 1979.

Shackley, Theodore G. *The Third Option*. New York: Reader's Digest/McGraw-Hill, 1981.

Sheehan, Neil. *A Bright and Shining Lie*. Baltimore: Johns Hopkins University Press, 1983.

Shultz, Richard H., Jr. *Secret War Against Hanoi*. New York: HarperCollins, 1999.

Snepp, Frank. *Decent Interval, an Insider's Account of Saigon's Indecent End Told by the CIA's Chief Strategy Analyst in Vietnam.* New York: Random House, 1977.

———. *Irreparable Harm.* New York: Random House, 1999.

Stein, Jeff. *A Murder in Wartime.* New York: St. Martin's Press, 1992.

Stockwell, John. *In Search of Enemies.* New York: W. W. Norton, 1978.

Summers, Harry G., Jr. *Historical Atlas of the Vietnam War.* New York: Houghton Mifflin, 1995.

———. *Vietnam War Almanac.* New York: Facts on File, 1985.

Terzani, Tisio. *Gia Phong!* London: Angus and Robertson, 1976.

Theroux, Paul. *The Great Railway Bazaar.* Boston: Houghton Mifflin, 1975.

Todd, Oliver. *Cruel April: The Fall of Saigon.* New York: W. W. Norton, 1990.

Wallace, Patricia Ward. *Politics of Conscience: A Biography of Margaret Chase Smith.* Westport, Conn.: Praeger Publishers, 1995.

INDEX

. . . .